NON SANZ DROICT.

MEASVRE,
For Meaſure.

William Shakespeare

Measure
for
Measure

With New and Updated
Critical Essays
and a Revised Bibliography

Edited by S. Nagarajan

THE SIGNET CLASSIC SHAKESPEARE
General Editor: Sylvan Barnet

A SIGNET CLASSIC

SIGNET CLASSIC
Published by New American Library, a division of
Penguin Putnam Inc., 375 Hudson Street, New York, New York 10014, U.S.A.
Penguin Books Ltd, 80 Strand, London WC2R 0RL, England
Penguin Books Australia Ltd, Ringwood, Victoria, Australia
Penguin Books Canada Ltd, 10 Alcorn Avenue, Toronto, Ontario, Canada
M4V 3B2
Penguin Books (N.Z.) Ltd, 182–190 Wairau Road, Auckland 10, New Zealand

Penguin Books Ltd, Registered Offices: Harmondsworth, Middlesex, England

Published by Signet Classic, an imprint of New American Library,
a division of Penguin Putnam Inc.

The Signet Classic Edition of *Measure for Measure* was first published in 1964,
and an updated edition was published in 1988.

First Signet Classic Printing (Second Revised Edition), December 1998
10   9   8   7   6   5   4

 REGISTERED TRADEMARK—MARCA REGISTRADA

Library of Congress Catalog Card Number: 98-24316

Printed in the United States of America

BOOKS ARE AVAILABLE AT QUANTITY DISCOUNTS WHEN USED TO PROMOTE PROD-
UCTS OR SERVICES. FOR INFORMATION PLEASE WRITE TO PREMIUM MARKETING DIVI-
SION, PENGUIN PUTNAM INC., 375 HUDSON STREET, NEW YORK, NEW YORK 10014.

Contents

Shakespeare: An Overview

Biographical Sketch

Between the record of his baptism in Stratford on 26 April 1564 and the record of his burial in Stratford on 25 April 1616, some forty official documents name Shakespeare, and many others name his parents, his children, and his grandchildren. Further, there are at least fifty literary references to him in the works of his contemporaries. More facts are known about William Shakespeare than about any other playwright of the period except Ben Jonson. The facts should, however, be distinguished from the legends. The latter, inevitably more engaging and better known, tell us that the Stratford boy killed a calf in high style, poached deer and rabbits, and was forced to flee to London, where he held horses outside a playhouse. These traditions are only traditions; they may be true, but no evidence supports them, and it is well to stick to the facts.

Mary Arden, the dramatist's mother, was the daughter of a substantial landowner; about 1557 she married John Shakespeare, a tanner, glove-maker, and trader in wool, grain, and other farm commodities. In 1557 John Shakespeare was a member of the council (the governing body of Stratford), in 1558 a constable of the borough, in 1561 one of the two town chamberlains, in 1565 an alderman (entitling him to the appellation of "Mr."), in 1568 high bailiff— the town's highest political office, equivalent to mayor. After 1577, for an unknown reason he drops out of local politics. What *is* known is that he had to mortgage his wife's property, and that he was involved in serious litigation.

The birthday of William Shakespeare, the third child and the eldest son of this locally prominent man, is unrecorded, but the Stratford parish register records that the infant was baptized on 26 April 1564. (It is quite possible that he was born on 23 April, but this date has probably been assigned by tradition because it is the date on which, fifty-two years later, he died, and perhaps because it is the feast day of St. George, patron saint of England.) The attendance records of the Stratford grammar school of the period are not extant, but it is reasonable to assume that the son of a prominent local official attended the free school—it had been established for the purpose of educating males precisely of his class—and received substantial training in Latin. The masters of the school from Shakespeare's seventh to fifteenth years held Oxford degrees; the Elizabethan curriculum excluded mathematics and the natural sciences but taught a good deal of Latin rhetoric, logic, and literature, including plays by Plautus, Terence, and Seneca.

On 27 November 1582 a marriage license was issued for the marriage of Shakespeare and Anne Hathaway, eight years his senior. The couple had a daughter, Susanna, in May 1583. Perhaps the marriage was necessary, but perhaps the couple had earlier engaged, in the presence of witnesses, in a formal "troth plight" which would render their children legitimate even if no further ceremony were performed. In February 1585, Anne Hathaway bore Shakespeare twins, Hamnet and Judith.

That Shakespeare was born is excellent; that he married and had children is pleasant; but that we know nothing about his departure from Stratford to London or about the beginning of his theatrical career is lamentable and must be admitted. We would gladly sacrifice details about his children's baptism for details about his earliest days in the theater. Perhaps the poaching episode is true (but it is first reported almost a century after Shakespeare's death), or perhaps he left Stratford to be a schoolmaster, as another tradition holds; perhaps he was moved (like Petruchio in *The Taming of the Shrew*) by

> Such wind as scatters young men through the world,
> To seek their fortunes farther than at home
> Where small experience grows.   (1.2.49–51)

In 1592, thanks to the cantankerousness of Robert Greene, we have our first reference, a snarling one, to Shakespeare as an actor and playwright. Greene, a graduate of St. John's College, Cambridge, had become a playwright and a pamphleteer in London, and in one of his pamphlets he warns three university-educated playwrights against an actor who has presumed to turn playwright:

> There is an upstart crow, beautified with our feathers, that with his *tiger's heart wrapped in a player's hide* supposes he is as well able to bombast out a blank verse as the best of you, and being an absolute Johannes-factotum [i.e., jack-of-all-trades] is in his own conceit the only Shake-scene in a country.

The reference to the player, as well as the allusion to Aesop's crow (who strutted in borrowed plumage, as an actor struts in fine words not his own), makes it clear that by this date Shakespeare had both acted and written. That Shakespeare is meant is indicated not only by *Shake-scene* but also by the parody of a line from one of Shakespeare's plays, *3 Henry VI*: "O, tiger's heart wrapped in a woman's hide" (1.4.137). If in 1592 Shakespeare was prominent enough to be attacked by an envious dramatist, he probably had served an apprenticeship in the theater for at least a few years.

In any case, although there are no extant references to Shakespeare between the record of the baptism of his twins in 1585 and Greene's hostile comment about "Shake-scene" in 1592, it is evident that during some of these "dark years" or "lost years" Shakespeare had acted and written. There are a number of subsequent references to him as an actor. Documents indicate that in 1598 he is a "principal comedian," in 1603 a "principal tragedian," in 1608 he is one of the "men players." (We do not have, however, any solid information about which roles he may have played; later traditions say he played Adam in *As You Like It* and the ghost in *Hamlet*, but nothing supports the assertions. Probably his role as dramatist came to supersede his role as actor.) The profession of actor was not for a gentleman, and it occasionally drew the scorn of university men like Greene who resented writing speeches for persons less educated than themselves, but it was respectable enough; players, if prosperous, were in effect members of the bourgeoisie, and there is nothing to suggest that Stratford considered William Shakespeare less than a solid citizen. When, in 1596, the Shakespeares were granted a coat of arms—i.e., the right to be considered gentlemen—the grant was made to Shakespeare's father, but probably William Shakespeare had arranged the matter on his own behalf. In subsequent transactions he is occasionally styled a gentleman.

Although in 1593 and 1594 Shakespeare published two narrative poems dedicated to the Earl of Southampton, *Venus and Adonis* and *The Rape of Lucrece*, and may well have written most or all of his sonnets in the middle nineties, Shakespeare's literary activity seems to have been almost entirely devoted to the theater. (It may be significant that the two narrative poems were written in years when the plague closed the theaters for several months.) In 1594 he was a charter member of a theatrical company called the Chamberlain's Men, which in 1603 became the royal company, the King's Men, making Shakespeare the king's playwright. Until he retired to Stratford (about 1611, apparently), he was with this remarkably stable company. From 1599 the company acted primarily at the Globe theater, in which Shakespeare held a one-tenth interest. Other Elizabethan dramatists are known to have acted, but no other is known also to have been entitled to a share of the profits.

Shakespeare's first eight published plays did not have his name on them, but this is not remarkable; the most popular play of the period, Thomas Kyd's *The Spanish Tragedy*, went through many editions without naming Kyd, and Kyd's authorship is known only because a book on the profession of acting happens to quote (and attribute to Kyd) some lines on the interest of Roman emperors in the drama. What is remarkable is that after 1598 Shakespeare's name commonly appears on printed plays—some of which are not his. Presumably his name was a drawing card, and publishers used it to attract potential buyers. Another indication of his popularity comes from Francis Meres, author of *Palladis Tamia: Wit's Treasury* (1598). In this anthology of snippets accompanied by an essay on literature, many playwrights are mentioned, but Shakespeare's name occurs more often than any other, and Shakespeare is the only playwright whose plays are listed.

From his acting, his play writing, and his share in a playhouse, Shakespeare seems to have made considerable money. He put it to work, making substantial investments in Stratford real estate. As early as 1597 he bought New Place, the second-largest house in Stratford. His family moved in soon afterward, and the house remained in the family until a granddaughter died in 1670. When Shakespeare made his will in 1616, less than a month before he died, he sought to leave his property intact to his descendants. Of small bequests to relatives and to friends (including three actors, Richard Burbage, John Heminges, and Henry Condell), that to his wife of the second-best bed has provoked the most comment. It has sometimes been taken as a sign of an unhappy marriage (other supposed signs are the apparently hasty marriage, his wife's seniority of eight years, and his residence in London without his family). Perhaps the second-best bed was the bed the couple had slept in, the best bed being reserved for visitors. In any case, had Shakespeare not excepted it, the bed would have gone (with the rest of his household possessions) to his daughter and her husband.

On 25 April 1616 Shakespeare was buried within the chancel of the church at Stratford. An unattractive monument to his memory, placed on a wall near the grave, says that he died on 23 April. Over the grave itself are the lines, perhaps by Shakespeare, that (more than his literary fame) have kept his bones undisturbed in the crowded burial ground where old bones were often dislodged to make way for new:

> Good friend, for Jesus' sake forbear
> To dig the dust enclosed here.
> Blessed be the man that spares these stones
> And cursed be he that moves my bones.

A Note on the Anti-Stratfordians, Especially Baconians and Oxfordians

Not until 1769—more than a hundred and fifty years after Shakespeare's death—is there any record of anyone expressing doubt about Shakespeare's authorship of the plays and poems. In 1769, however, Herbert Lawrence nominated Francis Bacon (1561–1626) in *The Life and Adventures of Common Sense*. Since then, at least two dozen other nominees have been offered, including Christopher Marlowe, Sir Walter Raleigh, Queen Elizabeth I, and Edward de Vere, 17th earl of Oxford. The impulse behind all anti-Stratfordian movements is the scarcely concealed snobbish opinion that "the man from Stratford" simply could not have written the plays because he was a country fellow without a university education and without access to high society. Anyone, the argument goes, who used so many legal terms, medical terms, nautical terms, and so forth, and who showed some familiarity with classical writing, must have attended a university, and anyone who knew so much about courtly elegance and courtly deceit must himself have moved among courtiers. The plays do indeed reveal an author whose interests were exceptionally broad, but specialists in any given field—law, medicine, arms and armor, and so on—soon find that the plays do not reveal deep knowledge in specialized matters; indeed, the playwright often gets technical details wrong.

The claim on behalf of Bacon, forgotten almost as soon as it was put forth in 1769, was independently reasserted by Joseph C. Hart in 1848. In 1856 it was reaffirmed by W. H. Smith in a book, and also by Delia Bacon in an article; in 1857 Delia Bacon published a book, arguing that Francis Bacon had directed a group of intellectuals who wrote the plays.

Francis Bacon's claim has largely faded, perhaps because it was advanced with such evident craziness by Ignatius Donnelly, who in *The Great Cryptogram* (1888) claimed to break a code in the plays that proved Bacon had written not only the plays attributed to Shakespeare but also other Renaissance works, for instance the plays of Christopher Marlowe and the essays of Montaigne.

Consider the last two lines of the Epilogue in *The Tempest*:

As you from crimes would pardoned be,
Let your indulgence set me free.

What was Shakespeare—sorry, Francis Bacon, Baron Verulam—*really* saying in these two lines? According to Baconians, the lines are an anagram reading, "Tempest of Francis Bacon, Lord Verulam; do ye ne'er divulge me, ye words." Ingenious, and it is a pity that in the quotation the letter *a* appears only twice in the cryptogram, whereas in the deciphered message it appears three times. Oh, no problem; just alter "Verulam" to "Verul'm" and it works out very nicely.

Most people understand that with sufficient ingenuity one can torture any text and find in it what one wishes. For instance: Did Shakespeare have a hand in the King James Version of the Bible? It was nearing completion in 1610, when Shakespeare was forty-six years old. If you look at the 46th Psalm and count forward for forty-six words, you will find the word *shake*. Now if you go to the end of the psalm and count backward forty-six words, you will find the word *spear*. Clear evidence, according to some, that Shakespeare slyly left his mark in the book.

Bacon's candidacy has largely been replaced in the twentieth century by the candidacy of Edward de Vere (1550–1604), 17th earl of Oxford. The basic ideas behind the Oxford theory, advanced at greatest length by Dorothy and Charlton Ogburn in *This Star of England* (1952, rev. 1955), a book of 1297 pages, and by Charlton Ogburn in *The Mysterious William Shakespeare* (1984), a book of 892 pages, are these: (1) The man from Stratford could not possibly have had the mental equipment and the experience to have written the plays—only a courtier could have written them; (2) Oxford had the requisite background (social position, education, years at Queen Elizabeth's court); (3) Oxford did not wish his authorship to be known for two basic reasons: writing for the public theater was a vulgar pursuit, and the plays show so much courtly and royal disreputable behavior that they would have compromised Oxford's position at court. Oxfordians offer countless details to support the claim. For example, Hamlet's phrase "that ever I was born to set it right" (1.5.89) barely conceals "E. Ver, I was born to set it right," an unambiguous announcement of de Vere's authorship, according to *This Star of England* (p. 654). A second example: Consider Ben

Jonson's poem entitled "To the Memory of My Beloved Master William Shakespeare," prefixed to the first collected edition of Shakespeare's plays in 1623. According to Oxfordians, when Jonson in this poem speaks of the author of the plays as the "swan of Avon," he is alluding not to William Shakespeare, who was born and died in Stratford-on-Avon and who throughout his adult life owned property there; rather, he is alluding to Oxford, who, the Ogburns say, used "William Shakespeare" as his pen name, and whose manor at Bilton was on the Avon River. Oxfordians do not offer any evidence that Oxford took a pen name, and they do not mention that Oxford had sold the manor in 1581, forty-two years before Jonson wrote his poem. Surely a reference to the Shakespeare who was born in Stratford, who had returned to Stratford, and who had died there only seven years before Jonson wrote the poem is more plausible. And exactly why Jonson, who elsewhere also spoke of Shakespeare as a playwright, and why Heminges and Condell, who had acted with Shakespeare for about twenty years, should speak of Shakespeare as the author in their dedication in the 1623 volume of collected plays is never adequately explained by Oxfordians. Either Jonson, Heminges and Condell, and numerous others were in on the conspiracy, or they were all duped—equally unlikely alternatives. Another difficulty in the Oxford theory is that Oxford died in 1604, and some of the plays are clearly indebted to works and events later than 1604. Among the Oxfordian responses are: At his death Oxford left some plays, and in later years these were touched up by hacks, who added the material that points to later dates. *The Tempest*, almost universally regarded as one of Shakespeare's greatest plays and pretty clearly dated to 1611, does indeed date from a period after the death of Oxford, but it is a crude piece of work that should not be included in the canon of works by Oxford.

The anti-Stratfordians, in addition to assuming that the author must have been a man of rank and a university man, usually assume two conspiracies: (1) a conspiracy in Elizabethan and Jacobean times, in which a surprisingly large number of persons connected with the theater knew that the actor Shakespeare did not write the plays attributed to him but for some reason or other pretended that he did; (2) a conspiracy of today's Stratfordians, the professors who teach Shakespeare in the colleges and universities, who are said to have a vested interest in preserving Shakespeare as the author of the plays they teach. In fact, (1) it is inconceivable that the secret of Shakespeare's non-authorship could have been preserved by all of the people who supposedly were in on the conspiracy, and (2) academic fame awaits any scholar today who can disprove Shakespeare's authorship.

The Stratfordian case is convincing not only because hundreds or even thousands of anti-Stratford arguments—of the sort that say "ever I was born" has the secret double meaning "E. Ver, I was born"—add up to nothing at all but also because irrefutable evidence connects the man from Stratford with the London theater and with the authorship of particular plays. The anti-Stratfordians do not seem to understand that it is not enough to dismiss the Stratford case by saying that a fellow from the provinces simply couldn't have written the plays. Nor do they understand that it is not enough to dismiss all of the evidence connecting Shakespeare with the plays by asserting that it is perjured.

The Shakespeare Canon

We return to William Shakespeare. Thirty-seven plays as well as some nondramatic poems are generally held to constitute the Shakespeare canon, the body of authentic works. The exact dates of composition of most of the works are highly uncertain, but evidence of a starting point and/or of a final limiting point often provides a framework for informed guessing. For example, *Richard II* cannot be earlier than 1595, the publication date of some material to which it is indebted; *The Merchant of Venice* cannot be later than 1598, the year Francis Meres mentioned it. Sometimes arguments for a date hang on an alleged topical allusion, such as the lines about the unseasonable weather in *A Midsummer Night's Dream*, 2.1.81–117, but such an allusion, if indeed it is an allusion to an event in the real world, can be variously interpreted, and in any case there is always the possibility that a topical allusion was inserted years later, to bring the play up to date. (The issue of alterations in a text between the time that Shakespeare drafted it and the time that it was printed—alterations due to censorship or playhouse practice or Shakespeare's own second thoughts—will be discussed in "The Play Text as a Collaboration" later in this overview.) Dates are often attributed on the basis of style, and although conjectures about style usually rest on other conjectures (such as Shakespeare's development as a playwright, or the appropriateness of lines to character), sooner or later one must rely on one's literary sense. There is no documentary proof, for example, that *Othello* is not as early as *Romeo and Juliet*, but one feels that *Othello* is a later, more mature work, and because the first record of its performance is 1604, one is glad enough to set its composition at that date and not push it back into Shakespeare's early years. (*Romeo and Juliet* was first published in 1597, but evidence suggests that it was written a little earlier.) The following chronology, then, is indebted not only to facts but also to informed guesswork and sensitivity. The dates, necessarily imprecise for some works, indicate something like a scholarly consensus concerning the time of original composition. Some plays show evidence of later revision.

Plays. The first collected edition of Shakespeare, published in 1623, included thirty-six plays. These are all accepted as Shakespeare's, though for one of them, *Henry VIII*, he is thought to have had a collaborator. A thirty-seventh play, *Pericles*, published in 1609 and attributed to Shakespeare on the title page, is also widely accepted as being partly by Shakespeare even though it is not included in the 1623 volume. Still another play not in the 1623 volume, *The Two Noble Kinsmen*, was first published in 1634, with a title page attributing it to John Fletcher and Shakespeare. Probably most students of the subject now believe that Shakespeare did indeed have a hand in it. Of the remaining plays attributed at one time or another to Shakespeare, only one, *Edward III*, anonymously published in 1596, is now regarded by some scholars as a serious candidate. The prevailing opinion, however, is that this rather simple-minded play is not Shakespeare's; at most he may have revised some passages, chiefly scenes with the Countess of

Salisbury. We include *The Two Noble Kinsmen* but do not include *Edward III* in the following list.

1588–94	*The Comedy of Errors*
1588–94	*Love's Labor's Lost*
1589–91	*2 Henry VI*
1590–91	*3 Henry VI*
1589–92	*1 Henry VI*
1592–93	*Richard III*
1589–94	*Titus Andronicus*
1593–94	*The Taming of the Shrew*
1592–94	*The Two Gentlemen of Verona*
1594–96	*Romeo and Juliet*
1595	*Richard II*
1595–96	*A Midsummer Night's Dream*
1596–97	*King John*
1594–96	*The Merchant of Venice*
1596–97	*1 Henry IV*
1597	*The Merry Wives of Windsor*
1597–98	*2 Henry IV*
1598–99	*Much Ado About Nothing*
1598–99	*Henry V*
1599	*Julius Caesar*
1599–1600	*As You Like It*
1599–1600	*Twelfth Night*
1600–1601	*Hamlet*
1601–1602	*Troilus and Cressida*
1602–1604	*All's Well That Ends Well*
1603–1604	*Othello*
1604	*Measure for Measure*
1605–1606	*King Lear*
1605–1606	*Macbeth*
1606–1607	*Antony and Cleopatra*
1605–1608	*Timon of Athens*
1607–1608	*Coriolanus*
1607–1608	*Pericles*
1609–10	*Cymbeline*
1610–11	*The Winter's Tale*
1611	*The Tempest*

| 1612–13 | *Henry VIII* |
| 1613 | *The Two Noble Kinsmen* |

Poems. In 1989 Donald W. Foster published a book in which he argued that "A Funeral Elegy for Master William Peter," published in 1612, ascribed only to the initials W.S., *may* be by Shakespeare. Foster later published an article in a scholarly journal, *PMLA* 111 (1996), in which he asserted the claim more positively. The evidence begins with the initials, and includes the fact that the publisher and the printer of the elegy had published Shakespeare's *Sonnets* in 1609. But such facts add up to rather little, especially because no one has found any connection between Shakespeare and William Peter (an Oxford graduate about whom little is known, who was murdered at the age of twenty-nine). The argument is based chiefly on statistical examinations of word patterns, which are said to correlate with Shakespeare's known work. Despite such correlations, however, many readers feel that the poem does not sound like Shakespeare. True, Shakespeare has a great range of styles, but his work is consistently imaginative and interesting. Many readers find neither of these qualities in "A Funeral Elegy."

1592–93	*Venus and Adonis*
1593–94	*The Rape of Lucrece*
1593–1600	*Sonnets*
1600–1601	*The Phoenix and the Turtle*

Shakespeare's English

1. Spelling and Pronunciation. From the philologist's point of view, Shakespeare's English is modern English. It requires footnotes, but the inexperienced reader can comprehend substantial passages with very little help, whereas for the same reader Chaucer's Middle English is a foreign language. By the beginning of the fifteenth century the chief grammatical changes in English had taken place, and the final unaccented -*e* of Middle English had been lost (though it survives even today in spelling, as in *name*); during the fifteenth century the dialect of London, the commercial and political center, gradually displaced the provincial dialects, at least in writing; by the end of the century, printing had helped to regularize and stabilize the language, especially spelling. Elizabethan spelling may seem erratic to us (there were dozens of spellings of *Shakespeare*, and a simple word like *been* was also spelled *beene* and *bin*), but it had much in common with our spelling. Elizabethan spelling was conservative in that for the most part it reflected an older pronunciation (Middle English) rather than the sound of the language as it was then spoken, just as our spelling continues to reflect medieval pronunciation—most obviously in the now silent but formerly pronounced letters in a word such as *knight*. Elizabethan pronunciation, though not identical with ours, was much closer to ours than to that of the Middle Ages. Incidentally, though no one can be certain about what Elizabethan English sounded like, specialists tend to believe it was rather like the speech of a modern stage Irishman (*time* apparently was pronounced *toime*, *old* pronounced *awld*, *day* pronounced *die*, and *join* pronounced *jine*) and not at all like the Oxford speech that most of us think it was.

An awareness of the difference between our pronunciation and Shakespeare's is crucial in three areas—in accent, or number of syllables (many metrically regular lines may look irregular to us); in rhymes (which may not look like rhymes); and in puns (which may not look like puns). Examples will be useful. Some words that were at least on occasion stressed differently from today are *aspèct*, *còmplete*, *fòrlorn*, *revènue*, and *sepùlcher*. Words that sometimes had an additional syllable are *emp[e]ress*, *Hen[e]ry*, *mon[e]th*, and *villain* (three syllables, *vil-lay-in*). An additional syllable is often found in possessives, like *moon*'s (pronounced *moones*) and in words ending in *-tion* or *-sion*. Words that had one less syllable than they now have are *needle* (pronounced *neel*) and *violet* (pronounced *vilet*). Among rhymes now lost are *one* with *loan*, *love* with *prove*, *beast* with *jest*, *eat* with *great*. (In reading, trust your sense of metrics and your ear, more than your eye.) An example of a pun that has become obliterated by a change in pronunciation is Falstaff's reply to Prince Hal's "Come, tell us your reason" in *1 Henry IV*: "Give you a reason on compulsion? If reasons were as plentiful as blackberries, I would give no man a reason upon compulsion, I" (2.4.237–40). The *ea* in *reason* was pronounced rather like a long *a*, like the *ai* in *raisin*, hence the comparison with blackberries.

Puns are not merely attempts to be funny; like metaphors they often involve bringing into a meaningful relationship areas of experience normally seen as remote. In *2 Henry IV*, when Feeble is conscripted, he stoically says, "I care not. A man can die but once. We owe God a death" (3.2.242–43), punning on *debt*, which was the way *death* was pronounced. Here an enormously significant fact of life is put into simple commercial imagery, suggesting its commonplace quality. Shakespeare used the same pun earlier in *1 Henry IV*, when Prince Hal says to Falstaff, "Why, thou owest God a death," and Falstaff replies, " 'Tis not due yet: I would be loath to pay him before his day. What need I be so forward with him that calls not on me?" (5.1.126–29).

Sometimes the puns reveal a delightful playfulness; sometimes they reveal aggressiveness, as when, replying to Claudius's "But now, my cousin Hamlet, and my son," Hamlet says, "A little more than kin, and less than kind!" (1.2.64–65). These are Hamlet's first words in the play, and we already hear him warring verbally against Claudius. Hamlet's "less than kind" probably means (1) Hamlet is not of Claudius's family or nature, *kind* having the sense it still has in our word *mankind*; (2) Hamlet is not kindly (affectionately) disposed toward Claudius; (3) Claudius is not naturally (but rather unnaturally, in a legal sense incestuously) Hamlet's father. The puns evidently were not put in as sops to the groundlings; they are an important way of communicating a complex meaning.

2. *Vocabulary.* A conspicuous difficulty in reading Shakespeare is rooted in the fact that some of his words are no longer in common use—for example, words concerned with armor, astrology, clothing, coinage, hawking, horsemanship, law, medicine, sailing, and war. Shakespeare had a large vocabulary—something near thirty thousand words— but it was not so much a vocabulary of big words as a vocabulary drawn from a wide range of life, and it is partly

his ability to call upon a great body of concrete language that gives his plays the sense of being in close contact with life. When the right word did not already exist, he made it up. Among words thought to be his coinages are *accommodation, all-knowing, amazement, bare-faced, countless, dexterously, dislocate, dwindle, fancy-free, frugal, indistinguishable, lackluster, laughable, overawe, premeditated, sea change, star-crossed*. Among those that have not survived are the verb *convive*, meaning to feast together, and *smilet*, a little smile.

Less overtly troublesome than the technical words but more treacherous are the words that seem readily intelligible to us but whose Elizabethan meanings differ from their modern ones. When Horatio describes the Ghost as an "erring spirit," he is saying not that the ghost has sinned or made an error but that it is wandering. Here is a short list of some of the most common words in Shakespeare's plays that often (but not always) have a meaning other than their most usual modern meaning:

'a	he
abuse	deceive
accident	occurrence
advertise	inform
an, and	if
annoy	harm
appeal	accuse
artificial	skillful
brave	fine, splendid
censure	opinion
cheer	(1) face (2) frame of mind
chorus	a single person who comments on the events
closet	small private room
competitor	partner
conceit	idea, imagination
cousin	kinsman
cunning	skillful
disaster	evil astrological influence
doom	judgment
entertain	receive into service

envy	malice
event	outcome
excrement	outgrowth (of hair)
fact	evil deed
fancy	(1) love (2) imagination
fell	cruel
fellow	(1) companion (2) low person (often an insulting term if addressed to someone of approximately equal rank)
fond	foolish
free	(1) innocent (2) generous
glass	mirror
hap, haply	chance, by chance
head	army
humor	(1) mood (2) bodily fluid thought to control one's psychology
imp	child
intelligence	news
kind	natural, acting according to nature
let	hinder
lewd	base
mere(ly)	utter(ly)
modern	commonplace
natural	a fool, an idiot
naughty	(1) wicked (2) worthless
next	nearest
nice	(1) trivial (2) fussy
noise	music
policy	(1) prudence (2) stratagem
presently	immediately
prevent	anticipate
proper	handsome
prove	test
quick	alive
sad	serious
saw	proverb
secure	without care, incautious
silly	innocent

sensible	capable of being perceived by the senses
shrewd	sharp
so	provided that
starve	die
still	always
success	that which follows
tall	brave
tell	count
tonight	last night
wanton	playful, careless
watch	keep awake
will	lust
wink	close both eyes
wit	mind, intelligence

All glosses, of course, are mere approximations; sometimes one of Shakespeare's words may hover between an older meaning and a modern one, and as we have seen, his words often have multiple meanings.

3. Grammar. A few matters of grammar may be surveyed, though it should be noted at the outset that Shakespeare sometimes made up his own grammar. As E.A. Abbott says in *A Shakespearian Grammar,* "Almost any part of speech can be used as any other part of speech": a noun as a verb ("he childed as I fathered"); a verb as a noun ("She hath made compare"); or an adverb as an adjective ("a seldom pleasure"). There are hundreds, perhaps thousands, of such instances in the plays, many of which at first glance would not seem at all irregular and would trouble only a pedant. Here are a few broad matters.

Nouns: The Elizabethans thought the *-s* genitive ending for nouns (as in *man's*) derived from *his*; thus the line " 'gainst the count his galleys I did some service," for "the count's galleys."

Adjectives: By Shakespeare's time adjectives had lost the endings that once indicated gender, number, and case. About the only difference between Shakespeare's adjectives and ours is the use of the now redundant *more* or *most* with the comparative ("some more fitter place") or superlative

("This was the most unkindest cut of all"). Like double comparatives and double superlatives, double negatives were acceptable; Mercutio "will not budge for no man's pleasure."

Pronouns: The greatest change was in pronouns. In Middle English *thou, thy,* and *thee* were used among familiars and in speaking to children and inferiors; *ye, your,* and *you* were used in speaking to superiors (servants to masters, nobles to the king) or to equals with whom the speaker was not familiar. Increasingly the "polite" forms were used in all direct address, regardless of rank, and the accusative *you* displaced the nominative *ye.* Shakespeare sometimes uses *ye* instead of *you,* but even in Shakespeare's day *ye* was archaic, and it occurs mostly in rhetorical appeals.

Thou, thy, and *thee* were not completely displaced, however, and Shakespeare occasionally makes significant use of them, sometimes to connote familiarity or intimacy and sometimes to connote contempt. In *Twelfth Night* Sir Toby advises Sir Andrew to insult Cesario by addressing him as *thou:* "If thou thou'st him some thrice, it shall not be amiss" (3.2.46–47). In *Othello* when Brabantio is addressing an unidentified voice in the dark he says, "What are you?" (1.1.91), but when the voice identifies itself as the foolish suitor Roderigo, Brabantio uses the contemptuous form, saying, "I have charged thee not to haunt about my doors" (93). He uses this form for a while, but later in the scene, when he comes to regard Roderigo as an ally, he shifts back to the polite *you,* beginning in line 163, "What said she to you?" and on to the end of the scene. For reasons not yet satisfactorily explained, Elizabethans used *thou* in addresses to God—"O God, thy arm was here," the king says in *Henry V* (4.8.108)—and to supernatural characters such as ghosts and witches. A subtle variation occurs in *Hamlet.* When Hamlet first talks with the Ghost in 1.5, he uses *thou,* but when he sees the Ghost in his mother's room, in 3.4, he uses *you,* presumably because he is now convinced that the Ghost is not a counterfeit but is his father.

Perhaps the most unusual use of pronouns, from our point of view, is the neuter singular. In place of our *its, his* was often used, as in "How far that little candle throws *his* beams." But the use of a masculine pronoun for a neuter noun came to seem unnatural, and so *it* was used for the possessive as well as the nominative: "The hedge-sparrow fed the cuckoo so long / That it had it head bit off by it young." In the late sixteenth century the possessive form *its* developed, apparently by analogy with the *-s* ending used to indicate a genitive noun, as in *book*'s, but *its* was not yet common usage in Shakespeare's day. He seems to have used *its* only ten times, mostly in his later plays. Other usages, such as "you have seen Cassio and she together" or the substitution of *who* for *whom*, cause little problem even when noticed.

Verbs, Adverbs, and Prepositions: Verbs cause almost no difficulty: The third person singular present form commonly ends in *-s*, as in modern English (e.g., "He blesses"), but sometimes in *-eth* (Portia explains to Shylock that mercy "blesseth him that gives and him that takes"). Broadly speaking, the *-eth* ending was old-fashioned or dignified or "literary" rather than colloquial, except for the words *doth, hath,* and *saith.* The *-eth* ending (regularly used in the King James Bible, 1611) is very rare in Shakespeare's dramatic prose, though not surprisingly it occurs twice in the rather formal prose summary of the narrative poem *Lucrece.* Sometimes a plural subject, especially if it has collective force, takes a verb ending in *-s*, as in "My old bones aches." Some of our strong or irregular preterites (such as *broke*) have a different form in Shakespeare (*brake*); some verbs that now have a weak or regular preterite (such as *helped*) in Shakespeare have a strong or irregular preterite (*holp*). Some adverbs that today end in *-ly* were not inflected: "grievous sick," "wondrous strange." Finally, prepositions often are not the ones we expect: "We are such stuff as dreams are made on," "I have a king here to my flatterer."

Again, none of the differences (except meanings that have substantially changed or been lost) will cause much difficulty. But it must be confessed that for some elliptical passages there is no widespread agreement on meaning. Wise editors resist saying more than they know, and when they are uncertain they add a question mark to their gloss.

Shakespeare's Theater

In Shakespeare's infancy, Elizabethan actors performed wherever they could—in great halls, at court, in the courtyards of inns. These venues implied not only different audiences but also different playing conditions. The innyards must have made rather unsatisfactory theaters: on some days they were unavailable because carters bringing goods to London used them as depots; when available, they had to be rented from the innkeeper. In 1567, presumably to avoid such difficulties, and also to avoid regulation by the Common Council of London, which was not well disposed toward theatricals, one John Brayne, brother-in-law of the carpenter turned actor James Burbage, built the Red Lion in an eastern suburb of London. We know nothing about its shape or its capacity; we can say only that it may have been the first building in Europe constructed for the purpose of giving plays since the end of antiquity, a thousand years earlier. Even after the building of the Red Lion theatrical activity continued in London in makeshift circumstances, in marketplaces and inns, and always uneasily. In 1574 the Common Council required that plays and playing places in London be licensed because

> sundry great disorders and inconveniences have been found to ensue to this city by the inordinate haunting of great multitudes of people, specially youth, to plays, interludes, and shows, namely occasion of frays and quarrels, evil practices of incontinency in great inns having chambers and secret places adjoining to their open stages and galleries.

The Common Council ordered that innkeepers who wished licenses to hold performance put up a bond and make contributions to the poor.

The requirement that plays and innyard theaters be licensed, along with the other drawbacks of playing at inns and presumably along with the success of the Red Lion, led James Burbage to rent a plot of land northeast of the city walls, on property outside the jurisdiction of the city. Here he built England's second playhouse, called simply the Theatre. About all that is known of its construction is that it was wood. It soon had imitators, the most famous being the Globe (1599), essentially an amphitheater built across the Thames (again outside the city's jurisdiction), constructed with timbers of the Theatre, which had been dismantled when Burbage's lease ran out.

Admission to the theater was one penny, which allowed spectators to stand at the sides and front of the stage that jutted into the yard. An additional penny bought a seat in a covered part of the theater, and a third penny bought a more comfortable seat and a better location. It is notoriously difficult to translate prices into today's money, since some things that are inexpensive today would have been expensive in the past and vice versa—a pipeful of tobacco (imported, of course) cost a lot of money, about three pennies, and an orange (also imported) cost two or three times what a chicken cost—but perhaps we can get some idea of the low cost of the penny admission when we realize that a penny could also buy a pot of ale. An unskilled laborer made about five or sixpence a day, an artisan about twelve pence a day, and the hired actors (as opposed to the sharers in the company, such as Shakespeare) made about ten pence a performance. A printed play cost five or sixpence. Of course a visit to the theater (like a visit to a baseball game today) usually cost more than the admission since the spectator probably would also buy food and drink. Still, the low entrance fee meant that the theater was available to all except the very poorest people, rather as movies and most athletic events are today. Evidence indicates that the audience ranged from apprentices who somehow managed to scrape together the minimum entrance fee and to escape from their masters for a few hours, to prosperous members of the middle class and aristocrats who paid the additional fee for admission to the galleries. The exact proportion of men to women cannot be determined, but women of all classes certainly were present. Theaters were open every afternoon but Sundays for much of the year, except in times of plague, when they were closed because of fear of infection. By the way, no evidence suggests the presence of toilet facilities. Presumably the patrons relieved themselves by making a quick trip to the fields surrounding the playhouses.

There are four important sources of information about the

structure of Elizabethan public playhouses—drawings, a
contract, recent excavations, and stage directions in the
plays. Of drawings, only the so-called de Witt drawing (c.
1596) of the Swan—really his friend Aernout van Buchell's
copy of Johannes de Witt's drawing—is of much significance. The drawing, the only extant representation of the
interior of an Elizabethan theater, shows an amphitheater of
three tiers, with a stage jutting from a wall into the yard or

Johannes de Witt, a Continental visitor to London, made a drawing
of the Swan theater in about the year 1596. The original drawing is
lost; this is Aernout van Buchell's copy of it.

center of the building. The tiers are roofed, and part of the stage is covered by a roof that projects from the rear and is supported at its front on two posts, but the groundlings, who paid a penny to stand in front of the stage or at its sides, were exposed to the sky. (Performances in such a playhouse were held only in the daytime; artificial illumination was not used.) At the rear of the stage are two massive doors; above the stage is a gallery.

The second major source of information, the contract for the Fortune (built in 1600), specifies that although the Globe (built in 1599) is to be the model, the Fortune is to be square, eighty feet outside and fifty-five inside. The stage is to be forty-three feet broad, and is to extend into the middle of the yard, i.e., it is twenty-seven and a half feet deep.

The third source of information, the 1989 excavations of the Rose (built in 1587), indicate that the Rose was fourteen-sided, about seventy-two feet in diameter with an inner yard almost fifty feet in diameter. The stage at the Rose was about sixteen feet deep, thirty-seven feet wide at the rear, and twenty-seven feet wide downstage. The relatively small dimensions and the tapering stage, in contrast to the rectangular stage in the Swan drawing, surprised theater historians and have made them more cautious in generalizing about the Elizabethan theater. Excavations at the Globe have not yielded much information, though some historians believe that the fragmentary evidence suggests a larger theater, perhaps one hundred feet in diameter.

From the fourth chief source, stage directions in the plays, one learns that entrance to the stage was by the doors at the rear (*"Enter one citizen at one door, and another at the other"*). A curtain hanging across the doorway—or a curtain hanging between the two doorways—could provide a place where a character could conceal himself, as Polonius does, when he wishes to overhear the conversation between Hamlet and Gertrude. Similarly, withdrawing a curtain from the doorway could "discover" (reveal) a character or two. Such discovery scenes are very rare in Elizabethan drama, but a good example occurs in *The Tempest* (5.1.171), where a stage direction tells us, *"Here Prospero discovers Ferdinand and Miranda playing at chess."* There was also some sort of playing space "aloft" or "above" to represent, for instance, the top of a city's walls or a room above the street. Doubtless each theater had its own peculiarities, but perhaps we can talk about a "typical" Elizabethan theater if we realize that no theater need exactly fit the description, just as no mother is the average mother with 2.7 children.

This hypothetical theater is wooden, round, or polygonal (in *Henry V* Shakespeare calls it a "wooden *O*") capable of holding some eight hundred spectators who stood in the yard around the projecting elevated stage—these spectators were the "groundlings"—and some fifteen hundred additional spectators who sat in the three roofed galleries. The stage, protected by a "shadow" or "heavens" or roof, is entered from two doors; behind the doors is the "tiring house" (attiring house, i.e., dressing room), and above the stage is some sort of gallery that may sometimes hold spectators but can be used (for example) as the bedroom from which Romeo—according to a stage direction in one text—"goeth down." Some evidence suggests that a throne can be lowered onto the platform stage, perhaps from the "shadow"; certainly characters can descend from the stage through a trap or traps into the cellar or "hell." Sometimes this space beneath the stage accommodates a sound-effects man or musician (in *Antony and Cleopatra "music of the hautboys* [oboes] *is under the stage"*) or an actor (in *Hamlet* the *"Ghost cries under the stage"*). Most characters simply walk on and off through the doors, but because there is no curtain in front of the platform, corpses will have to be carried off (Hamlet obligingly clears the stage of Polonius's corpse, when he says, "I'll lug the guts into the neighbor room"). Other characters may have fallen at the rear, where a curtain on a doorway could be drawn to conceal them.

Such may have been the "public theater," so called because its inexpensive admission made it available to a wide range of the populace. Another kind of theater has been called the "private theater" because its much greater admission charge (sixpence versus the penny for general admission at the public theater) limited its audience to the wealthy or the prodigal. The private theater was basically a large room, entirely roofed and therefore artificially illuminated, with a stage at one end. The theaters thus were distinct in two ways: One was essentially an amphitheater that catered to the general public; the other was a hall that catered to the wealthy. In 1576 a hall theater was established in Blackfriars, a Dominican priory in London that had been suppressed in 1538 and confiscated by the Crown and thus was not under the city's jurisdiction. All the actors in this Blackfriars theater were boys about eight to thirteen years old (in the public theaters similar boys played female parts; a boy Lady Macbeth played to a man Macbeth). Near the end of this section on Shakespeare's theater we will talk at some length about possible implications in this convention of using boys to play female roles, but for the moment we should say that it doubtless accounts for the relative lack of female roles in Elizabethan drama. Thus, in *A Midsummer Night's Dream*, out of twenty-one named roles, only four are female; in *Hamlet*, out of twenty-four, only two (Gertrude and Ophelia) are female. Many of Shakespeare's characters have fathers but no mothers—for instance, King Lear's daughters. We need not bring in Freud to explain the disparity; a dramatic company had only a few boys in it.

To return to the private theaters, in some of which all of the performers were children—the "eyrie of . . . little eyases" (nest of unfledged hawks—2.2.347–48) which Rosencrantz mentions when he and Guildenstern talk with Hamlet. The theater in Blackfriars had a precarious existence, and ceased operations in 1584. In 1596 James Burbage, who had already made theatrical history by building the Theatre, began to construct a second Blackfriars theater. He died in 1597, and for several years this second Blackfriars theater was used by a troupe of boys, but in 1608 two of Burbage's sons and five other actors (including Shakespeare) became joint operators of the theater, using it in the winter when the open-air Globe was unsuitable. Perhaps such a smaller theater, roofed, artificially illuminated, and with a tradition of a wealthy audience, exerted an influence in Shakespeare's late plays.

Performances in the private theaters may well have had intermissions during which music was played, but in the public theaters the action was probably uninterrupted, flowing from scene to scene almost without a break. Actors would enter, speak, exit, and others would immediately enter and establish (if necessary) the new locale by a few properties and by words and gestures. To indicate that the scene took place at night, a player or two would carry a torch. Here are some samples of Shakespeare establishing the scene:

This is Illyria, lady.   (*Twelfth Night,* 1.2.2)

Well, this is the Forest of Arden.   (*As You Like It,* 2.4.14)

This castle has a pleasant seat; the air
Nimbly and sweetly recommends itself
Unto our gentle senses.   (*Macbeth,* 1.6.1–3)

The west yet glimmers with some streaks of day.
                                        (*Macbeth,* 3.3.5)

Sometimes a speech will go far beyond evoking the minimal setting of place and time, and will, so to speak, evoke the social world in which the characters move. For instance, early in the first scene of *The Merchant of Venice* Salerio suggests an explanation for Antonio's melancholy. (In the following passage, *pageants* are decorated wagons, floats, and *cursy* is the verb "to curtsy," or "to bow.")

Your mind is tossing on the ocean,
There where your argosies with portly sail—
Like signiors and rich burghers on the flood,
Or as it were the pageants of the sea—
Do overpeer the petty traffickers
That cursy to them, do them reverence,
As they fly by them with their woven wings.   (1.1.8–14)

Late in the nineteenth century, when Henry Irving produced the play with elaborate illusionistic sets, the first scene showed a ship moored in the harbor, with fruit vendors and dock laborers, in an effort to evoke the bustling and exotic life of Venice. But Shakespeare's words give us this exotic, rich world of commerce in his highly descriptive language when Salerio speaks of "argosies with portly sail" that fly with "woven wings"; equally important, through Salerio Shakespeare conveys a sense of the orderly, hierarchical society in which the lesser ships, "the petty traffickers," curtsy and thereby "do . . . reverence" to their superiors, the merchant prince's ships, which are "Like signiors and rich burghers."

On the other hand, it is a mistake to think that except for verbal pictures the Elizabethan stage was bare. Although Shakespeare's Chorus in *Henry V* calls the stage an "unworthy scaffold" (Prologue 1.10) and urges the spectators to "eke out our performance with your mind" (Prologue 3.35), there was considerable spectacle. The last act of *Macbeth,* for instance, has five stage directions calling for *"drum and colors,"* and another sort of appeal to the eye is indicated by the stage direction *"Enter Macduff, with Macbeth's head."* Some scenery and properties may have been substantial; doubtless a throne was used, but the pillars supporting the roof would have served for the trees on which Orlando pins his poems in *As You Like It.*

Having talked about the public theater—"this wooden *O*"—at some length, we should mention again that Shakespeare's plays were performed also in other locales. Alvin Kernan, in *Shakespeare, the King's Playwright: Theater in the Stuart Court 1603–1613* (1995) points out that "several of [Shakespeare's] plays contain brief theatrical performances, set always in a court or some noble house. When Shakespeare portrayed a theater, he did not, except for the choruses in *Henry V*, imagine a public theater" (p. 195). (Examples include episodes in *The Taming of the Shrew*, *A Midsummer Night's Dream*, *Hamlet*, and *The Tempest*.)

A Note on the Use of Boy Actors in Female Roles

Until fairly recently, scholars were content to mention that the convention existed; they sometimes also mentioned that it continued the medieval practice of using males in female roles, and that other theaters, notably in ancient Greece and in China and Japan, also used males in female roles. (In classical Noh drama in Japan, males still play the female roles.) Prudery may have been at the root of the academic failure to talk much about the use of boy actors, or maybe there really is not much more to say than that it was a convention of a male-centered culture (Stephen Greenblatt's view, in *Shakespearean Negotiations* [1988]). Further, the very nature of a convention is that it is not thought about: Hamlet is a Dane and Julius Caesar is a Roman, but in Shakespeare's plays they speak English, and we in the audience never give this odd fact a thought. Similarly, a character may speak in the presence of others and we understand, again without thinking about it, that he or she is not heard by the figures on the stage (the aside); a character alone on the stage may speak (the soliloquy), and we do not take the character to be unhinged; in a realistic (box) set, the fourth wall, which allows us to see what is going on, is miraculously missing. The no-nonsense view, then, is that the boy actor was an accepted convention, accepted unthinkingly—just as today we know that Kenneth Branagh is not Hamlet, Al Pacino is not Richard III, and Denzel Washington is not the Prince of Aragon. In this view, the audience takes the performer for the role, and that is that; such is the argument we now make for race-free casting, in which African-Americans and Asians can play roles of persons who lived in medieval Denmark and ancient Rome. But gender perhaps is different, at least today. It is a matter of abundant academic study: The Elizabethan theater is now sometimes called a transvestite theater, and we hear much about cross-dressing.

Shakespeare himself in a very few passages calls attention to the use of boys in female roles. At the end of *As You Like It* the boy who played Rosalind addresses the audience, and says, "O men, . . . if I were a woman, I would kiss as many of you as had beards that pleased me." But this is in the Epilogue; the plot is over, and the actor is stepping out of the play and into the audience's everyday world. A second reference to the practice of boys playing female roles occurs in *Antony and Cleopatra*, when Cleopatra imagines that she and Antony will be the subject of crude plays, her role being performed by a boy:

> The quick comedians
> Extemporally will stage us, and present
> Our Alexandrian revels: Antony
> Shall be brought drunken forth, and I shall see
> Some squeaking Cleopatra boy my greatness.   (5.2.216–20)

In a few other passages, Shakespeare is more indirect. For instance, in *Twelfth Night* Viola, played of course by a boy, disguises herself as a young man and seeks service in the house of a lord. She enlists the help of a Captain, and (by way of explaining away her voice and her beardlessness) says,

> I'll serve this duke
> Thou shalt present me as an eunuch to him.   (1.2.55–56)

In *Hamlet*, when the players arrive in 2.2, Hamlet jokes with the boy who plays a female role. The boy has grown since Hamlet last saw him: "By'r Lady, your ladyship is nearer to heaven than when I saw you last by the altitude of a chopine" (a lady's thick-soled shoe). He goes on: "Pray God your voice . . . be not cracked" (434–38).

Exactly how sexual, how erotic, this material was and is, is now much disputed. Again, the use of boys may have been unnoticed, or rather not thought about—an unexamined convention—by most or all spectators most of the time, perhaps *all* of the time, except when Shakespeare calls the convention to the attention of the audience, as in the passages just quoted. Still, an occasional bit seems to invite erotic thoughts. The clearest example is the name that Rosalind takes in *As You Like It*, Ganymede—the beautiful youth whom Zeus abducted. Did boys dressed to play female roles carry homoerotic appeal for straight men (Lisa Jardine's view, in *Still Harping on Daughters* [1983]), or for gay men, or for some or all women in the audience? Further, when the boy actor played a woman who (for the purposes of the plot) disguised herself as a male, as Rosalind, Viola, and Portia do—so we get a boy playing a woman playing a man—what sort of appeal was generated, and for what sort of spectator?

Some scholars have argued that the convention empowered women by letting female characters display a freedom unavailable in Renaissance patriarchal society; the convention, it is said, undermined rigid gender distinctions. In this view, the convention (along with plots in which female characters for a while disguised themselves as young men) allowed Shakespeare to say what some modern gender

critics say: Gender is a constructed role rather than a bio-
logical given, something we make, rather than a fixed binary
opposition of male and female (see Juliet Dusinberre, in
Shakespeare and the Nature of Women [1975]). On the other
hand, some scholars have maintained that the male disguise
assumed by some female characters serves only to reaffirm
traditional social distinctions since female characters who
don male garb (notably Portia in *The Merchant of Venice*
and Rosalind in *As You Like It*) return to their female garb
and at least implicitly (these critics say) reaffirm the status
quo. (For this last view, see Clara Claiborne Park, in an
essay in *The Woman's Part*, ed. Carolyn Ruth Swift Lenz et
al. [1980].) Perhaps no one answer is right for all plays; in
As You Like It cross-dressing empowers Rosalind, but in
Twelfth Night cross-dressing comically traps Viola.

Shakespeare's Dramatic Language: Costumes, Gestures and Silences; Prose and Poetry

Because Shakespeare was a dramatist, not merely a poet,
he worked not only with language but also with costume,
sound effects, gestures, and even silences. We have already
discussed some kinds of spectacle in the preceding section,
and now we will begin with other aspects of visual language:
a theater, after all, is literally a "place for seeing." Consider
the opening stage direction in *The Tempest*, the first play in
the first published collection of Shakespeare's plays: "*A
tempestuous noise of thunder and Lightning heard: Enter a
Ship-master, and a Boteswain.*"

Costumes: What did that shipmaster and that boatswain
wear? Doubtless they wore something that identified them
as men of the sea. Not much is known about the costumes
that Elizabethan actors wore, but at least three points are
clear: (1) many of the costumes were splendid versions of
contemporary Elizabethan dress; (2) some attempts were
made to approximate the dress of certain occupations and of
antique or exotic characters such as Romans, Turks, and
Jews; (3) some costumes indicated that the wearer was

supernatural. Evidence for elaborate Elizabethan clothing can be found in the plays themselves and in contemporary comments about the "sumptuous" players who wore the discarded clothing of noblemen, as well as in account books that itemize such things as "a scarlet cloak with two broad gold laces, with gold buttons down the sides."

The attempts at approximation of the dress of certain occupations and nationalities also can be documented from the plays themselves, and it derives additional confirmation from a drawing of the first scene of Shakespeare's *Titus Andronicus*—the only extant Elizabethan picture of an identifiable episode in a play. (See pp. xxxviii–xxxix.) The drawing, probably done in 1594 or 1595, shows Queen Tamora pleading for mercy. She wears a somewhat medieval-looking robe and a crown; Titus wears a toga and a wreath, but two soldiers behind him wear costumes fairly close to Elizabethan dress. We do not know, however, if the drawing represents an actual stage production in the public theater, or perhaps a private production, or maybe only a reader's visualization of an episode. Further, there is some conflicting evidence: In *Julius Caesar* a reference is made to Caesar's doublet (a close-fitting jacket), which, if taken literally, suggests that even the protagonist did not wear Roman clothing; and certainly the lesser characters, who are said to wear hats, did not wear Roman garb.

It should be mentioned, too, that even ordinary clothing can be symbolic: Hamlet's "inky cloak," for example, sets him apart from the brightly dressed members of Claudius's court and symbolizes his mourning; the fresh clothes that are put on King Lear partly symbolize his return to sanity. Consider, too, the removal of disguises near the end of some plays. For instance, Rosalind in *As You Like It* and Portia and Nerissa in *The Merchant of Venice* remove their male attire, thus again becoming fully themselves.

Gestures and Silences: Gestures are an important part of a dramatist's language. King Lear kneels before his daughter Cordelia for a benediction (4.7.57–59), an act of humility that contrasts with his earlier speeches banishing her and that contrasts also with a comparable gesture, his ironic

kneeling before Regan (2.4.153–55). Northumberland's
failure to kneel before King Richard II (3.3.71–72) speaks
volumes. As for silences, consider a moment in *Coriolanus:*
Before the protagonist yields to his mother's entreaties
(5.3.182), there is this stage direction: *"Holds her by the
hand, silent."* Another example of "speech in dumbness"
occurs in *Macbeth,* when Macduff learns that his wife and
children have been murdered. He is silent at first, as Malcolm's speech indicates: "What, man! Ne'er pull your hat
upon your brows. Give sorrow words" (4.3.208–09). (For
a discussion of such moments, see Philip C. McGuire's
Speechless Dialect: Shakespeare's Open Silences [1985].)

Of course when we think of Shakespeare's work, we think
primarily of his language, both the poetry and the prose.

Prose: Although two of his plays (*Richard II* and *King John*)
have no prose at all, about half the others have at least one
quarter of the dialogue in prose, and some have notably
more: *1 Henry IV* and *2 Henry IV,* about half; *As You Like It*

and *Twelfth Night*, a little more than half; *Much Ado About Nothing*, more than three quarters; and *The Merry Wives of Windsor*, a little more than five sixths. We should remember that despite Molière's joke about M. Jourdain, who was amazed to learn that he spoke prose, most of us do not speak prose. Rather, we normally utter repetitive, shapeless, and often ungrammatical torrents; prose is something very different—a sort of literary imitation of speech at its most coherent.

Today we may think of prose as "natural" for drama; or even if we think that poetry is appropriate for high tragedy we may still think that prose is the right medium for comedy. Greek, Roman, and early English comedies, however, were written in verse. In fact, prose was not generally considered a literary medium in England until the late fifteenth century; Chaucer tells even his bawdy stories in verse. By the end of the 1580s, however, prose had established itself on the English comic stage. In tragedy, Marlowe made some use of prose, not simply in the speeches of clownish servants but even in the speech of a tragic hero, Doctor Faustus. Still, before Shakespeare, prose normally was used in the theater only for special circumstances: (1) letters and proclamations, to set them off from the poetic dialogue; (2) mad characters, to indicate that normal thinking has become disordered; and (3) low comedy, or speeches uttered by clowns even when they are not being comic. Shakespeare made use of these conventions, but he also went far beyond them. Sometimes he begins a scene in prose and then shifts into verse as the emotion is heightened; or conversely, he may shift from verse to prose when a speaker is lowering the emotional level, as when Brutus speaks in the Forum.

Shakespeare's prose usually is not prosaic. Hamlet's prose includes not only small talk with Rosencrantz and Guildenstern but also princely reflections on "What a piece of work is a man" (2.2.312). In conversation with Ophelia, he shifts from light talk in verse to a passionate prose denunciation of women (3.1.103), though the shift to prose here is perhaps also intended to suggest the possibility of madness. (Consult Brian Vickers, *The Artistry of Shakespeare's Prose* [1968].)

Poetry: Drama in rhyme in England goes back to the Middle Ages, but by Shakespeare's day rhyme no longer dominated poetic drama; a finer medium, blank verse (strictly speaking, unrhymed lines of ten syllables, with the stress on every second syllable) had been adopted. But before looking at unrhymed poetry, a few things should be said about the chief uses of rhyme in Shakespeare's plays. (1) A couplet (a pair of rhyming lines) is sometimes used to convey emotional heightening at the end of a blank verse speech; (2) characters sometimes speak a couplet as they leave the stage, suggesting closure; (3) except in the latest plays, scenes fairly often conclude with a couplet, and sometimes, as in *Richard II*, 2.1.145–46, the entrance of a new character within a scene is preceded by a couplet, which wraps up the earlier portion of that scene; (4) speeches of two characters occasionally are linked by rhyme, most notably in *Romeo and Juliet*, 1.5.95–108, where the lovers speak a sonnet between them; elsewhere a taunting reply occasionally rhymes with the previous speaker's last line; (5) speeches with sententious or gnomic remarks are sometimes in rhyme, as in the duke's speech in *Othello* (1.3.199–206); (6) speeches of sardonic mockery are sometimes in rhyme—for example, Iago's speech on women in *Othello* (2.1.146–58)—and they sometimes conclude with an emphatic couplet, as in Bolingbroke's speech on comforting words in *Richard II* (1.3.301–2); (7) some characters are associated with rhyme, such as the fairies in *A Midsummer Night's Dream*; (8) in the early plays, especially *The Comedy of Errors* and *The Taming of the Shrew*, comic scenes that in later plays would be in prose are in jingling rhymes; (9) prologues, choruses, plays-within-the-play, inscriptions, vows, epilogues, and so on are often in rhyme, and the songs in the plays are rhymed.

Neither prose nor rhyme immediately comes to mind when we first think of Shakespeare's medium: It is blank verse, unrhymed iambic pentameter. (In a mechanically exact line there are five iambic feet. An iambic foot consists of two syllables, the second accented, as in *away*; five feet make a pentameter line. Thus, a strict line of iambic pentameter contains ten syllables, the even syllables being stressed more heavily than the odd syllables. Fortunately, Shakespeare usually varies the line somewhat.) The first speech in *A Midsummer Night's Dream*, spoken by Duke Theseus to his betrothed, is an example of blank verse:

> Now, fair Hippolyta, our nuptial hour
> Draws on apace. Four happy days bring in
> Another moon; but, O, methinks, how slow
> This old moon wanes! She lingers my desires,
> Like to a stepdame, or a dowager,
> Long withering out a young man's revenue.   (1.1.1–6)

As this passage shows, Shakespeare's blank verse is not mechanically unvarying. Though the predominant foot is the iamb (as in *apace* or *desires*), there are numerous variations. In the first line the stress can be placed on "fair," as the regular metrical pattern suggests, but it is likely that "Now" gets almost as much emphasis; probably in the second line "Draws" is more heavily emphasized than "on," giving us a trochee (a stressed syllable followed by an unstressed one); and in the fourth line each word in the phrase "This old moon wanes" is probably stressed fairly heavily, conveying by two spondees (two feet, each of two stresses) the oppressive tedium that Theseus feels.

In Shakespeare's early plays much of the blank verse is end-stopped (that is, it has a heavy pause at the end of each line), but he later developed the ability to write iambic pentameter verse paragraphs (rather than lines) that give the illusion of speech. His chief techniques are (1) enjambing, i.e., running the thought beyond the single line, as in the first three lines of the speech just quoted; (2) occasionally replacing an iamb with another foot; (3) varying the position of the chief pause (the caesura) within a line; (4) adding an occasional unstressed syllable at the end of a line, traditionally called a feminine ending; (5) and beginning or ending a speech with a half line.

Shakespeare's mature blank verse has much of the rhythmic flexibility of his prose; both the language, though richly figurative and sometimes dense, and the syntax seem natural. It is also often highly appropriate to a particular character. Consider, for instance, this speech from *Hamlet*, in which Claudius, King of Denmark ("the Dane"), speaks to Laertes:

> And now, Laertes, what's the news with you?
> You told us of some suit. What is't, Laertes?
> You cannot speak of reason to the Dane
> And lose your voice. What wouldst thou beg, Laertes,
> That shall not be my offer, not thy asking?   (1.2.42–46)

Notice the short sentences and the repetition of the name "Laertes," to whom the speech is addressed. Notice, too, the shift from the royal "us" in the second line to the more intimate "my" in the last line, and from "you" in the first three lines to the more intimate "thou" and "thy" in the last two lines. Claudius knows how to ingratiate himself with Laertes.

For a second example of the flexibility of Shakespeare's blank verse, consider a passage from *Macbeth*. Distressed by the doctor's inability to cure Lady Macbeth and by the imminent battle, Macbeth addresses some of his remarks to the doctor and others to the servant who is arming him. The entire speech, with its pauses, interruptions, and irresolution (in "Pull't off, I say," Macbeth orders the servant to remove the armor that the servant has been putting on him), catches Macbeth's disintegration. (In the first line, *physic* means "medicine," and in the fourth and fifth lines, *cast the water* means "analyze the urine.")

> Throw physic to the dogs, I'll none of it.
> Come, put mine armor on. Give me my staff.
> Seyton, send out.—Doctor, the thanes fly from me.—
> Come, sir, dispatch. If thou couldst, doctor, cast
> The water of my land, find her disease
> And purge it to a sound and pristine health,
> I would applaud thee to the very echo,
> That should applaud again.—Pull't off, I say.—
> What rhubarb, senna, or what purgative drug,
> Would scour these English hence? Hear'st thou of them?
>
> (5.3.47–56)

Blank verse, then, can be much more than unrhymed iambic pentameter, and even within a single play Shakespeare's blank verse often consists of several styles, depending on the speaker and on the speaker's emotion at the moment.

The Play Text as a Collaboration

Shakespeare's fellow dramatist Ben Jonson reported that the actors said of Shakespeare, "In his writing, whatsoever he penned, he never blotted out line," i.e., never crossed out material and revised his work while composing. None of Shakespeare's plays survives in manuscript (with the possible exception of a scene in *Sir Thomas More*), so we cannot fully evaluate the comment, but in a few instances the published work clearly shows that he revised his manuscript. Consider the following passage (shown here in facsimile) from the best early text of *Romeo and Juliet*, the Second Quarto (1599):

Ro. Would I were sleepe and peace so sweet to rest
The grey eyde morne smiles on the frowning night,
Checkring the Easterne Clouds with streaks of light,
And darknesse sleckted like a drunkard reeles,
From forth daies pathway, made by *Tytans* wheeles.
Hence will I to my ghostly Friers close cell,
His helpe to craue, and my deare hap to tell.

                                                Exit.

Enter Frier alone with a basket.   (night,
Fri. The grey-eyed morne smiles on the frowning
Checking the Easterne clowdes with streaks of light:
And fleckeld darknesse like a drunkard reeles,
From forth daies path, and *Titans* burning wheeles:
Now ere the sun aduance his burning eie,

Romeo rather elaborately tells us that the sun at dawn is
dispelling the night (morning is smiling, the eastern clouds
are checked with light, and the sun's chariot—Titan's
wheels—advances), and he will seek out his spiritual father,
the Friar. He exits and, oddly, the Friar enters and says pretty
much the same thing about the sun. Both speakers say that
"the gray-eyed morn smiles on the frowning night," but there
are small differences, perhaps having more to do with the
business of printing the book than with the author's
composition: For Romeo's "checkring," "fleckted," and
"pathway," we get the Friar's "checking," "fleckeld," and
"path." (Notice, by the way, the inconsistency in Elizabethan
spelling: Romeo's "clouds" become the Friar's "clowdes.")
     Both versions must have been in the printer's copy, and it
seems safe to assume that both were in Shakespeare's manuscript. He must have written one version—let's say he first
wrote Romeo's closing lines for this scene—and then he
decided, no, it's better to give this lyrical passage to the
Friar, as the opening of a new scene, but he neglected to
delete the first version. Editors must make a choice, and they
may feel that the reasonable thing to do is to print the text as
Shakespeare intended it. But how can we know what he
intended? Almost all modern editors delete the lines from

Romeo's speech, and retain the Friar's lines. They don't do this because they know Shakespeare's intention, however. They give the lines to the Friar because the first published version (1597) of *Romeo and Juliet* gives only the Friar's version, and this text (though in many ways inferior to the 1599 text) is thought to derive from the memory of some actors, that is, it is thought to represent a performance, not just a script. Maybe during the course of rehearsals Shakespeare—an actor as well as an author—unilaterally decided that the Friar should speak the lines; if so (remember that we don't know this to be a fact) his final intention was to give the speech to the Friar. Maybe, however, the actors talked it over and settled on the Friar, with or without Shakespeare's approval. On the other hand, despite the 1597 version, one might argue (if only weakly) on behalf of giving the lines to Romeo rather than to the Friar, thus: (1) Romeo's comment on the coming of the daylight emphasizes his separation from Juliet, and (2) the figurative language seems more appropriate to Romeo than to the Friar. Having said this, in the Signet edition we have decided in this instance to draw on the evidence provided by earlier text and to give the lines to the Friar, on the grounds that since Q1 reflects a production, in the theater (at least on one occasion) the lines were spoken by the Friar.

A playwright sold a script to a theatrical company. The script thus belonged to the company, not the author, and author and company alike must have regarded this script not as a literary work but as the basis for a play that the actors would create on the stage. We speak of Shakespeare as the author of the plays, but readers should bear in mind that the texts they read, even when derived from a single text, such as the First Folio (1623), are inevitably the collaborative work not simply of Shakespeare with his company—doubtless during rehearsals the actors would suggest alterations—but also with other forces of the age. One force was governmental censorship. In 1606 parliament passed "an Act to restrain abuses of players," prohibiting the utterance of oaths and the name of God. So where the earliest text of *Othello* gives us "By heaven" (3.3.106), the first Folio gives "Alas," presumably reflecting the compliance of stage practice with the law. Similarly, the 1623 version of *King Lear* omits the oath "Fut" (probably from "By God's foot") at 1.2.142, again presumably reflecting the line as it was spoken on the stage. Editors who seek to give the reader the play that Shakespeare initially conceived—the "authentic" play conceived by the solitary Shakespeare— probably will restore the missing oaths and references to God. Other editors, who see the play as a collaborative work, a construction made not only by Shakespeare but also by actors and compositors and even government censors, may claim that what counts is the play as it was actually performed. Such editors regard the censored text as legitimate, since it is the play that was (presumably) finally put on. A performed text, they argue, has more historical reality than a text produced by an editor who has sought to get at what Shakespeare initially wrote. In this view, the text of a play is rather like the script of a film; the script is not the film, and the play text is not the performed play. Even if we want to talk about the play that Shakespeare "intended," we will find ourselves talking about a script that he handed over to a company with the intention that it be implemented by actors. The "intended" play is the one that the actors—we might almost say "society"—would help to construct.

Further, it is now widely held that a play is also the work of readers and spectators, who do not simply receive meaning, but who create it when they respond to the play. This idea is fully in accord with contemporary post-structuralist critical thinking, notably Roland Barthes's "The Death of the Author," in *Image-Music-Text* (1977) and Michel Foucault's "What Is an Author?," in *The Foucault Reader* (1984). The gist of the idea is that an author is not an isolated genius; rather, authors are subject to the politics and other social structures of their age. A dramatist especially is a worker in a collaborative project, working most obviously with actors—parts may be written for particular actors—but working also with the audience. Consider the words of Samuel Johnson, written to be spoken by the actor David Garrick at the opening of a theater in 1747:

The stage but echoes back the public voice;
The drama's laws, the drama's patrons give,
For we that live to please, must please to live.

The audience—the public taste as understood by the playwright—helps to determine what the play is. Moreover, even members of the public who are not part of the playwright's immediate audience may exert an influence through censorship. We have already glanced at governmental censorship, but there are also other kinds. Take one of Shakespeare's most beloved characters, Falstaff, who appears in three of Shakespeare's plays, the two parts of *Henry IV* and *The Merry Wives of Windsor*. He appears with this name in the earliest printed version of the first of these plays, *1 Henry IV*, but we know that Shakespeare originally called him (after an historical figure) Sir John Oldcastle. Oldcastle appears in Shakespeare's source (partly reprinted in the Signet edition of *1 Henry IV*), and a trace of the name survives in Shakespeare's play, 1.2.43–44, where Prince Hal punningly addresses Falstaff as "my old lad of the castle." But for some reason—perhaps because the family of the historical Oldcastle complained—Shakespeare had to change the name. In short, the play as we have it was (at least in this detail) subject to some sort of censorship. If we think that a text should present what we take to be the author's intention, we probably will want to replace *Falstaff* with *Oldcastle*. But if we recognize that a play is a collaboration, we may welcome the change, even if it was forced on Shakespeare. Somehow *Falstaff*, with its hint of *false-staff*, i.e., inadequate prop, seems just right for this fat knight who, to our delight, entertains the young prince with untruths. We can go as far as saying that, at least so far as a play is concerned, an insistence on the author's original intention (even if we could know it) can sometimes impoverish the text.

The tiny example of Falstaff's name illustrates the point that the text we read is inevitably only a version—something in effect produced by the collaboration of the playwright with his actors, audiences, compositors, and editors—of a fluid text that Shakespeare once wrote, just as the *Hamlet* that we see on the screen starring Kenneth Branagh is not the *Hamlet* that Shakespeare saw in an open-air playhouse starring Richard Burbage. *Hamlet* itself, as we shall note in a moment, also exists in several versions. It is not surprising that there is now much talk about the *instability* of Shakespeare's texts.

Because he was not only a playwright but was also an actor and a shareholder in a theatrical company, Shakespeare probably was much involved with the translation of the play from a manuscript to a stage production. He may or may not have done some rewriting during rehearsals, and he may or may not have been happy with cuts that were made. Some plays, notably *Hamlet* and *King Lear*, are so long that it is most unlikely that the texts we read were acted in their entirety. Further, for both of these plays we have more than one early text that demands consideration. In *Hamlet*, the Second Quarto (1604) includes some two hundred lines not found in the Folio (1623). Among the passages missing from the Folio are two of Hamlet's reflective speeches, the "dram of evil" speech (1.4.13–38) and "How all occasions do inform against me" (4.4.32–66). Since the Folio has more numerous and often fuller stage directions, it certainly looks as though in the Folio we get a theatrical version of the play, a text whose cuts were probably made—this is only a hunch, of course—not because Shakespeare was changing his conception of Hamlet but because the playhouse demanded a modified play. (The problem is complicated, since the Folio not only cuts some of the Quarto but adds some material. Various explanations have been offered.)

Or take an example from *King Lear*. In the First and Second Quarto (1608, 1619), the final speech of the play is given to Albany, Lear's surviving son-in-law, but in the First Folio version (1623), the speech is given to Edgar. The Quarto version is in accord with tradition—usually the highest-ranking character in a tragedy speaks the final words. Why does the Folio give the speech to Edgar? One possible answer is this: The Folio version omits some of Albany's speeches in earlier scenes, so perhaps it was decided (by Shakespeare? by the players?) not to give the final lines to so pale a character. In fact, the discrepancies are so many between the two texts, that some scholars argue we do not simply have texts showing different theatrical productions. Rather, these scholars say, Shakespeare substantially revised the play, and we really have two versions of *King Lear* (and of *Othello* also, say some)—two different plays—not simply two texts, each of which is in some ways imperfect.

In this view, the 1608 version of *Lear* may derive from Shakespeare's manuscript, and the 1623 version may derive from his later revision. The Quartos have almost three hundred lines not in the Folio, and the Folio has about a hundred lines not in the Quartos. It used to be held that all the texts were imperfect in various ways and from various causes— some passages in the Quartos were thought to have been set from a manuscript that was not entirely legible, other passages were thought to have been set by a compositor who was new to setting plays, and still other passages were thought to have been provided by an actor who misremembered some of the lines. This traditional view held that an editor must draw on the Quartos and the Folio in order to get Shakespeare's "real" play. The new argument holds (although not without considerable strain) that we have two authentic plays, Shakespeare's early version (in the Quarto) and Shakespeare's—or his theatrical company's—revised version (in the Folio). Not only theatrical demands but also Shakespeare's own artistic sense, it is argued, called for extensive revisions. Even the titles vary: Q1 is called *True Chronicle Historie of the life and death of King Lear and his three Daughters*, whereas the Folio text is called *The Tragedie of King Lear*. To combine the two texts in order to produce what the editor thinks is the play that Shakespeare intended to write is, according to this view, to produce a text that is false to the history of the play. If the new view is correct, and we do have texts of two distinct versions of *Lear* rather than two imperfect versions of one play, it supports in a textual way the poststructuralist view that we cannot possibly have an unmediated vision of (in this case) a play by Shakespeare; we can only recognize a plurality of visions.

Editing Texts

Though eighteen of his plays were published during his lifetime, Shakespeare seems never to have supervised their publication. There is nothing unusual here; when a playwright sold a play to a theatrical company he surrendered his ownership to it. Normally a company would not publish the play, because to publish it meant to allow competitors to acquire the piece. Some plays did get published: Apparently hard-up actors sometimes pieced together a play for a publisher; sometimes a company in need of money sold a play; and sometimes a company allowed publication of a play that no longer drew audiences. That Shakespeare did not concern himself with publication is not remarkable; of his contemporaries, only Ben Jonson carefully supervised the publication of his own plays.

In 1623, seven years after Shakespeare's death, John Heminges and Henry Condell (two senior members of Shakespeare's company, who had worked with him for about twenty years) collected his plays—published and unpublished—into a large volume, of a kind called a folio. (A folio is a volume consisting of large sheets that have been folded once, each sheet thus making two leaves, or four pages. The size of the page of course depends on the size of the sheet—a folio can range in height from twelve to sixteen inches, and in width from eight to eleven; the pages in the 1623 edition of Shakespeare, commonly called the First Folio, are approximately thirteen inches tall and eight inches wide.) The eighteen plays published during Shakespeare's lifetime had been issued one play per volume in small formats called quartos. (Each sheet in a quarto has been folded twice, making four leaves, or eight pages, each page being about nine inches tall and seven inches wide, roughly the size of a large paperback.)

Heminges and Condell suggest in an address "To the great variety of readers" that the republished plays are presented in better form than in the quartos:

> Before you were abused with diverse stolen and surreptitious copies, maimed and deformed by the frauds and stealths of injurious impostors that exposed them; even those, are now offered to your view cured and perfect of their limbs, and all the rest absolute in their numbers, as he [i.e., Shakespeare] conceived them.

There is a good deal of truth to this statement, but some of the quarto versions are better than others; some are in fact preferable to the Folio text.

Whoever was assigned to prepare the texts for publication

in the first Folio seems to have taken the job seriously and yet not to have performed it with uniform care. The sources of the texts seem to have been, in general, good unpublished copies or the best published copies. The first play in the collection, *The Tempest*, is divided into acts and scenes, has unusually full stage directions and descriptions of spectacle, and concludes with a list of the characters, but the editor was not able (or willing) to present all of the succeeding texts so fully dressed. Later texts occasionally show signs of carelessness: in one scene of *Much Ado About Nothing* the names of actors, instead of characters, appear as speech prefixes, as they had in the Quarto, which the Folio reprints; proofreading throughout the Folio is spotty and apparently was done without reference to the printer's copy; the pagination of *Hamlet* jumps from 156 to 257. Further, the proofreading was done while the presses continued to print, so that each play in each volume contains a mix of corrected and uncorrected pages.

Modern editors of Shakespeare must first select their copy; no problem if the play exists only in the Folio, but a considerable problem if the relationship between a Quarto and the Folio—or an early Quarto and a later one—is unclear. In the case of *Romeo and Juliet*, the First Quarto (Q1), published in 1597, is vastly inferior to the Second (Q2), published in 1599. The basis of Q1 apparently is a version put together from memory by some actors. Not surprisingly, it garbles many passages and is much shorter than Q2. On the other hand, occasionally Q1 makes better sense than Q2. For instance, near the end of the play, when the parents have assembled and learned of the deaths of Romeo and Juliet, in Q2 the Prince says (5.3.208–9),

Come, *Montague:* for thou art early vp
To see thy sonne and heire, now earling downe.

The last three words of this speech surely do not make sense, and many editors turn to Q1, which instead of "now earling downe" has "more early downe." Some modern editors take only "early" from Q1, and print "now early down"; others take "more early," and print "more early down." Further, Q1 (though, again, quite clearly a garbled and abbreviated text) includes some stage directions that are not found in Q2, and today many editors who base their text on Q2 are glad to add these stage directions, because the directions help to give us a sense of what the play looked like on Shakespeare's stage. Thus, in 4.3.58, after Juliet drinks the potion, Q1 gives us this stage direction, not in Q2: *"She falls upon her bed within the curtains."*

In short, an editor's decisions do not end with the choice of a single copy text. First of all, editors must reckon with Elizabethan spelling. If they are not producing a facsimile, they probably modernize the spelling, but ought they to preserve the old forms of words that apparently were pronounced quite unlike their modern forms—*lanthorn, alablaster*? If they preserve these forms are they really preserving Shakespeare's forms or perhaps those of a compositor in the printing house? What is one to do when one finds *lanthorn* and *lantern* in adjacent lines? (The editors of this series in general, but not invariably, assume that words should be spelled in their modern form, unless, for instance, a rhyme is involved.) Elizabethan punctuation, too, presents problems. For example, in the First Folio, the only text for the play, Macbeth rejects his wife's idea that he can wash the blood from his hand (2.2.60–62):

> No: this my Hand will rather
> The multitudinous Seas incarnardine,
> Making the Greene one, Red.

Obviously an editor will remove the superfluous capitals, and will probably alter the spelling to "incarnadine," but what about the comma before "Red"? If we retain the comma, Macbeth is calling the sea "the green one." If we drop the comma, Macbeth is saying that his bloody hand will make the sea ("the Green") *uniformly* red.

An editor will sometimes have to change more than spelling and punctuation. Macbeth says to his wife (1.7.46–47):

> I dare do all that may become a man,
> Who dares no more, is none.

For two centuries editors have agreed that the second line is unsatisfactory, and have emended "no" to "do": "Who dares do more is none." But when in the same play (4.2.21–22) Ross says that fearful persons

> Floate vpon a wilde and violent Sea
> Each way, and moue,

need we emend the passage? On the assumption that the compositor misread the manuscript, some editors emend "each way, and move" to "and move each way"; others emend "move" to "none" (i.e., "Each way and none"). Other editors, however, let the passage stand as in the original. The editors of the Signet Classic Shakespeare have restrained themselves from making abundant emendations. In their minds they hear Samuel Johnson on the dangers of emendation: "I have adopted the Roman sentiment, that it is more honorable to save a citizen than to kill an enemy." Some departures (in addition to spelling, punctuation, and lineation) from the copy text have of course been made, but the original readings are listed in a note following the play, so that readers can evaluate the changes for themselves.

Following tradition, the editors of the Signet Classic Shakespeare have prefaced each play with a list of characters, and throughout the play have regularized the names of the speakers. Thus, in our text of *Romeo and Juliet*, all speeches by Juliet's mother are prefixed "Lady Capulet," although the 1599 Quarto of the play, which provides our copy text, uses at various points seven speech tags for this one character: *Capu. Wi.* (i.e., Capulet's wife), *Ca. Wi., Wi., Wife, Old La.* (i.e., Old Lady), *La.,* and *Mo.* (i.e., Mother). Similarly, in *All's Well That Ends Well*, the character whom we regularly call "Countess" is in the Folio (the copy text) variously identified as *Mother, Countess, Old Countess, Lady,* and *Old Lady*. Admittedly there is some loss in regularizing, since the various prefixes may give us a hint of the way Shakespeare (or a scribe who copied Shakespeare's manuscript) was thinking of the character in a particular scene—for instance, as a mother, or as an old lady. But too much can be made of these differing prefixes, since the social relationships implied are *not* always relevant to the given scene.

We have also added line numbers and in many cases act and scene divisions as well as indications of locale at the beginning of scenes. The Folio divided most of the plays into acts and some into scenes. Early eighteenth-century editors increased the divisions. These divisions, which provide a convenient way of referring to passages in the plays, have been retained, but when not in the text chosen as the basis for the Signet Classic text they are enclosed within square brackets, [ ], to indicate that they are editorial additions. Similarly, though no play of Shakespeare's was equipped with indications of the locale at the heads of scene divisions, locales have here been added in square brackets for the convenience of readers, who lack the information that costumes, properties, gestures, and scenery afford to spectators. Spectators can tell at a glance they are in the throne room, but without an editorial indication the reader may be puzzled for a while. It should be mentioned, incidentally, that there are a few authentic stage directions—perhaps Shakespeare's, perhaps a prompter's—that suggest locales, such as *"Enter Brutus in his orchard,"* and *"They go up into the Senate house."* It is hoped that the bracketed additions in the Signet text will provide readers with the sort of help provided by these two authentic directions, but it is equally hoped that the reader will remember that the stage was not loaded with scenery.

Shakespeare on the Stage

Each volume in the Signet Classic Shakespeare includes a brief stage (and sometimes film) history of the play. When we read about earlier productions, we are likely to find them eccentric, obviously wrongheaded—for instance, Nahum Tate's version of *King Lear*, with a happy ending, which held the stage for about a century and a half, from the late seventeenth century until the end of the first quarter of the nineteenth. We see engravings of David Garrick, the greatest actor of the eighteenth century, in eighteenth-century garb as King Lear, and we smile, thinking how absurd the production must have been. If we are more thoughtful, we say, with the English novelist L. P. Hartley, "The past is a foreign country: they do things differently there." But if the eighteenth-century staging is a foreign country, what of the plays of the late sixteenth and seventeenth centuries? A foreign language, a foreign theater, a foreign audience.

Probably all viewers of Shakespeare's plays, beginning with Shakespeare himself, at times have been unhappy with the plays on the stage. Consider three comments about production that we find in the plays themselves, which suggest Shakespeare's concerns. The Chorus in *Henry V* complains that the heroic story cannot possibly be adequately staged:

> But pardon, gentles all,
> The flat unraisèd spirits that hath dared
> On this unworthy scaffold to bring forth
> So great an object. Can this cockpit hold
> The vasty fields of France? Or may we cram
> Within this wooden *O* the very casques
> That did affright the air at Agincourt?
> . . . .
> Piece out our imperfections with your thoughts.
>
> (Prologue 1.8–14,23)

Second, here are a few sentences (which may or may not represent Shakespeare's own views) from Hamlet's longish lecture to the players:

> Speak the speech, I pray you, as I pronounced it to you, trippingly on the tongue. But if you mouth it, as many of our players do, I had as lief the town crier spoke my lines. . . . O, it offends me to the soul to hear a robustious periwig-pated fellow tear a passion to tatters, to very rags, to split the ears of the groundlings. . . . And let those that play your clowns speak no more than is set down for them, for there be of them that will themselves laugh, to set on some quantity of barren spectators to laugh too, though in the meantime some necessary question of the play be then to be considered. That's villainous and shows a most pitiful ambition in the fool that uses it. (3.2.1–47)

Finally, we can quote again from the passage cited earlier in this introduction, concerning the boy actors who played the female roles. Cleopatra imagines with horror a theatrical version of her activities with Antony:

> The quick comedians
> Extemporally will stage us, and present
> Our Alexandrian revels: Antony
> Shall be brought drunken forth, and I shall see
> Some squeaking Cleopatra boy my greatness
> I' th' posture of a whore.   (5.2.216–21)

It is impossible to know how much weight to put on such passages—perhaps Shakespeare was just being modest about his theater's abilities—but it is easy enough to think that he was unhappy with some aspects of Elizabethan production. Probably no production can fully satisfy a playwright, and for that matter, few productions can fully satisfy *us;* we regret this or that cut, this or that way of costuming the play, this or that bit of business.

One's first thought may be this: Why don't they just do "authentic" Shakespeare, "straight" Shakespeare, the play as Shakespeare wrote it? But as we read the plays—words written to be performed—it sometimes becomes clear that we do not know *how* to perform them. For instance, in *Antony and Cleopatra* Antony, the Roman general who has succumbed to Cleopatra and to Egyptian ways, says, "The nobleness of life / Is to do thus" (1.1.36–37). But what is "thus"? Does Antony at this point embrace Cleopatra? Does he embrace and kiss her? (There are, by the way, very few scenes of kissing on Shakespeare's stage, possibly because boys played the female roles.) Or does he make a sweeping gesture, indicating the Egyptian way of life?

This is not an isolated example; the plays are filled with lines that call for gestures, but we are not sure what the gestures should be. *Interpretation* is inevitable. Consider a passage in *Hamlet.* In 3.1, Polonius persuades his daughter, Ophelia, to talk to Hamlet while Polonius and Claudius eavesdrop. The two men conceal themselves, and Hamlet encounters Ophelia. At 3.1.131 Hamlet suddenly says to her, "Where's your father?" Why does Hamlet, apparently out of nowhere—they have not been talking about Polonius—ask this question? Is this an example of the "antic disposition" (fantastic behavior) that Hamlet earlier (1.5.172) had told Horatio and others—including us—he would display? That is, is the question about the whereabouts of her father a seemingly irrational one, like his earlier question (3.1.103) to Ophelia, "Ha, ha! Are you honest?" Or, on the other hand, has Hamlet (as in many productions) suddenly glimpsed Polonius's foot protruding from beneath a drapery at the rear? That is, does Hamlet ask the question because he has suddenly seen something suspicious and now is testing Ophelia? (By the way, in productions that do give Hamlet a physical cue, it is almost always Polonius rather than Claudius who provides the clue. This itself is an act of interpretation on the part of the director.) Or (a third possibility) does Hamlet get a clue from Ophelia, who inadvertently betrays the spies by nervously glancing at their place of hiding? This is the interpretation used in the BBC television version, where Ophelia glances in fear toward the hiding place just after Hamlet says "Why wouldst thou be a breeder of sinners?" (121–22). Hamlet, realizing that he is being observed, glances here and there *before* he asks "Where's your father?" The question thus is a climax to what he has been doing while speaking the preceding lines. Or (a fourth interpretation) does Hamlet suddenly, without the aid of any clue whatsoever, intuitively (insightfully, mysteriously, wonderfully) sense that someone is spying? Directors must decide, of course—and so must readers.

Recall, too, the preceding discussion of the texts of the plays, which argued that the texts—though they seem to be before us in permanent black on white—are unstable. The Signet text of *Hamlet*, which draws on the Second Quarto (1604) and the First Folio (1623) is considerably longer than any version staged in Shakespeare's time. Our version, even if spoken very briskly and played without any intermission, would take close to four hours, far beyond "the two hours' traffic of our stage" mentioned in the Prologue to *Romeo and Juliet*. (There are a few contemporary references to the duration of a play, but none mentions more than three hours.) Of Shakespeare's plays, only *The Comedy of Errors*, *Macbeth*, and *The Tempest* can be done in less than three hours without cutting. And even if we take a play that exists only in a short text, *Macbeth*, we cannot claim that we are experiencing the very play that Shakespeare conceived, partly because some of the Witches' songs almost surely are non-Shakespearean additions, and partly because we are not willing to watch the play performed without an intermission and with boys in the female roles.

Further, as the earlier discussion of costumes mentioned, the plays apparently were given chiefly in contemporary, that is, in Elizabethan dress. If today we give them in the costumes that Shakespeare probably saw, the plays seem not contemporary but curiously dated. Yet if we use our own dress, we find lines of dialogue that are at odds with what we see; we may feel that the language, so clearly not our own, is inappropriate coming out of people in today's dress. A common solution, incidentally, has been to set the plays in the nineteenth century, on the grounds that this attractively distances the plays (gives them a degree of foreignness, allowing for interesting costumes) and yet doesn't put them into a museum world of Elizabethan England.

Inevitably our productions are adaptations, *our* adaptations, and inevitably they will look dated, not in a century but in twenty years, or perhaps even in a decade. Still, we cannot escape from our own conceptions. As the director Peter Brook has said, in *The Empty Space* (1968):

> It is not only the hair-styles, costumes and make-ups that look dated. All the different elements of staging—the shorthands of behavior that stand for emotions; gestures, gesticulations and tones of voice—are all fluctuating on an invisible stock exchange all the time. . . . A living theatre that thinks it can stand aloof from anything as trivial as fashion will wilt. (p. 16)

As Brook indicates, it is through today's hairstyles, costumes, makeup, gestures, gesticulations, tones of voice—this includes our *conception* of earlier hairstyles, costumes, and so forth if we stage the play in a period other than our own—that we inevitably stage the plays.

It is a truism that every age invents its own Shakespeare, just as, for instance, every age has invented its own classical world. Our view of ancient Greece, a slave-holding society in which even free Athenian women were severely circum-scribed, does not much resemble the Victorians' view of ancient Greece as a glorious democracy, just as, perhaps, our view of Victorianism itself does not much resemble theirs. We cannot claim that the Shakespeare on our stage is the true Shakespeare, but in our stage productions we find a Shakespeare that speaks to us, a Shakespeare that our ances-tors doubtless did not know but one that seems to us to be the true Shakespeare—at least for a while.

Our age is remarkable for the wide variety of kinds of staging that it uses for Shakespeare, but one development deserves special mention. This is the now common practice of race-blind or color-blind or nontraditional casting, which allows persons who are not white to play in Shakespeare. Previously blacks performing in Shakespeare were limited to a mere three roles, Othello, Aaron (in *Titus Andronicus*), and the Prince of Morocco (in *The Merchant of Venice*), and there were no roles at all for Asians. Indeed, African-Americans rarely could play even one of these three roles, since they were not welcome in white companies. Ira Aldridge (c.1806–1867), a black actor of undoubted talent, was forced to make his living by performing Shakespeare in England and in Europe, where he could play not only Othello but also—in whiteface—other tragic roles such as King Lear. Paul Robeson (1898–1976) made theatrical his-tory when he played Othello in London in 1930, and there was some talk about bringing the production to the United States, but there was more talk about whether American audiences would tolerate the sight of a black man—a real black man, not a white man in blackface—kissing and then killing a white woman. The idea was tried out in summer stock in 1942, the reviews were enthusiastic, and in the fol-lowing year Robeson opened on Broadway in a production that ran an astounding 296 performances. An occasional all-black company sometimes performed Shakespeare's plays, but otherwise blacks (and other minority members) were in effect shut out from performing Shakespeare. Only since about 1970 has it been common for nonwhites to play major roles along with whites. Thus, in a 1996–97 production of *Antony and Cleopatra*, a white Cleopatra, Vanessa Red-grave, played opposite a black Antony, David Harewood.

Multiracial casting is now especially common at the New York Shakespeare Festival, founded in 1954 by Joseph Papp, and in England, where even siblings such as Claudio and Isabella in *Measure for Measure* or Lear's three daughters may be of different races. Probably most viewers today soon stop worrying about the lack of realism, and move beyond the color of the performers' skin to the quality of the performance.

Nontraditional casting is not only a matter of color or race; it includes sex. In the past, occasionally a distinguished woman of the theater has taken on a male role—Sarah Bernhardt (1844–1923) as Hamlet is perhaps the most famous example—but such performances were widely regarded as eccentric. Although today there have been some performances involving cross-dressing (a drag *As You Like It* staged by the National Theatre in England in 1966 and in the United States in 1974 has achieved considerable fame in the annals of stage history), what is more interesting is the casting of women in roles that traditionally are male but that need not be. Thus, a 1993–94 English production of *Henry V* used a woman—*not* cross-dressed—in the role of the governor of Harfleur. According to Peter Holland, who reviewed the production in *Shakespeare Survey* 48 (1995), "having a female Governor of Harfleur feminized the city and provided a direct response to the horrendous threat of rape and murder that Henry had offered, his language and her body in direct connection and opposition" (p. 210). Ten years from now the device may not play so effectively, but today it speaks to us. Shakespeare, born in the Elizabethan Age, has been dead nearly four hundred years, yet he is, as Ben Jonson said, "not of an age but for all time." We must understand, however, that he is "for all time" precisely because each age finds in his abundance something for itself and something of itself.

And here we come back to two issues discussed earlier in this introduction—the instability of the text and, curiously, the Bacon/Oxford heresy concerning the authorship of the plays. *Of course* Shakespeare wrote the plays, and we should daily fall on our knees to thank him for them—and yet there is something to the idea that he is not their only author. Every editor, every director and actor, and every reader to some degree shapes them, too, for when we edit, direct, act, or read, we inevitably become Shakespeare's collaborator and re-create the plays. The plays, one might say, are so cunningly contrived that they guide our responses, tell us how we ought to feel, and make a mark on us, but (for better or for worse) we also make a mark on them.

—SYLVAN BARNET
Tufts University

Introduction

Measure for Measure was first published in 1623 in the Folio of Shakespeare's work. It was probably written in 1604, for it is on record that a play called *Mesure for Mesure*, by "Shaxberd," was performed before King James I on 26 December of that year, when it was presumably a new play. It was thus composed just before the writing of the great tragedies in which Shakespeare's powers were at their height. It does not seem to have been performed again till 1662, and in fact, till recently, it was not popular on the stage in spite of its theatrical craftsmanship.

It was not popular with the older critics, either. Coleridge, to whom we owe some of our most penetrating Shakespeare criticism, found it "a hateful work," indeed "the only painful play" that Shakespeare ever wrote. Its comedy disgusted him and its tragedy seemed merely horrible. His sense of justice was also revolted by the pardon of Angelo, the corrupt deputy who is virtually guilty of both rape and murder. The heroine, Isabella, was to Coleridge an unamiable character who primly preferred her own chastity to her brother's life. That brother himself, Claudio, was a weak, vacillating youth who expected his sister to save him from the consequences of his own immorality. The play slithered through to an unearned happy ending which was entirely unconvincing. In general, the opinion of the nineteenth century was that *Measure for Measure* was essentially a dark comedy, full of bitter satire and cynicism, reflecting some obscure phase of tragedy or disillusionment in the personal life of Shakespeare himself.

In the first quarter of this century, a far different view of the play was favored. The twin myths of Shakespeare's personal sorrows and of a general gloom during the early years

of the seventeenth century were discredited. It was argued
that the play should be read as a dramatic parable embodying
some of the noblest precepts of Christianity. This interpretation might have claimed a consistency of impression for
the play that was not quite warranted, but it had the merit of
not confusing art with life and of recognizing that there
is a strong non-naturalistic element in the play. Other critics felt that the play, though it had some superb moments,
changed course halfway through and that its form could
not accommodate the questions that it raised so compel-
lingly. As for its religious significance, such as it was, it
could be traced to Shakespeare's sources in drama and folklore. The Italian storybook that gave Shakespeare his plot
contains several tales on the theme of a woman forgiving
an enemy who has done her an irreparable wrong, and the
folklore of Shakespeare's day had popularized the legend
of the good monarch, who moves among his people in disguise in order to see things for himself and to protect the
good and punish the wicked. There is a third, more recent,
interpretation of the play, especially popular on the modern
stage. It prefers to see the play as a modern representation of
the hidden, explosive sources of desire in men and women,
of different, incompatible, and mutually incomprehensible
levels of social reality, the touch-and-go, hit-or-miss nature
of Establishment justice, the abundance of social energy at
the lower strata of society, and of the way money can inter-
fere with sex and marriage. The play is seen as an open-
ended problem play that raises more questions than it
answers and permits divergent interpretations of more or
less equal validity. Ambiguity is the very essence of the
play's meaning.

  To help us toward a plausible interpretation of the play,
we may briefly look at its sources, and what Shakespeare
made of them. The chief one is almost certainly George
Whetstone's *Promos and Cassandra* (1578), a tedious,
though earnest, play in two parts of five acts each. Whetstone made a prose version of the story for his collection of
stories called the *Heptameron of Civil Discourses* (1582). In
addition to these works, Shakespeare very probably knew
the Italian source of Whetstone, the *Hecatommithi* (1565) of
Giraldi Cinthio, and Cinthio's dramatized version of the

story, *Epitia* (1583). In Whetstone's play, Cassandra pleads with Promos for the life of her brother, Andrugio, who has been condemned to death for fornication. Promos agrees to pardon Andrugio if Cassandra will lie with him. She refuses, but ultimately consents when her brother appeals to her sisterly affection. After she has kept her side of the bargain, Promos goes back on his word, and commands the jailer to behead Andrugio and present the head to Cassandra. The compassionate jailer happens to know the truth and conceals Andrugio, presenting Cassandra with the head of a recently executed felon. Cassandra wants to commit suicide, but decides to appeal to the King first and to seek vengeance on Promos. The King finds that the complaint is true and orders that Promos should marry her and then be put to death. But as soon as the marriage is solemnized, Cassandra finds herself "tied in the greatest bonds of affection to her husband." She now becomes "an earnest suitor for his life" with the King, but in vain. In the meanwhile, her brother, who has been living under a disguise, comes to know of her predicament and reveals himself to the King. Promos is pardoned, and everything ends happily.

When Shakespeare took up this tale for dramatic treatment, he made certain far-reaching changes. In the first place, Cassandra's compelled acceptance of the loathsome and virtually illusory choice thrust on her by Promos hurts the moral feelings of the reader beyond healing, and her last-minute marriage, by royal fiat, to the violator of her honor merely adds insult to injury. Even in Shakespeare's day, Puritan moralists, to specify a single group, held that there were wrongs which no marriage could redress. They demanded that sexual misdemeanor should be severely punished, even with death. The sudden change of Cassandra's affections from hatred to love as soon as she is married to Promos is also rather incredible. Very properly, therefore, Shakespeare made his heroine refuse to yield to Angelo. But since the story required that Angelo's condition should somehow be met, he created the character of Mariana and substituted her for Isabella by means of an old folktale device (found even in the Old Testament), which was presumably acceptable to the original audience. He had already used "the bed trick," as it is usually called, in what may be

an earlier play, *All's Well That Ends Well.* The "bed trick"
does not commend itself to modern taste, and does not also
quite agree with the realistic context of the play, but we must
remember that Mariana is deeply in love with Angelo, and
the consummation of her love leads to her marriage with him
at the end. Our sympathies are so fully engaged in her behalf
that we want her to be happy, and wink at this otherwise
dubious mode of securing her happiness.

Shakespeare also altered the significance of the brother's
offense. In Whetstone's play, Andrugio is guilty of fornication; committed, as in Shakespeare's play, with the volun-
tary consent of the girl. Cassandra attributes her brother's
offense partly to the irresistible force of love and partly to
his youth. In *Measure for Measure*, however, Claudio explains the reason for his arrest differently:

> From too much liberty, my Lucio, liberty.
> As surfeit is the father of much fast,
> So every scope by the immoderate use
> Turns to restraint. Our natures do pursue,
> Like rats that ravin down their proper bane,
> A thirsty evil, and when we drink, we die. (1.2.128–33)

In our very nature there is something that drives us into acts
of too much liberty, which we loathe even while we indulge
in them.

> For that which I do, I allow not: for what I would, that do I not;
> but what I hate, that do I. . . . For I know that in me (that is, in my
> flesh) dwelleth no good thing: for to will is present with me; but
> how to perform that which is good I find not. For the good that I
> would, I do not: but the evil which I would not, that I do. . . . I find
> then a law, that, when I would do good, evil is present with me.
> For I delight in the law of God after the inward man. But I see
> another law in my members, warring against the law of my mind
> and bringing me into captivity to the law of sin which is in my
> members.   (Romans 7:15, 18, 19, 21–23)

Claudio is angry and disgusted with himself. Juliet is con-
trite, but there is no self-disgust in her conversation with the

Duke-Friar. (Claudio is so disgusted with himself that he does not say anything to Juliet. In many stage productions they embrace each other in the last scene of the play.) But he does not know what to do with this problem. His friend Lucio, described in the original list of actors as a "fantastic," does not see that there is a problem. Lucio's view of the matter is reflected in the imagery of his speech when he describes Claudio's offense:

> Your brother and his lover have embraced;
> As those that feed grow full, as blossoming time
> That from the seedness the bare fallow brings
> To teeming foison, even so her plenteous womb
> Expresseth his full tilth and husbandry.   (1.4.40–44)

Juliet's "fertility" was realized by Claudio's "tilth." *Not* to do as Claudio did is to be guilty of a lack of "husbandry." There is enough truth in this view of human sex to make it superficially attractive, but we are put on our guard by being shown its consequences. (In Shakespeare's London, prostitution and sexually transmitted diseases were widespread problems. Many of the wealthier citizens had invested in brothels.) Lucio has seduced Mistress Kate Keepdown and has abandoned her and the child. (Incidentally, the child has been looked after by a bawd, a fact which should make us distrust theories of Shakespeare's cynicism in *Measure for Measure*. The Duke forces Lucio to marry Kate and make "an honest woman of her.") Lucio has degenerated into a coarse sensualist, bent on his own pleasures and reckless of all the essential obligations of a decent life in society. Even his interest in Claudio's pardon is not quite disinterested. "I pray she may"—that is, Isabella may persuade Angelo—he tells Claudio, "as well for the encouragement of the like, which else would stand under grievous imposition, as for the enjoying of thy life, who I would be sorry should be thus foolishly lost at a game of tick-tack" (1.2.191–95). There is of course a middle ground which may occasionally shift a little this way or that, depending upon the circumstances, between license and Puritan extremism.

Shakespeare enlarged the role of the overlord in the story

to make him a disguised spectator of and later an active participant in the action of the play. Duke Vincentio has been rather slack in his princely duties, loving his subjects not wisely but too well, but otherwise he is a scholar, a statesman, and a soldier. We are told further that his supreme concern has always been to know himself. When he contributes, in his indirect way, to the debate initiated by Claudio, he implies that self-restraint is both essential and possible. When he goes to the prison, disguised as a friar, to console "the afflicted spirits" (2.3.4) there, he requests the Provost to inform him of the nature of the crimes committed by the condemned prisoners so that he may "minister to them accordingly" (7–8). With Claudio the ministration (admittedly somewhat chilly) takes the form of setting him free from "the deceiving promises of life" (3.2.249) and of creating in him a calm resolution to face the approaching end. Sir Thomas More, the Tudor statesman and saint about whom Shakespeare perhaps helped to write a play, declares in his little treatise, *The Four Last Things*, which he wrote to teach "the art of dying well," that nothing can more effectively withdraw the human soul from the wretched affections of the body than a sincere remembrance of death. "The thirsty evil" (1.2.133) which Claudio bemoans is the consequence of an excessive attachment to life, itself the result of our forgetting our "glassy essence" (2.2.120). Some of the Duke's actions have been strongly criticized, but we must bear in mind the circumstances and the effect that they secure. For example, his concealment from Isabella that her brother is alive is certainly cruel, but it endows her denunciation of Angelo in the last act with a passionate sincerity that it might not have acquired otherwise.

Shakespeare made Isabella a novice of Saint Clare. Why he did so is not quite obvious, for his young women do not need any "motivation" to justify their preference for chastity. Chastity is an absolute value with them. Isabella's novitiate should perhaps be regarded as her answer to the problem of the "prompture of the blood" (2.4.178), of which she seems to have some personal knowledge if one may judge from the accents of her admission to Angelo that women, no less than men, are frail:

Ay, as the glasses where they view themselves,
Which are as easy broke as they make forms.
Women! Help heaven! Men their creation mar
In profiting by them. Nay, call us ten times frail;
For we are soft as our complexions are,
And credulous to false prints.   (125–30)

Her denunciation of her brother when he timidly suggests
that she should yield to Angelo no doubt grates on our
ears—Sir Arthur Quiller-Couch was moved to declare that
there was something rancid in her chastity—but her harshness reflects her bitterness at being asked to abet the "prompture of the blood." It is significant that the only conventual
rule that we hear of in the play relates to receiving male visitors, and that Isabella should desire a stricter restraint upon
the votarists of Saint Clare, though that order has the reputation of being the strictest women's order of the Roman
Catholic Church. She has been criticized for agreeing too
readily to the bed trick, but she does so partly for the sake of
Mariana. At the end of the play, the Duke makes her a proposal which, he says, "much imports your good" (5.1.538),
surely not a material good, for she is not presented as a girl
with whom such frivolous considerations would weigh. Presumably she accepts the Duke's proposal; in Shakespeare's
day, it was perfectly in order for a novice to go back to secular life. Though the play itself is ambiguous on the point, it
is attractive to believe that Isabella made the discovery that
the "prompture of the blood" could be resolved in the married state also. The lack of any previous courtship between
the Duke and Isabella has troubled some commentators and
inspired some ingenious stage business, but perhaps more to
the point is the appropriateness of the match indicated by the
Duke's proposal, given the state of Vienna and the roles and
characters of the Duke and Isabella.

Halfway through the play, Isabella meets Mariana. Mariana plays a small but significant part in the design of the
drama. In spite of Angelo's "unjust unkindness" (3.1.244),
which should "in all reason" (245) have quenched her love
for him, she continues to cherish him. But she will not substitute herself for Isabella until "the friar," whose advice has
often stilled her "brawling discontent" (4.1.9), assures her

that it is no sin. In the last act she pleads that her husband's evil is a passing cloud which will leave him purer than before. Her love is dedicated entirely to the welfare of the beloved's soul, and we may describe it, without undue exaggeration, as a humble human instance of the divine love which found out the remedy when all the souls that were, were forfeit. Mariana's love has transcended the problem of the "prompture of the blood." We know that Isabella is deeply moved by the story of Mariana's love, and it is her appeal that Angelo's very evil may be the cause of his regeneration, which in the end wins Isabella over to plead for him. Perhaps Isabella learned the secret of a soul-centered love from Mariana.

Between Isabella and Angelo there is a curious superficial resemblance. Angelo has lived in retirement, and evidently prefers it to the public office which he is summoned to. He has tried to "blunt his natural edge" with "profits of the mind, study and fast" (1.4.60–61). A due sincerity governs his deeds till he looks on Isabella. But the "prompture of the blood" finally overcomes him. Isabella's very virtue corrupts him, while the strumpet with all her double vigor, art and nature, could never once stir him. He has identified virtue wholly with a mode of external conduct. His seemingly virtuous conduct does not represent a transformed will, but is a mere factitious creation, a state whereon he has studied, not a habit of the soul. He himself points out that the problem of "we would" and "we would not" (4.4.36) arises when we forget our "grace," a word which may well have a specific Christian sense in view of Isabella's charge that he is not "new made" (2.2.78). It is characteristic of him that he should mistake Mariana's love for levity. His ear, coarsened by the strident jazz of a code that is throttling the instincts, cannot catch the quiet melody of an ethic that observes the very rhythm of the blood. So "the natural guiltiness" (139) lurks within, subverting virtue itself to cause his fall. "Sin, taking occasion by the commandment, deceived me, and by it slew me" (Romans 7:11). The sentence of death that the Duke passes on him frees Angelo from an intolerable, meaningless existence, and he welcomes it. He is a new-made man after he is pardoned. To detest him and to disagree with his pardon is natural, for the process of his contrition is rather hurried, but we must try to understand his predicament.

Angelo's ignorance of the inwardness of virtue is also the cause of the excessive legalism of his rule. (Juliet is "the fornicatress," and she must not be provided with any unnecessary comforts.) At bottom, the criticism of the rule of law as Angelo interprets it is that it is ultimately futile. Its severity is aimless, and its achievements are transitory. It only fills up the prison and provides full employment to Abhorson. "There is so great a fever on goodness, that the dissolution of it must cure it" (3.2.225–26), says the disguised Duke to Escalus. The time has come when nothing but a total dissolution of the fever that afflicts goodness can restore it to its pristine health. The laws are no doubt "the needful bits and curbs to headstrong weeds" (1.3.20), but they can at best regulate conduct; they cannot change the "old man" in us. And as long as that change does not take place, sensuality will prevail in Vienna, openly or covertly. In Vincentio's city immorality has become so rampant that syphilis (no antibiotics then!) has become a matter for jokes.

The wise old Escalus, the most genial character in the play, tries to deal with the problem in his gentle, humanitarian way, but even he is shocked when he discovers that Mistress Overdone is still forfeit in the same kind after double and treble admonition. Pompey refuses to change at all. He is an unashamed rascal who puts the law in place with his remark that his pimping would be legal if the law, which is contrary to human nature, is changed. (Shakespeare has a gift for making his rascals likable even while we reject them on moral grounds.) The Duke himself, as it happens, intervenes to save Claudio's life precisely at the moment when Claudio sues to be rid of it; that is, when Claudio is cured of his malady. In dealing with Barnardine again, the Duke reveals his essentially spiritual approach to the problem of law and justice. Barnardine is a murderer and has a stubborn soul that apprehends no further than this life, and he has squared his life accordingly. When the Duke pardons all his earthly faults, he entrusts him to a friar for advice. Barnardine is so full of a coarse animal vitality that it is difficult to imagine his being put to death.

With Angelo, however, he decides on "measure for measure." "Judge not, that ye be not judged. For with what judgment ye judge, ye shall be judged: and with what measure ye mete, it shall be measured to you again" (Matthew 7:1–2). He also reminds Isabella that her brother's ghost cries out for vengeance. In condemning Angelo, the Duke thus seems to observe the law of the Old Testament—an eye for an eye and a tooth for a tooth. But actually he is testing Isabella's adherence to the New Law, which commands that one's enemy shall be loved as a friend, and that good shall be returned for evil. How superbly she answers the test! She does not plead for Angelo's pardon, for she has seen that Mariana's plea for mercy has been disallowed. With a boldness that takes away one's breath, she asserts that Angelo is not guilty at all. There are three charges against him. His "salt imagination" (5.1.404) wronged her honor; he violated sacred chastity; and he broke his promise that he would pardon Claudio if the foul ransom were paid. The first charge, the Duke himself has recommended should be pardoned because that "salt imagination" provided the opportunity of doing a service to Mariana. The second charge is not true because Mariana was Angelo's wife on a precontract. As for the "promise-breach" (408), it cannot be denied that Isabella did not in fact lie with Angelo or that her brother was guilty, after all, of the crime for which he was sentenced. The type of betrothal that Claudio and Juliet had entered upon did not in law give them any marital rights, whereas Mariana's contract with Angelo did, at least in law. The ducal friar may be faulted for promoting the bed trick, but he was facing a desperate situation that demanded an immediate and unorthodox way out. To borrow his own words, the doubleness of the benefit may be allowed to defend the deceit from reproof. Finally, it is true that Angelo intended to violate her, but the intention never became an act and law cannot take cognizance of thoughts. "Thoughts are no subjects, / Intents but merely thoughts" (456–57). Counsel for the defense submits therefore that the accused is not guilty on any count, does not need a pardon, and much less can be punished with "Measure still for Measure" (414). The prosperous art that she shows in playing with reason and discourse could hardly be stretched further.

Ye have heard that it hath been said, Thou shalt love thy neighbor, and hate thine enemy. But I say unto you, Love your enemies, bless them that curse you, do good to them that hurt you, and pray for them which despitefully use you and persecute you. That ye may be the children of your Father which is in heaven: for he maketh his sun to rise on the evil and on the good, and sendeth rain on the just and on the unjust. . . . Be ye therefore perfect, even as your Father which is in heaven is perfect. (Matthew 5:43–45, 48)

Such then are some of the themes and characters of the play before us. Shakespeare's contemporaries would have probably called it a tragicomedy, a form that was not unknown in earlier English drama and whose poetics was being discussed in Shakespeare's days. Tragicomedy is not a loose putting together of tragedy with comedy, but an independent form of dramatic composition with an aesthetic of its own. As the Italian playwright Giambattista Guarini, who had himself written a tragicomedy, set forth in his *Compendium of Tragicomic Poetry* (published in 1601): "He who makes a tragicomedy does not intend to compose separately either a tragedy or a comedy, but from the two a third thing that will be perfect of its kind, and may take from the others the parts that with most verisimilitude can stand together." From tragedy, said Guarini, tragicomedy takes the movement but not the disturbance of the feelings, the pleasure and not the sadness, the danger but not the death. From comedy, it takes laughter that is not excessive, modest amusement, feigned difficulty, happy reversal, and above all, the comic order. Speaking of the style proper to tragicomedy, Guarini said that the magnificent was its norm, combined not with the grave as in a tragedy, but with the polished. There is something in this description of tragicomedy that reminds us of *Measure for Measure*. For instance, our awareness of the immanence of the Duke, with his declared objective of testing whether power will change purpose effectively, prevents the first part of the play from the tragic course. The "intrigue" of the fourth act does not exist for its own sake, but serves to establish the control of the Duke over the action and to lead to a happy conclusion. The episode of Barnardine makes clear that the resolution to face death which "the friar" has preached to Claudio is far from the insensibility and desperateness of Barnardine, who will not "wake." The style of the play ranges from the passionate conjurations of Isabella, the tortured self-examinations of Angelo, the exploratory dialectic of Angelo and Isabella, the meditative analysis of the Duke and the surging thrill of terror in Claudio as he stands at the brink of the grave to the irreverent bawdry of Lucio and the petty cunning of Pompey's coiled speech with Escalus. The riotous gaiety of the subplot sets off the high seriousness of the main plot. Coleridge was obliged to acknowledge that *Measure for Measure* was Shakespearean throughout. It is indeed one of Shakespeare's most impressive achievements whether we consider the seriousness of the issues it deals with, its characterization, or its construction.

—S. NAGARAJAN
University of Hyderabad

Measure for Measure

Vincentio,°1 the Duke
Angelo, the Deputy
Escalus, an ancient Lord
Claudio, a young gentleman
Lucio,° a fantastic
Two Other Like Gentlemen
Provost°

Thomas } two friars
Peter

[A Justice]
[Varrius]
Elbow, a simple constable
Froth, a foolish gentleman
Clown [Pompey, servant to Mistress Overdone]
Abhorson, an executioner
Barnardine, a dissolute prisoner
Isabella, sister to Claudio
Mariana, betrothed to Angelo
Juliet, beloved of Claudio
Francisca, a nun
Mistress Overdone,° a bawd
[Lords, Officers, Citizens, Boy, and Attendants]

Scene: Vienna]

¹The degree sign° indicates a footnote, which is keyed to the text by line number. Text references are printed in **boldface** type, the annotation follows in roman type

°**Vincentio** The name occurs only here
°**Lucio** (Italian, "light")
°**Provost** (Officer charged with the apprehension and custody of offenders)
°**Overdone** (**do** sometimes meant "copulate with," hence, "a worn-out whore")

Measure for Measure

ACT 1

Scene 1. [*The Duke's palace.*]

Enter Duke, Escalus, Lords, [and Attendants].

Duke. Escalus.

Escalus. My lord.

Duke. Of government the properties°1 to unfold,
  Would seem in me t' affect° speech and discourse,°
  Since I am put to know° that your own science°   *5*
  Exceeds, in that, the lists° of all advice
  My strength can give you. Then no more remains
  But that, to your sufficiency as your worth is able,°
  And let them work. The nature of our people,
  Our city's institutions,° and the terms°   *10*
  For common justice, y'are as pregnant in°
  As art and practice hath enrichèd any
  That we remember. There is our commission,
  From which we would not have you warp.° Call
    hither,

1.1.3 **properties** characteristics 4 **affect** be fond of 4 **discourse** talk
5 **put to know** given to understand 5 **science** knowledge 6 **lists**
limits 8 **to your sufficiency ... able** (perhaps a line is missing after
this line; the general sense is: use your natural ability and your authority
according to your discretion) 10 **institutions** established laws and cus-
toms 10 **terms** conditions for the administration of justice 11 **pregnant in** full of knowledge 14 **warp** deviate

15   I say, bid come before us Angelo.
                                    [*Exit an Attendant.*]
      What figure° of us, think you, he will bear?°
      For you must know, we have with special soul°
      Elected him our absence to supply;
      Lent him our terror, dressed him with our love,
20   And given his deputation all the organs°
      Of our own pow'r. What think you of it?

Escalus. If any in Vienna be of worth
      To undergo° such ample grace and honor,
      It is Lord Angelo.

                    Enter Angelo.

Duke.   Look where he comes.

25 *Angelo.* Always obedient to your Grace's will,
      I come to know your pleasure.

Duke.   Angelo,
      There is a kind of character° in thy life,
      That to th' observer doth thy history
      Fully unfold. Thyself and thy belongings°
30   Are not thine own so proper° as to waste
      Thyself upon thy virtues, they on thee.
      Heaven doth with us as we with torches do.°
      Not light them for themselves; for if our virtues
      Did not go forth of us, 'twere all alike
      As if we had them not. Spirits are not finely
35   touched
      But to fine issues,° nor Nature never lends
      The smallest scruple° of her excellence
      But like a thrifty goddess she determines

---

16 **figure** image 16 **bear** represent 17 **soul** thought 20 **organs**
means of action 23 **undergo** enjoy 27 **character** secret handwriting 29 **belongings** endowments 30 **proper** exclusively 32 **Heav-
en ... do** (see Luke 11:33: "No man, when he hath lighted a candle,
putteth it in a secret place, neither under a bushel, but on a candlestick that they which come in may see the light." Also Matthew 7:16:
"Ye shall know them by their fruits") 35–36 **Spirits ... issues** i.e.,
great qualities are bestowed only so that they may lead to great
achievements 37 **scruple** 1/24 oz.

Herself the glory of a creditor,
Both thanks and use.° But I do bend° my speech   40
To one that can my part in him advertise.°
Hold therefore, Angelo:
In our remove° be thou at full ourself;
Mortality and mercy in Vienna
Live in thy tongue and heart. Old Escalus,   45
Though first in question,° is thy secondary.°
Take thy commission.

Angelo.   Now, good my lord,
Let there be some more test made of my mettle°
Before so noble and so great a figure
Be stamped upon it.

Duke.   No more evasion.   50
We have with a leavened° and preparèd choice
Proceeded to you; therefore take your honors.
Our haste from hence is of so quick condition
That it prefers itself,° and leaves unquestioned°
Matters of needful value. We shall write to you,   55
As time and our concernings shall importune,
How it goes with us, and do look to know
What doth befall you here. So fare you well.
To th' hopeful execution do I leave you
Of your commissions.

Angelo.   Yet give leave, my lord,   60
That we may bring° you something on the way.

Duke. My haste may not admit it;
Nor need you, on mine honor, have to do
With any scruple; your scope is as mine own,
So to enforce or qualify the laws   65
As to your soul seems good. Give me your hand.
I'll privily away; I love the people,
But do not like to stage me to their eyes.
Though it do well, I do not relish well

40 **use** interest   40 **bend** address   41 **advertise** display prominently
43 **remove** absence   46 **question** consideration   46 **secondary** sub-
ordinate   48 **mettle** (pun on "metal," i.e., material)   51 **leavened**
i.e., long-pondered   54 **prefers itself** takes precedence   54 **unques-
tioned** unexamined   61 **bring** escort

70 │ Their loud applause and aves° vehement.
    │ Nor do I think the man of safe discretion
    └ That does affect it. Once more, fare you well.

Angelo. The heavens give safety to your purposes.

Escalus. Lead forth and bring you back in happiness.

75 *Duke.* I thank you; fare you well.   *Exit.*

Escalus. I shall desire you, sir, to give me leave
      To have free speech with you; and it concerns me
      To look into the bottom of my place.°
      A pow'r I have, but of what strength and nature,
80   I am not yet instructed.

Angelo. 'Tis so with me. Let us withdraw together,
      And we may soon our satisfaction have
      Touching that point.

Escalus.   I'll wait upon your honor.
                                          Exeunt.

Scene 2. [*A street.*]

Enter Lucio and two other Gentlemen.

Lucio. If the Duke, with the other dukes, come not
      to composition° with the King of Hungary,° why
      then all the dukes fall upon the King.

First Gentleman. Heaven grant us its peace, but not
5   the King of Hungary's!

Second Gentleman. Amen.

Lucio. Thou conclud'st like the sanctimonious pirate,
      that went to sea with the Ten Commandments, but
      scraped one out of the table.

---

70 **aves** salutations   78 **To look ... place** i.e., to examine carefully
the range of my authority   1.2.2 **composition** agreement   2 **Hungary**
(perhaps a pun on "hungry")

Second Gentleman. "Thou shalt not steal"?   ₁₀

Lucio. Ay, that he razed.

First Gentleman. Why, 'twas a commandment to command the captain and all the rest from their functions: they put forth to steal. There's not a soldier of us all that, in the thanksgiving before meat,° do   15 relish the petition well that prays for peace.

Second Gentleman. I never heard any soldier dislike it.

Lucio. I believe thee, for I think thou never wast where grace was said.   20

Second Gentleman. No? A dozen times at least.

First Gentleman. What, in meter?

Lucio. In any proportion,° or in any language.

First Gentleman. I think, or in any religion.

Lucio. Ay, why not? Grace is grace, despite of all   25 controversy: as, for example, thou thyself art a wicked villain, despite of all grace.

First Gentleman. Well, there went but a pair of shears between us.°

Lucio. I grant; as there may between the lists° and   30 the velvet. Thou art the list.

First Gentleman. And thou the velvet. Thou art good velvet; thou'rt a three-piled° piece, I warrant thee. I had as lief be a list of an English kersey,° as be piled, as thou art piled, for a French velvet.° Do   35 I speak feelingly° now?

Lucio. I think thou dost; and, indeed, with most pain-

15 **meat** food in general   23 **proportion** length   28–29 **there . . . us** i.e., we are cut from the same cloth   30 **lists** selvage or border of a cloth (usually of a different material from the body)   33 **three-piled** (1) pile of a treble thickness (2) "piled" (bald) as a result of venereal disease   34 **kersey** coarse cloth (therefore "plain and honest")   35 **French velvet** (1) excellent velvet (2) French prostitute (syphilis was also known as "the French disease")   35–36 **Do . . . feelingly** i.e., do I touch you there?

ful feeling° of thy speech. I will, out of thine own
confession, learn to begin thy health; but, whilst I
40 live, forget to drink after thee.°

First Gentleman. I think I have done myself wrong,
have I not?

Second Gentleman. Yes, that thou hast, whether thou
art tainted or free.

Enter Bawd [Mistress Overdone].

45 *Lucio.* Behold, behold, where Madam Mitigation
comes! I have purchased as many diseases under
her roof as come to—

Second Gentleman. To what, I pray?

Lucio. Judge.

50 *Second Gentleman.* To three thousand dolors° a year.

First Gentleman. Ay, and more.

Lucio. A French crown° more.

First Gentleman. Thou art always figuring diseases in
me, but thou art full of error. I am sound.

55 *Lucio.* Nay, not as one would say, healthy, but so
sound as things that are hollow. Thy bones are
hollow; impiety° has made a feast of thee.

First Gentleman. How now! Which of your hips has
the most profound sciatica?

60 *Mistress Overdone.* Well, well; there's one yonder arrested and carried to prison was worth five thousand of you all.

Second Gentleman. Who's that, I pray thee?

Mistress Overdone. Marry,° sir, that's Claudio,
65 Signior Claudio.

38 **feeling** personal experience   39–40 **learn … thee** drink to your
health but not after you from the same cup (to avoid the infection)   50 **dolors** "sorrows" with a pun on "dollars," the English name
for the German thaler and the Spanish peso of eight reals   52 **French
crown** (1) *écu* (2) head that has gone bald from venereal disease   57 **im-
piety** immorality   64 **Marry** (a light oath, from "by the Virgin Mary")

First Gentleman. Claudio to prison? 'Tis not so.

Mistress Overdone. Nay, but I know 'tis so. I saw
him arrested; saw him carried away, and which
is more, within these three days his head to be
chopped off.   70

Lucio. But, after all this fooling, I would not have it
so. Art thou sure of this?

Mistress Overdone. I am too sure of it; and it is for
getting Madam Julietta with child.

Lucio. Believe me, this may be. He promised to meet   75
me two hours since, and he was ever precise in
promise-keeping.

Second Gentleman. Besides, you know, it draws
something near to the speech we had to such a
purpose.   80

First Gentleman. But, most of all, agreeing with the
proclamation.

Lucio. Away! Let's go learn the truth of it.
                          Exit [Lucio with Gentlemen].

Mistress Overdone. Thus, what with the war, what
with the sweat,° what with the gallows, and what   85
with poverty, I am custom-shrunk.

                   Enter Clown [Pompey].

How now? What's the news with you?

Pompey. Yonder man is carried to prison.

Mistress Overdone. Well; what has he done?

Pompey. A woman.   90

Mistress Overdone. But what's his offense?

Pompey. Groping for trouts in a peculiar° river.

Mistress Overdone. What? Is there a maid with child
by him?

85 **sweat** sweating sickness, plague   92 **peculiar** private

95   *Pompey.* No, but there's a woman with maid by him.
     You have not heard of the proclamation, have you?

Mistress Overdone. What proclamation, man?

Pompey. All houses° in the suburbs° of Vienna must
     be plucked down.

100 *Mistress Overdone.* And what shall become of those
     in the city?

Pompey. They shall stand for seed:° they had gone
     down too, but that a wise burgher put in° for them.

Mistress Overdone. But shall all our houses of resort
105 in the suburbs be pulled down?

Pompey. To the ground, mistress.

Mistress Overdone. Why, here's a change indeed in
     the commonwealth! What shall become of me?

Pompey. Come, fear not you; good counselors lack
110 no clients. Though you change your place, you
     need not change your trade; I'll be your tapster°
     still. Courage, there will be pity taken on you; you
     that have worn your eyes almost out in the service,
     you will be considered.

115 *Mistress Overdone.* What's to do here, Thomas
     Tapster? Let's withdraw.

Pompey. Here comes Signior Claudio, led by the
     provost to prison; and there's Madam Juliet.

                                        Exeunt.

          *Enter Provost, Claudio, Juliet, Officers, Lucio,
                    and two Gentlemen.*

Claudio. Fellow, why dost thou show me thus to th'
     world?
120 Bear me to prison, where I am committed.

Provost. I do it not in evil disposition,

98 **houses** (of prostitution)   98 **suburbs** (in Shakespeare's London, the
area of the brothels)   102 **stand for seed** be left standing for the continua-
tion of prostitution   103 **put in** intercede (in Shakespeare's London, many
burghers invested in brothels)   111 **tapster** bartender, waiter (here, pimp)

  But from Lord Angelo, by special charge.

Claudio. Thus can the demigod Authority
Make us pay down for our offense by weight.
The words of heaven: on whom it will, it will;   125
On whom it will not, so. Yet still 'tis just.°

Lucio. Why, how now, Claudio! Whence comes this
restraint?

Claudio. From too much liberty, my Lucio, liberty.
As surfeit is the father of much fast,
So every scope by the immoderate use   130
Turns to restraint. Our natures do pursue,
Like rats that ravin down their proper bane,°
A thirsty evil, and when we drink, we die.

Lucio. If I could speak so wisely under an arrest, I
would send for certain of my creditors. And yet, to 135
say the truth, I had as lief have the foppery° of
freedom as the mortality° of imprisonment. What's
thy offense, Claudio?

Claudio. What but to speak of would offend again.

Lucio. What, is't murder?   140

Claudio. No.

Lucio. Lechery?

Claudio. Call it so.

Provost. Away, sir, you must go.

Claudio. One word, good friend. Lucio, a word with
you.   145

Lucio. A hundred, if they'll do you any good.
Is lechery so looked after?

Claudio. Thus stands it with me: upon a true contract°

125–26 **The words ... just** (see Romans 9:15,18. "For he saith to
Moses, I will have mercy on whom I will have mercy, and I will
have compassion on whom I will have compassion.... Therefore
hath he mercy on whom he will have mercy, and whom he will he hard-
eneth")   132 **ravin ... bane** greedily devour what is poisonous to
them   136 **foppery** foolishness   137 **mortality** deadliness   148 **true
contract** (which would have led to a church marriage)

I got possession of Julietta's bed.
150 You know the lady, she is fast my wife,
Save that we do the denunciation° lack
Of outward order. This we came not to,
Only for propagation° of a dower
Remaining in the coffer of her friends.°
155 From whom we thought it meet to hide our love
Till time had made them for us.° But it chances
The stealth of our most mutual entertainment
With character too gross is writ on Juliet.

Lucio. With child, perhaps?

Claudio.   Unhappily, even so.
160 And the new deputy now for the Duke—
Whether it be the fault and glimpse of newness,°
Or whether that the body public be
A horse whereon the governor doth ride,
Who, newly in the seat, that it may know
165 He can command, lets it straight feel the spur;
Whether the tyranny be in his place,
Or in his eminence° that fills it up,
I stagger in°—but this new governor
Awakes me all the enrollèd° penalties
170 Which have, like unscoured armor, hung by th' wall
So long, that nineteen zodiacs° have gone round,
And none of them been worn; and, for a name,
Now puts the drowsy and neglected act
Freshly on me. 'Tis surely for a name.

175 *Lucio.* I warrant it is, and thy head stands so tickle°
on thy shoulders, that a milkmaid,° if she be in love,
may sigh it off. Send after the Duke, and appeal
to him.

Claudio. I have done so, but he's not to be found.
180 I prithee, Lucio, do me this kind service:
This day my sister should the cloister enter,

151 **denunciation** formal announcement 153 **propagation** increase
154 **friends** relatives and well-wishers 156 **made them for us** won
them over to our side 161 **fault and glimpse of newness** i.e., weakness
arising from the sudden vision of new authority 167 **eminence** sense
of superiority 168 **stagger in** am not sure 169 **enrollèd** inscribed
in the rolls of the laws 171 **zodiacs** i.e., years 175 **tickle** insecure
176 **milkmaid** (proverbial for love sickness)

And there receive her approbation.°
Acquaint her with the danger of my state;
Implore her, in my voice, that she make friends
To the strict deputy; bid herself assay° him.   *185*
I have great hope in that; for in her youth
There is a prone° and speechless dialect,
Such as move men; beside, she hath prosperous art
When she will play with reason and discourse,
And well she can persuade.   *190*

Lucio. I pray she may; as well for the encouragement
of the like, which else would stand under grievous
imposition, as for the enjoying of thy life, who I
would be sorry should be thus foolishly lost at a
game of tick-tack.° I'll to her.   *195*

Claudio. I thank you, good friend Lucio.

Lucio. Within two hours.

Claudio.   Come, officer, away!

                                              Exeunt.

Scene 3. [*A monastery.*]

Enter Duke and Friar Thomas

Duke. No, holy father; throw away that thought;
Believe not that the dribbling dart° of love
Can pierce a complete° bosom. Why I desire thee
To give me secret harbor, hath a purpose
More grave and wrinkled° than the aims and ends   *5*
Of burning youth.

---

182 **approbation** novitiate   185 **assay** test, i.e., attempt to persuade
187 **prone** winning, submissive   195 **tick-tack** (literally, a game using
a board into which pegs were fitted)   1.3.2 **dribbling dart** arrow feebly
shot   3 **complete** protected, independent   5 **wrinkled** mature, aged

Friar Thomas.   May your Grace speak of it?

Duke. My holy sir, none better knows than you
     How I have ever loved the life removed,
     And held in idle price to haunt assemblies
10   Where youth and cost, witless bravery° keeps.
     I have delivered to Lord Angelo,
     A man of stricture° and firm abstinence,
     My absolute power and place here in Vienna,
     And he supposes me traveled to Poland;
15   For so I have strewed it in the common ear,°
     And so it is received. Now, pious sir,
     You will demand of me why I do this.

Friar Thomas. Gladly, my lord.

Duke. We have strict statutes and most biting laws,
20   The needful bits and curbs to headstrong weeds,
     Which for this fourteen° years we have let slip,
     Even like an o'ergrown lion in a cave,
     That goes not out to prey. Now, as fond fathers,
     Having bound up the threat'ning twigs of birch,
25   Only to stick it in their children's sight
     For terror, not to use; in time the rod
     Becomes more mocked than feared; so our decrees,
     Dead to infliction,° to themselves are dead,
     And Liberty° plucks Justice by the nose;
30   The baby beats the nurse, and quite athwart
     Goes all decorum.

Friar Thomas.   It rested in your Grace
     To unloose this tied-up Justice when you pleased,
     And it in you more dreadful would have seemed
     Than in Lord Angelo.

Duke.   I do fear, too dreadful:
35   Sith° 'twas my fault to give the people scope,
     'Twould be my tyranny to strike and gall° them

---

10 **witless bravery** senseless show   12 **stricture** strictness   15 **common ear** the ear of the people   21 **fourteen** (in 1.2.171 the time has been "nineteen" years. Doubtless the printer's copy in both lines had either xiv or xix and in one line was misread)   28 **Dead to infliction** utterly unenforced   29 **Liberty** license   35 **Sith** since   36 **gall** wound

For what I bid them do; for we bid this be done
When evil deeds have their permissive pass,
And not the punishment. Therefore, indeed, my
    father,
I have on Angelo imposed the office,   40
Who may, in th' ambush° of my name, strike home,
And yet my nature never in the fight
To do it slander. And to behold his sway,
I will, as 'twere a brother of your order,
Visit both prince and people. Therefore, I prithee,   45
Supply me with the habit° and instruct me
How I may formally in person bear
Like a true friar. Moe° reasons for this action
At our more leisure shall I render you;
Only, this one: Lord Angelo is precise,°   50
Stands at a guard with envy;° scarce confesses
That his blood flows, or that his appetite
Is more to bread than stone. Hence shall we see,
If power change purpose, what our seemers be.
                                    Exit [with Friar].

Scene 4. [*A nunnery.*]

Enter Isabella and Francisca, a nun.

Isabella. And have you nuns no farther privileges?

Francisca. Are not these large enough?

Isabella. Yes, truly. I speak not as desiring more,
    But rather wishing a more strict restraint
    Upon the sisterhood, the votarists of Saint Clare.°   5

Lucio. (*Within*) Ho! Peace be in this place!

---

41 **in th' ambush** under cover 46 **habit** garment 48 **Moe** more
50 **precise** fastidiously strict 51 **Stands … envy** defies all malicious
criticism 1.4.5 **Saint Clare** (a notably strict order of nuns founded by
Isabella, sister of St. Louis of France)

Isabella.   Who's that which calls?

Francisca. It is a man's voice. Gentle Isabella,
    Turn you the key, and know his business of him.
    You may, I may not: you are yet unsworn.
    When you have vowed, you must not speak with
10   men
    But in the presence of the prioress:
    Then, if you speak, you must not show your face,
    Or, if you show your face, you must not speak.
    He calls again; I pray you, answer him.   [*Exit.*]

15 *Isabella.* Peace and prosperity! Who is't that calls?

[*Enter Lucio.*]

Lucio. Hail, virgin—if you be, as those cheek-roses
    Proclaim you are no less! Can you so stead° me
    As bring me to the sight of Isabella,
    A novice of this place and the fair sister
20   To her unhappy brother, Claudio?

Isabella. Why "her unhappy brother"? Let me ask,
    The rather for I now must make you know
    I am that Isabella and his sister.

Lucio. Gentle and fair, your brother kindly greets you.
25   Not to be weary° with you, he's in prison.

Isabella. Woe me! For what?

Lucio. For that which, if myself might be his judge,
    He should receive his punishment in thanks:
    He hath got his friend with child.

Isabella. Sir! Make me not your story.°

30 *Lucio.*   'Tis true.
    I would not, though 'tis my familiar sin
    With maids to seem the lapwing,° and to jest,
    Tongue far from heart, play with all virgins so.
    I hold you as a thing enskied and sainted,
35   By your renouncement, an immortal spirit;

17 **stead** help   25 **weary** tiresome   30 **story** subject for mirth   32 **lap-
wing** pewit (a bird that runs away from its nest to mislead intruders)

And to be talked with in sincerity,
As with a saint.

Isabella. You do blaspheme the good in mocking me.

Lucio. Do not believe it. Fewness and truth,° 'tis thus:
Your brother and his lover have embraced;   40
As those that feed grow full, as blossoming time
That from the seedness° the bare fallow brings
To teeming foison,° even so her plenteous womb
Expresseth his full tilth and husbandry.

Isabella. Someone with child by him? My cousin
Juliet?   45

Lucio. Is she your cousin?

Isabella. Adoptedly, as schoolmaids change their names
By vain, though apt, affection.

Lucio.   She it is.

Isabella. O, let him marry her.

Lucio.   This is the point:
The Duke is very strangely gone from hence;   50
Bore many gentlemen, myself being one,
In hand and hope of action,° but we do learn
By those that know the very nerves of state,
His givings-out were of an infinite distance
From his true-meant design. Upon his place,   55
And with full line of his authority,
Governs Lord Angelo, a man whose blood
Is very snow-broth; one who never feels
The wanton stings and motions of the sense,
But doth rebate° and blunt his natural edge   60
With profits of the mind, study and fast.
He—to give fear to use and liberty,°
Which have for long run by the hideous law,
As mice by lions—hath picked out an act,

39 **Fewness and truth** briefly and truly   42 **seedness** sowing   43
foison harvest   51–52 **Bore ... action** deluded ... with the hope
of military action   60 **rebate** dull (accent second syllable)   62 **use
and liberty** habitual license

65 Under whose heavy sense° your brother's life
Falls into forfeit; he arrests him on it,
And follows close the rigor of the statute,
To make him an example. All hope is gone,
Unless you have the grace by your fair prayer
70 To soften Angelo. And that's my pith of business
'Twixt you and your poor brother.

Isabella.   Doth he so?
Seek his life?

Lucio.   Has censured° him
Already, and, as I hear, the provost hath
A warrant for's execution.

75 *Isabella.* Alas, what poor ability's in me
To do him good?

Lucio.   Assay the pow'r you have.

Isabella. My power? Alas, I doubt—

Lucio.   Our doubts are traitors,
And makes° us lose the good we oft might win,
By fearing to attempt. Go to Lord Angelo,
80 And let him learn to know, when maidens sue,
Men give like gods; but when they weep and kneel,
All their petitions are as freely theirs
As they themselves would owe° them.

Isabella. I'll see what I can do.

Lucio.   But speedily.

85 *Isabella.* I will about it straight,
No longer staying but to give the Mother
Notice of my affair. I humbly thank you;
Commend me to my brother; soon at night
I'll send him certain word of my success.°

Lucio. I take my leave of you.

90 *Isabella.*   Good sir, adieu.

                              Exeunt.

65 **sense** interpretation   72 **censured** pronounced judgment on   78
makes (a plural subject sometimes takes a verb ending in -s)   83 **owe**
own   89 **success** outcome

ACT 2

Scene 1. [*A room.*]

Enter Angelo, Escalus, and Servants, Justice.

Angelo. We must not make a scarecrow of the law,
　　Setting it up to fear the birds of prey,
　　And let it keep one shape, till custom make it
　　Their perch and not their terror.

Escalus. 　　　　　　　　　　Ay, but yet
　　Let us be keen, and rather cut° a little,　　　　　　　5
　　Than fall,° and bruise to death. Alas, this gentleman
　　Whom I would save had a most noble father.
　　Let but your honor know,
　　Whom I believe to be most strait° in virtue,
　　That, in the working of your own affections,°　　　10
　　Had time cohered with place or place with wishing,
　　Or that the resolute acting of your blood
　　Could have attained th' effect of your own purpose,
　　Whether you had not sometime in your life
　　Erred in this point which now you censure him,　　15
　　And pulled the law upon you.

Angelo. 'Tis one thing to be tempted, Escalus,
　　Another thing to fall. I not deny,

2 1 5 **cut** prune   6 **fall** let the ax fall   9 **strait** strict   10 **affections** passions

19

The jury, passing on the prisoner's life,
20   May in the sworn twelve have a thief or two
        Guiltier than him they try. What's open made to
            Justice,
        That Justice seizes. What knows the laws
        That thieves do pass on thieves? 'Tis very preg-
            nant,°
        The jewel that we find, we stoop and take't
25   Because we see it; but what we do not see
        We tread upon, and never think of it.
        You may not so extenuate his offense
        For I have had such faults; but rather tell me,
        When I, that censure him, do so offend,
30   Let mine own judgment pattern out my death,
        And nothing come in partial. Sir, he must die.

Escalus. Be it as your wisdom will.

Angelo.   Where is the provost?

                    Enter Provost.

Provost. Here, if it like your honor.

Angelo.   See that Claudio
        Be executed by nine tomorrow morning.
35   Bring him his confessor, let him be prepared,
        For that's the utmost of his pilgrimage,
                                        [*Exit Provost.*]

Escalus. Well, Heaven forgive him, and forgive us all.
        Some rise by sin, and some by virtue fall:
        Some run from breaks of ice,° and answer none;
40   And some condemnèd for a fault° alone.

            Enter Elbow, Froth, Clown [Pompey], Officers.

Elbow. Come, bring them away. If these be good peo-
        ple in a commonweal that do nothing but use their
        abuses in common houses, I know no law. Bring
        them away.

23 **pregnant** clear   39 **Some . . . ice** some escape even after gross vio-
lations of chastity (° the passage is much disputed)   40 **fault** (1) small
crack in the ice (2) act of sex

Angelo. How now, sir! What's your name? And what's   45
the matter?

Elbow. If it please your honor, I am the poor Duke's
constable, and my name is Elbow. I do lean upon
justice, sir, and do bring in here before your good
honor two notorious benefactors.   50

Angelo. Benefactors? Well, what benefactors are they?
Are they not malefactors?

Elbow. If it please your honor, I know not well what
they are, but precise villains they are, that I am
sure of, and void of all profanation° in the world   55
that good Christians ought to have.

Escalus. This comes off well; here's a wise officer.

Angelo. Go to: what quality° are they of? Elbow is
your name? Why dost thou not speak, Elbow?

Pompey. He cannot, sir; he's out at elbow.°   60

Angelo. What are you, sir?

Elbow. He, sir! A tapster, sir, parcel-bawd,° one that
serves a bad woman whose house, sir, was, as they
say, plucked down in the suburbs, and now she
professes a hothouse,° which, I think, is a very ill   65
house too.

Escalus. How know you that?

Elbow. My wife, sir, whom I detest° before Heaven
and your honor—

Escalus. How! Thy wife?   70

Elbow. Ay, sir—whom, I thank Heaven, is an honest°
woman—

Escalus. Dost thou detest her therefore?

Elbow. I say, sir, I will detest myself also, as well as

55 **profanation** (profession)   58 **quality** profession   60 **out at elbow**
(1) somewhat seedy (2) speechless (out at the sound of his name)
62 **parcel-bawd** partly a bawd   65 **hothouse** bathhouse   68 **detest**
i.e., protest   71 **honest** chaste

75   she, that this house, if it be not a bawd's house, it
is pity of her life, for it is a naughty° house.

Escalus. How dost thou know that, constable?

Elbow. Marry, sir, by my wife, who, if she had been a
woman cardinally° given, might have been accused
80   in fornication, adultery, and all uncleanliness there.

Escalus. By the woman's means?

Elbow. Ay, sir, by Mistress Overdone's means; but as
she spit in his face, so she defied him.

Pompey. Sir, if it please your honor, this is not so.

85 *Elbow.* Prove it before these varlets here, thou honorable man; prove it.

Escalus. Do you hear how he misplaces?

Pompey. Sir, she came in great with child; and longing,
saving your honor's reverence, for stewed prunes.°
90   Sir, we had but two in the house, which at that very
distant time stood, as it were, in a fruit dish, a dish
of some threepence; your honors have seen such
dishes; they are not china dishes, but very good
dishes—

95 *Escalus.* Go to, go to; no matter for the dish, sir.

Pompey. No, indeed, sir, not of a pin; you are therein
in the right; but to the point. As I say, this Mistress
Elbow, being, as I say, with child, and being great-
bellied, and longing, as I said, for prunes; and hav-
100   ing but two in the dish, as I said, Master Froth here,
this very man, having eaten the rest, as I said, and,
as I say, paying for them very honestly; for, as you
know, Master Froth, I could not give you threepence again.

105 *Froth.* No, indeed.

Pompey. Very well, you being then, if you be remem-

76 **naughty** immoral   79 **cardinally** i.e., carnally   89 **stewed prunes**
(supposed to be a favorite dish among prostitutes)

b'red, cracking the stones of the foresaid prunes—

Froth. Ay, so I did indeed.

Pompey. Why, very well; I telling you then, if you be remationemb'red, that such a one and such a one were past cure of the thing you wot° of, unless they kept very good diet, as I told you— 110

Froth. All this is true.

Pompey. Why, very well, then—

Escalus. Come, you are a tedious fool; to the purpose. What was done to Elbow's wife, that he hath cause to complain of? Come me to what was done to her. 115

Pompey. Sir, your honor cannot come to that yet.°

Escalus. No, sir, nor I mean it not.

Pompey. Sir, but you shall come to it, by your honor's leave. And, I beseech you, look into Master Froth here, sir, a man of fourscore pound a year, whose father died at Hallowmas.° Was't not at Hallowmas, Master Froth? 120

Froth. All-hallond Eve.° 125

Pompey. Why, very well; I hope here be truths. He, sir, sitting, as I say, in a lower chair, sir, 'twas in the Bunch of Grapes, where, indeed, you have a delight to sit, have you not?

Froth. I have so, because it is an open room, and good for winter. 130

Pompey. Why, very well, then; I hope here be truths.

Angelo. This will last out a night in Russia,
When nights are longest there. I'll take my leave,
And leave you to the hearing of the cause, 135
Hoping you'll find good cause to whip them all.

---

111 **wot** know   117–18 **Come me ... that yet** (the verbs carry a sexual innuendo)   123 **Hallowmas** All Saints' Day, November 1st 125 **All-hallond Eve** October 31st

Escalus. I think no less. Good morrow to your lord-
　　ship.　　　　　　　　　　　　　*Exit* [*Angelo*].
　　Now, sir, come on: what was done to Elbow's wife,
　　once more?

140 *Pompey.* Once, sir? There was nothing done to her
　　once.

Elbow. I beseech you, sir, ask him what this man did
　　to my wife.

Pompey. I beseech your honor, ask me.

145 *Escalus.* Well, sir; what did this gentleman to her?

Pompey. I beseech you, sir, look in this gentleman's
　　face. Good Master Froth, look upon his honor;
　　'tis for a good purpose. Doth your honor mark his
　　face?

150 *Escalus.* Ay, sir, very well.

Pompey. Nay, I beseech you, mark it well.

Escalus. Well, I do so.

Pompey. Doth your honor see any harm in his face?

Escalus. Why, no.

155 *Pompey.* I'll be supposed° upon a book,° his face is the
　　worst thing about him. Good, then; if his face be
　　the worst thing about him, how could Master Froth
　　do the constable's wife any harm? I would know
　　that of your honor.

160 *Escalus.* He's in the right. Constable, what say you
　　to it?

Elbow. First, and° it like you, the house is a re-
　　spected° house; next, this is a respected fellow;
　　and his mistress is a respected woman.

165 *Pompey.* By this hand, sir, his wife is a more respected
　　person than any of us all.

155 **supposed** i.e., deposed　155 **a book** (perhaps the Bible)　162 **and**
if 162–63 **respected** i.e., suspected

Elbow. Varlet, thou liest; thou liest, wicked varlet! The
time is yet to come that she was ever respected with
man, woman, or child.

Pompey. Sir, she was respected with him before he   170
married with her.

Escalus. Which is the wiser here, Justice or Iniquity?°
Is this true?

Elbow. O thou caitiff! O thou varlet! O thou wicked
Hannibal!° I respected with her before I was mar-   175
ried to her! If ever I was respected with her, or she
with me, let not your worship think me the poor
Duke's officer. Prove this, thou wicked Hannibal,
or I'll have mine action of batt'ry on thee.

Escalus. If he took you a box o' th' ear, you might   180
have your action of slander too.

Elbow. Marry, I thank your good worship for it. What
is't your worship's pleasure I shall do with this
wicked caitiff?

Escalus. Truly, officer, because he hath some offenses   185
in him that thou wouldst discover if thou couldst,
let him continue in his courses till thou know'st
what they are.

Elbow. Marry, I thank your worship for it. Thou seest,
thou wicked varlet, now, what's come upon thee.   190
Thou art to continue now, thou varlet; thou art to
continue.

Escalus. Where were you born, friend?

Froth. Here in Vienna, sir.

Escalus. Are you of fourscore pounds a year?   195

Froth. Yes, and't please you, sir.

Escalus. So. [*To Pompey*] What trade are you of, sir?

Pompey. A tapster, a poor widow's tapster.

172 **Justice or Iniquity** (personified characters in morality plays)
175 **Hannibal** i.e., cannibal, fleshmonger (?)

Escalus. Your mistress' name?

200 *Pompey.* Mistress Overdone.

Escalus. Hath she had any more than one husband?

Pompey. Nine, sir; Overdone by the last.

Escalus. Nine! Come hither to me, Master Froth.
Master Froth, I would not have you acquainted
205   with tapsters: they will draw you,° Master Froth,
and you will hang them. Get you gone, and let me
hear no more of you.

Froth. I thank your worship. For mine own part, I
never come into any room in a taphouse, but I am
210   drawn in.

Escalus. Well, no more of it, Master Froth; farewell.
                        [Exit Froth.]
Come you hither to me, Master Tapster. What's
your name, Master Tapster?

Pompey. Pompey.

215 *Escalus.* What else?

Pompey. Bum, sir.

Escalus. Troth, and your bum is the greatest thing
about you; so that, in the beastliest sense, you are
Pompey the Great. Pompey, you are partly a bawd,
220   Pompey, howsoever you color° it in being a tapster,
are you not? Come, tell me true; it shall be the better
for you.

Pompey. Truly, sir, I am a poor fellow that would live.

Escalus. How would you live, Pompey? By being a
225   bawd? What do you think of the trade, Pompey?
Is it a lawful trade?

Pompey. If the law would allow it, sir.

---

205 **draw you** (1) draw drinks for you (2) empty you, disembowel
you   220 **color** camouflage

Escalus. But the law will not allow it, Pompey; nor
  it shall not be allowed in Vienna.

Pompey. Does your worship mean to geld and splay   230
  all the youth of the city?

Escalus. No, Pompey.

Pompey. Truly, sir, in my poor opinion, they will to't,
  then. If your worship will take order for the drabs°
  and the knaves, you need not to fear the bawds.   235

Escalus. There is pretty orders beginning, I can tell
  you; it is but heading° and hanging.

Pompey. If you head and hang all that offend that
  way but for ten year together, you'll be glad to give
  out a commission for more heads; if this law hold   240
  in Vienna ten year, I'll rent the fairest house in it
  after threepence a bay;° if you live to see this come
  to pass, say Pompey told you so.

Escalus. Thank you, good Pompey; and, in requital
  of your prophecy, hark you: I advise you, let me   245
  not find you before me again upon any complaint
  whatsoever; no, not for dwelling where you do. If
  I do, Pompey, I shall beat you to your tent, and
  prove a shrewd Caesar to you; in plain dealing,
  Pompey, I shall have you whipped. So, for this   250
  time, Pompey, fare you well.

Pompey. I thank your worship for your good counsel;
  [*aside*] but I shall follow it as the flesh and fortune
  shall better determine.
  Whip me? No, no; let carman whip his jade.°   255
  The valiant heart's not whipped out of his trade.

                                        Exit.

Escalus. Come hither to me, Master Elbow; come
  hither, Master constable. How long have you been
  in this place of constable?

234 **drabs** prostitutes   237 **heading** beheading   242 **bay** space under
a single gable   255 **carman whip his jade** (the cartman whipped the
whore after carting her through the streets; a "jade" is literally a nag)

260 *Elbow.* Seven year and a half, sir.

Escalus. I thought, by the readiness in the office, you
had continued in it some time. You say, seven years
together?

Elbow. And a half, sir.

265 *Escalus.* Alas, it hath been great pains to you. They
do you wrong to put you so oft upon't.° Are there
not men in your ward sufficient to serve it?

Elbow. Faith, sir, few of any wit in such matters. As
they are chosen, they are glad to choose me for them;
270 I do it for some piece of money, and go through
with all.

Escalus. Look you bring me in the names of some
six or seven, the most sufficient° of your parish.

Elbow. To your worship's house, sir?

275 *Escalus.* To my house. Fare you well. [*Exit Elbow.*]
What's o'clock, think you?

Justice. Eleven, sir.

Escalus. I pray you home to dinner with me.

Justice. I humbly thank you.

280 *Escalus.* It grieves me for the death of Claudio,
But there's no remedy.

Justice. Lord Angelo is severe.

Escalus.   It is but needful:
Mercy is not itself, that oft looks so;
Pardon is still° the nurse of second woe.
285 But yet—poor Claudio! There is no remedy.
Come, sir.   *Exeunt.*

---

266 **put you so oft upon't** i.e., impose on you the task of being a constable   273 **sufficient** able, fit for office   284 **still** always

Scene 2. [*A room.*]

Enter Provost, [and a] Servant.

Servant. He's hearing of a cause; he will come straight:
I'll tell him of you.

Provost.   Pray you, do. [*Exit Servant.*] I'll know
His pleasure; maybe he will relent. Alas,
He hath but as offended in a dream.
All sects,° all ages smack of this vice; and he   5
To die for't!

Enter Angelo.

Angelo.   Now, what's the matter, provost?

Provost. Is it your will Claudio shall die tomorrow?

Angelo. Did not I tell thee yea? Hadst thou not order?
Why dost thou ask again?

Provost.   Lest I might be too rash.
Under your good correction, I have seen,   10
When, after execution, judgment hath
Repented o'er his doom.

Angelo.   Go to; let that be mine.°
Do you your office, or give up your place,
And you shall well be spared.

Provost.   I crave your honor's
     pardon.
What shall be done, sir, with the groaning Juliet?   15
She's very near her hour.

Angelo.   Dispose of her
To some more fitter place, and that with speed.

[*Re-enter Servant.*]

Servant. Here is the sister of the man condemned
    Desires access to you.

Angelo.   Hath he a sister?

20 *Provost.* Ay, my good lord, a very virtuous maid
    And to be shortly of a sisterhood,
    If not already.

Angelo.   Well, let her be admitted.

                      [*Exit Servant.*]

    See you the fornicatress be removed;
    Let her have needful, but not lavish, means;
    There shall be order for't.

Enter Lucio and Isabella.

25 *Provost.*   'Save your honor.

Angelo. Stay a little while. [*To Isabella*] Y'are wel-
    come: what's your will?

Isabella. I am a woeful suitor to your honor,
    Please but your honor hear me.

Angelo.   Well; what's your suit?

Isabella. There is a vice that most I do abhor,
30   And most desire should meet the blow of justice,
    For which I would not plead, but that I must,
    For which I must not plead, but that I am
    At war 'twixt will and will not.

Angelo.   Well: the matter?

Isabella. I have a brother is condemned to die.
35   I do beseech you, let it be his fault,°
    And not my brother.

Provost.   [*Aside*] Heaven give thee moving graces.

Angelo. Condemn the fault, and not the actor of it?
    Why, every fault's condemned ere it be done.

35 **let it be his fault** i.e., condemn his fault, not him

Mine were the very cipher of a function,
To fine the faults whose fine° stands in record,   40
And let go by the actor.

Isabella.   O just but severe law!
I had a brother, then. Heaven keep your honor.

Lucio. [*Aside to Isabella*] Give't not o'er so. To him
    again, entreat him,
Kneel down before him, hang upon his gown;
You are too cold; if you should need a pin,   45
You could not with more tame a tongue desire it.
To him, I say!

Isabella. Must he needs die?

Angelo.   Maiden, no remedy.

Isabella. Yes; I do think that you might pardon him,
And neither heaven nor man grieve at the mercy.   50

Angelo. I will not do't.

Isabella.   But can you, if you would?

Angelo. Look what° I will not, that I cannot do.

Isabella. But might you do't, and do the world no
    wrong,
If so your heart were touched with that remorse°
As mine is to him?

Angelo.   He's sentenced; 'tis too late.   55

Lucio. [*Aside to Isabella*] You are too cold.

Isabella. Too late? Why, no: I, that do speak a word,
May call it again. Well, believe this:
No ceremony° that to great ones 'longs,°
Not the king's crown, nor the deputed sword,   60
The marshal's truncheon, nor the judge's robe,
Become them with one half so good a grace
As mercy does.
If he had been as you, and you as he,

40 **fine . . . fine** penalize . . . penalty 52 **Look what** whatever 54 **remorse** compassion 59 **ceremony** insignia of greatness 59 **'longs** belongs

65 You would have slipped like him; but he, like you,
    Would not have been so stern.

Angelo.   Pray you, be gone.

Isabella. I would to heaven I had your potency,°
    And you were Isabel; should it then be thus?
    No; I would tell what 'twere to be a judge,
    And what a prisoner.

Lucio. [*Aside to Isabella*] Ay, touch him; there's the
70 vein.

Angelo. Your brother is a forfeit of the law,
    And you but waste your words.

Isabella.   Alas, alas!
    Why, all the souls that were were forfeit once;
    And He that might the vantage best have took
75 Found out the remedy. How would you be,
    If He, which is the top of judgment, should
    But judge you as you are? O, think on that,
    And mercy then will breathe within your lips,
    Like man new made.°

Angelo.   Be you content, fair maid;
80 It is the law, not I, condemn your brother.
    Were he my kinsman, brother, or my son,
    It should be thus with him; he must die tomorrow.

Isabella. Tomorrow! O, that's sudden! Spare him,
    spare him!
    He's not prepared for death. Even for our kitchens
85 We kill the fowl of season:° shall we serve heaven
    With less respect than we do minister
    To our gross selves? Good, good my lord, bethink
    you:
    Who is it that hath died for this offense?
    There's many have committed it.

Lucio. [*Aside to Isabella*]   Ay, well said.

Angelo. The law hath not been dead, though it hath
90 slept.

67 **potency** power   76–79 **If He . . . made** (see Matthew 7 1)   79 **man
new made** (see II Cor. 5.17)   85 **of season** in season

Those many had not dared to do that evil,
If the first that did th' edict infringe
Had answered for his deed. Now 'tis awake,
Takes note of what is done, and, like a prophet,
Looks in a glass, that shows what future evils,   95
Either new, or by remissness new conceived,°
And so in progress to be hatched and born,
Are now to have no successive degrees.°
But here they live, to end.

Isabella.   Yet show some pity.

Angelo. I show it most of all when I show justice,   100
For then I pity those I do not know,
Which a dismissed° offense would after gall;
And do him right that, answering one foul wrong,
Lives not to act another. Be satisfied;
Your brother dies tomorrow; be content.   105

Isabella. So you must be the first that gives this sen-
    tence,
And he, that suffers. O, it is excellent
To have a giant's strength; but it is tyrannous
To use it like a giant.

Lucio. [*Aside to Isabella*] That's well said.

Isabella. Could great men thunder   110
As Jove himself does, Jove would ne'er be quiet,
For every pelting,° petty officer
Would use his heaven for thunder.
Nothing but thunder. Merciful heaven,
Thou rather with thy sharp and sulfurous bolt   115
Splits the unwedgeable and gnarlèd oak
Than the soft myrtle. But man, proud man,
Dressed in a little brief authority,
Most ignorant of what he's most assured,

95–96 **future … conceived** i.e., evils that will take place in future,
but that are either now planned or may be planned later ("remissness": careless omission of duty)   98 **successive degrees** further stages
102 **dismissed** forgiven   112 **pelting** paltry

120 His glassy essence,° like an angry ape,
Plays such fantastic tricks before high heaven
As makes the angels weep; who, with our spleens,°
Would all themselves laugh mortal.

Lucio. [*Aside to Isabella*] O, to him, to him, wench!
He will relent;
He's coming; I perceive't.

125 Provost. [*Aside*] Pray heaven she win him.

Isabella. We cannot weigh our brother with ourself:
Great men may jest with saints; 'tis wit in them;
But in the less, foul profanation.

Lucio. Thou'rt i' th' right, girl; more o' that.

130 Isabella. That in the captain's but a choleric word,
Which in the soldier is flat blasphemy.

Lucio. [*Aside to Isabella*] Art avised° o' that? More
on't.

Angelo. Why do you put these sayings upon me?

Isabella. Because authority, though it err like others,
135 Hath yet a kind of medicine in itself,
That skins the vice° o' th' top; go to your bosom,
Knock there, and ask your heart what it doth know
That's like my brother's fault; if it confess
A natural guiltiness such as is his,
140 Let it not sound a thought upon your tongue
Against my brother's life.

Angelo. [*Aside*] She speaks, and 'tis
Such sense,° that my sense breeds° with it. [*Aloud*]
Fare you well.

Isabella. Gentle my lord, turn back.

Angelo. I will bethink me; come again tomorrow.

120 **glassy essence** the rational soul which reveals to man, as in a mirror,
what constitutes him a human being (?) fragile nature (?) 122 **spleens**
(the spleen was believed the seat of mirth and anger) 132 **avised** informed 136 **skins the vice** i.e., covers the sore of vice with a skin, but
does not heal it (or perhaps "skims off the visible layer of vice") 142
sense . . . sense meaning . . sensual desire 142 **breeds** rises

Isabella. Hark how I'll bribe you; good my lord, turn
     back.   *145*

Angelo. How? Bribe me?

Isabella. Ay, with such gifts that heaven shall share
     with you.

Lucio. [*Aside to Isabella*] You had marred all else.

Isabella. Not with fond sicles° of the tested gold,
     Or stones whose rate are either rich or poor   *150*
     As fancy values them; but with true prayers
     That shall be up at heaven, and enter there
     Ere sunrise, prayers from preservèd souls,
     From fasting maids whose minds are dedicate
     To nothing temporal.

Angelo.   Well; come to me tomorrow.   *155*

Lucio. [*Aside to Isabella*] Go to; 'tis well; away.

Isabella. Heaven keep your honor safe.

Angelo.   [*Aside*] Amen:
     For I am that way going to temptation,
     Where prayers cross.°

Isabella.   At what hour tomorrow
     Shall I attend your lordship?

Angelo.   At any time 'fore noon.   *160*

Isabella. 'Save your honor.

              [*Exeunt Isabella, Lucio, and Provost.*]

Angelo.   From thee, even from thy virtue!
     What's this? What's this? Is this her fault or mine?
     The tempter or the tempted, who sins most?
     Ha, not she. Nor doth she tempt; but it is I
     That, lying by the violet in the sun,   *165*
     Do as the carrion does, not as the flow'r,
     Corrupt with virtuous season.° Can it be

149 **fond sicles** foolish shekels   159 **cross** are at cross purposes   167
Corrupt with virtuous season go bad in the season that blossoms the
flower

That modesty may more betray our sense
Than woman's lightness? Having waste ground enough,
170   Shall we desire to raze the sanctuary,
And pitch our evils° there? O fie, fie, fie!
What dost thou, or what art thou, Angelo?
Dost thou desire her foully for those things
That make her good? O, let her brother live:
175   Thieves for their robbery have authority
When judges steal themselves. What, do I love her,
That I desire to hear her speak again,
And feast upon her eyes? What is't I dream on?
O cunning enemy, that, to catch a saint,
180   With saints dost bait thy hook! Most dangerous
Is that temptation that doth goad us on
To sin in loving virtue. Never could the strumpet,
With all her double vigor, art and nature,
Once stir my temper; but this virtuous maid
185   Subdues me quite. Ever till now,
When men were fond,° I smiled, and wond'red
how.   *Exit.*

Scene 3. [*The prison.*]

Enter Duke [disguised as a friar] and Provost.

Duke. Hail to you, provost—so I think you are.

Provost. I am the provost. What's your will, good
friar?

Duke. Bound by my charity and my blest order,
I come to visit the afflicted spirits
5   Here in the prison. Do me the common right
To let me see them, and to make me know

171 **evils** evil structures (e g, perhaps whorehouses or privies)
186 **fond** infatuated

The nature of their crimes, that I may minister
To them accordingly.

Provost. I would do more than that, if more were
    needful.

                Enter Juliet.

Look, here comes one: a gentlewoman of mine,   *10*
Who, falling in the flaws° of her own youth,
Hath blistered her report:° she is with child;
And he that got it, sentenced; a young man
More fit to do another such offense
Than die for this.   *15*

Duke. When must he die?

Provost.   As I do think, tomorrow.
    [*To Juliet*] I have provided for you; stay awhile,
And you shall be conducted.

Duke. Repent you, fair one, of the sin you carry?

Juliet. I do, and bear the shame most patiently.   *20*

Duke. I'll teach you how you shall arraign° your con-
    science,
And try your penitence, if it be sound
Or hollowly put on.

Juliet.   I'll gladly learn.

Duke. Love you the man that wronged you?

Juliet. Yes, as I love the woman that wronged him.   *25*

Duke. So, then, it seems your most offenseful act
    Was mutually committed?

Juliet.   Mutually.

Duke. Then was your sin of heavier kind than his.

Juliet. I do confess it, and repent it, father.

Duke. 'Tis meet so, daughter. But lest you do repent   *30*

2.3.11 **flaws** (1) sudden gusts of wind (2) outbursts of passion   12 **report**
reputation   21 **arraign** interrogate

As that the sin hath brought you to this shame—
Which sorrow is always toward ourselves, not
    heaven,
Showing we would not spare heaven as we love it,
But as we stand in fear—

35 *Juliet.* I do repent me, as it is an evil,
And take the shame with joy.

Duke.   There rest.
Your partner, as I hear, must die tomorrow,
And I am going with instruction to him.
Grace go with you, *Benedicite!*°   *Exit.*

40 *Juliet.* Must die tomorrow! O injurious love,
That respites° me a life, whose very comfort
Is still a dying horror.

Provost.   'Tis pity of him.   *Exeunt.*

Scene 4. [*A room.*]

Enter Angelo.

Angelo. When I would pray and think, I think and
    pray
To several° subjects: heaven hath my empty words,
Whilst my invention,° hearing not my tongue,
Anchors on Isabel: heaven in my mouth,
5 As if I did but only chew his name,
And in my heart the strong and swelling evil
Of my conception.° The state,° whereon I studied,
Is like a good thing, being often read,
Grown seared° and tedious; yea, my gravity,
10 Wherein, let no man hear me, I take pride,

39 **Benedicite** bless you   41 **respites** saves   2.4.2 **several** separate
3 **invention** imagination   7 **conception** thought   7 **state** attitude (?)
statecraft (?)   9 **seared** worn out

Could I with boot° change for an idle plume
Which the air beats for vain. O place, O form,
How often dost thou with thy case,° thy habit,°
Wrench awe from fools, and tie the wiser souls
To thy false seeming! Blood, thou art blood.   15
Let's write "good angel" on the devil's horn,
'Tis not the devil's crest.° How now, who's there?

Enter Servant.

Servant. One Isabel, a sister, desires access to you.

Angelo. Teach her the way. [*Exit Servant.*] O heavens,
Why does my blood thus muster to my heart,   20
Making both it unable for itself,
And dispossessing all my other parts
Of necessary fitness?
So play the foolish throngs with one that swounds,°
Come all to help him, and so stop the air   25
By which he should revive; and even so
The general,° subject to a well-wished king,
Quit their own part, and in obsequious fondness
Crowd to his presence, where their untaught love
Must needs appear offense.

Enter Isabella.

                        How now, fair maid?   30

Isabella. I am come to know your pleasure.

Angelo. That you might know it, would much better
    please me
Than to demand what 'tis. Your brother cannot
    live.

Isabella. Even so. Heaven keep your honor.

Angelo. Yet may he live awhile, and it may be,   35
    As long as you or I; yet he must die.

Isabella. Under your sentence?

11 **with boot** with profit   13 **case** circumstances or outward appearances   13 **habit** (1) behavior (2) garment   16–17 **Let's . . . crest** the
devil's horn is no longer the distinguishing mark of the devil, and we
may as well write 'Good Angel' on it   24 **swounds** swoons   27 **general** multitude (King James I seems to have disliked crowds)

Angelo. Yea.

Isabella. When? I beseech you that in his reprieve,
40   Longer or shorter, he may be so fitted
        That his soul sicken not.

Angelo. Ha! Fie, these filthy vices! It were as good
        To pardon him that hath from nature stol'n
        A man already made, as to remit
45   Their saucy sweetness° that do coin heaven's image
        In stamps that are forbid: 'tis all as easy
        Falsely to take away a life true made,
        As to put metal in restrainèd° means
        To make a false one.

50 *Isabella.* 'Tis set down so in heaven, but not in earth.

Angelo. Say you so? Then I shall pose° you quickly.
        Which had you rather: that the most just law
        Now took your brother's life; or, to redeem him,
        Give up your body to such sweet uncleanness
        As she that he hath stained?

55 *Isabella.*   Sir, believe this:
        I had rather give my body than my soul.

Angelo. I talk not of your soul; our compelled sins
        Stand more for number than for accompt.°

Isabella.   How say you?

Angelo. Nay, I'll not warrant that; for I can speak
60   Against the thing I say. Answer to this:
        I, now the voice of the recorded law,
        Pronounce a sentence on your brother's life;
        Might there not be a charity in sin
        To save this brother's life?

Isabella.   Please you to do't,
65   I'll take it as a peril to my soul,
        It is no sin at all, but charity.

44–45 **to remit ... sweetness** to pardon their lascivious pleasures
48 **restrainèd** forbidden   51 **pose** baffle (with a difficult question)
58 **Stand ... accompt** are enumerated but not counted against us

Angelo. Pleased you to do't at peril of your soul,
  Were equal poise° of sin and charity.

Isabella. That I do beg his life, if it be sin, ·
  Heaven let me bear it. You granting of my suit,   *70*
  If that be sin, I'll make it my morn prayer
  To have it added to the faults of mine,
  And nothing of your answer.

Angelo.   Nay, but hear me.
  Your sense pursues not mine; either you are ig-
    norant,
  Or seem so, crafty; and that's not good.   *75*

Isabella. Let me be ignorant, and in nothing good,
  But graciously to know I am no better.°

Angelo. Thus wisdom wishes to appear most bright
  When it doth tax° itself, as these black masks
  Proclaim an enshield° beauty ten times louder   *80*
  Than beauty could, displayed. But mark me;
  To be receivèd plain, I'll speak more gross:
  Your brother is to die.

Isabella. So.

Angelo. And his offense is so, as it appears,   *85*
  Accountant° to the law upon that pain.°

Isabella. True.

Angelo. Admit no other way to save his life—
  As I subscribe° not that, nor any other,
  But in the loss of question°—that you, his sister,   *90*
  Finding yourself desired of such a person
  Whose credit with the judge, or own great place,
  Could fetch your brother from the manacles
  Of the all-binding law; and that there were
  No earthly mean to save him, but that either   *95*
  You must lay down the treasures of your body
  To this supposed, or else to let him suffer:

---

68 **poise** balance   76–77 **in nothing ... better** (i.e., my only good
point is that I know through God's grace that I am a sinner)   79 **tax**
censure   80 **enshield** concealed   86 **Accountant** accountable   86 **pain**
punishment   89 **subscribe** assent   90 **But ... question** except to keep
alive the argument

What would you do?

Isabella. As much for my poor brother as myself:
100   That is, were I under the terms of death,
   Th' impression of keen whips I'd wear as rubies,
   And strip myself to death as to a bed
   That longing have been sick for, ere I'd yield
   My body up to shame.

Angelo.   Then must your brother die.

105 *Isabella.* And 'twere the cheaper way.
   Better it were a brother died at once
   Than that a sister, by redeeming him,
   Should die forever.

Angelo. Were not you, then, as cruel as the sentence
110   That you have slandered so?

Isabella. Ignomy in ransom and free pardon
   Are of two houses; lawful mercy
   Is nothing kin to foul redemption.

Angelo. You seemed of late to make the law a tyrant,
115   And rather proved the sliding of your brother
   A merriment than a vice.

Isabella. O, pardon me, my lord. It oft falls out,
   To have what we would have, we speak not what
     we mean.
   I something do excuse the thing I hate
120   For his advantage that I dearly love.

Angelo. We are all frail.

Isabella.   Else let my brother die,
   If not a fedary, but only he
   Owe and succeed thy weakness.°

Angelo. Nay, women are frail too.

Isabella. Ay, as the glasses where they view them-
125   selves,

122–23 **If ... weakness** (the meaning seems to be: "Let my brother
die if he is the only inheritor of human frailty instead of being a mere
accomplice in it")

Which are as easy broke as they make forms.°
Women! Help heaven! Men their creation mar
In profiting by them. Nay, call us ten times frail;
For we are soft as our complexions are,
And credulous° to false prints.

Angelo.   I think it well,   130
And from this testimony of your own sex—
Since, I suppose, we are made to be no stronger
Than faults may shake our frames—let me be bold:
I do arrest your words.° Be that you are,
That is, a woman; if you be more, you're none;°   135
If you be one, as you are well expressed°
By all external warrants, show it now,
By putting on the destined livery.°

Isabella. I have no tongue but one; gentle my lord,
Let me entreat you speak the former language.   140

Angelo. Plainly conceive, I love you.

Isabella. My brother did love Juliet,
And you tell me that he shall die for't.

Angelo. He shall not, Isabel, if you give me love.

Isabella. I know your virtue hath a license in't,   145
Which seems a little fouler than it is,
To pluck on° others.

Angelo.   Believe me, on mine honor,
My words express my purpose.

Isabella. Ha! Little honor to be much believed,
And most pernicious purpose. Seeming, seeming!   150
I will proclaim thee, Angelo; look for't:
Sign me a present pardon for my brother,
Or with an outstretched throat I'll tell the world
    aloud
What man thou art.

126 **forms** images, appearances   130 **credulous** receptive   134 **I do
arrest your words** I take you at your word   135 **if you . . . none** (if you
seek to go beyond the limits of your sex, you cease to be a woman)
136 **expressed** shown to be   138 **the destined livery** the dress that it is
the destiny of a woman to wear   147 **pluck on** draw on

Angelo.   Who will believe thee, Isabel?
155   My unsoiled name, th' austereness of my life,
       My vouch° against you, and my place i' th' state,
       Will so your accusation overweigh,
       That you shall stifle in your own report,
       And smell of calumny. I have begun,
160   And now I give my sensual race the rein.
       Fit thy consent to my sharp appetite,
       Lay by all nicety° and prolixious° blushes,
       That banish what they sue for; redeem thy brother
       By yielding up thy body to my will,°
165   Or else he must not only die the death,
       But thy unkindness shall his death draw out
       To ling'ring sufferance.° Answer me tomorrow,
       Or, by the affection° that now guides me most,
       I'll prove a tyrant to him. As for you,
170   Say what you can, my false o'erweighs your true.
                                               Exit.

Isabella. To whom should I complain? Did I tell this,
       Who would believe me? O perilous mouths,
       That bear in them one and the selfsame tongue,
       Either of condemnation or approof;°
175   Bidding the law make curtsy to their will,
       Hooking both right and wrong to th' appetite,
       To follow as it draws. I'll to my brother.
       Though he hath fall'n by prompture of the blood,
       Yet hath he in him such a mind of honor,
180   That, had he twenty heads to tender down
       On twenty bloody blocks, he'd yield them up,
       Before his sister should her body stoop
       To such abhorred pollution.
       Then, Isabel, live chaste, and, brother, die:
185   More than our brother is our chastity.
       I'll tell him yet of Angelo's request,
       And fit his mind to death, for his soul's rest.   *Exit.*

---

156 **vouch** testimony   162 **nicety** niceness   162 **prolixious** tediously
drawn-out   164 **will** carnal appetite   167 **sufferance** torture   168 **affection** passion   174 **approof** approval

ACT 3

Scene 1. [*The prison.*]

Enter Duke [as friar], Claudio, and Provost.

Duke. So then, you hope of pardon from Lord Angelo?

Claudio. The miserable have no other medicine
But only hope:
I have hope to live, and am prepared to die.

Duke. Be absolute° for death; either death or life   5
Shall thereby be the sweeter. Reason thus with life:
If I do lose thee, I do lose a thing
That none but fools would keep; a breath thou art,
Servile to all the skyey influences,°
That dost this habitation, where thou keep'st,°   10
Hourly afflict; merely, thou art death's fool,°
For him thou labor'st by thy flight to shun,
And yet run'st toward him still. Thou art not noble,
For all th' accommodations° that thou bear'st
Are nursed by baseness. Thou'rt by no means val-
iant,   15
For thou dost fear the soft and tender fork°
Of a poor worm. Thy best of rest is sleep,

3.1.5 **absolute** unconditionally prepared 9 **skyey influences** influence of the stars 10 **keep'st** dwellest 11 **fool** (the professional
jester in a nobleman's household whose job was to keep his master
amused) 14 **accommodations** comforts 16 **fork** forked tongue (of
a snake)

45

And that thou oft provok'st;° yet grossly fear'st
Thy death, which is no more. Thou art not thyself;

20 For thou exists on many a thousand grains
That issue out of dust. Happy thou art not,
For what thou hast not, still thou striv'st to get,
And what thou hast, forget'st. Thou art not certain,°
For thy complexion shifts to strange effects,

25 After the moon.° If thou art rich, thou'rt poor.
For, like an ass whose back with ingots bows,
Thou bear'st thy heavy riches but a journey,
And death unloads thee. Friend hast thou none,
For thine own bowels,° which do call thee sire,

30 The mere effusion of thy proper loins,°
Do curse the gout, serpigo,° and the rheum.°
For ending thee no sooner. Thou hast nor youth
    nor age,
But, as it were, an after-dinner's° sleep,
Dreaming on both; for all thy blessèd youth

35 Becomes as° agèd, and doth beg the alms
Of palsied eld,° and when thou art old and rich,
Thou has neither heat, affection,° limb, nor beauty,
To make thy riches pleasant. What's yet in this
That bears° the name of life? Yet in this life

40 Lie hid moe thousand deaths; yet death we fear,
That makes these odds all even.

Claudio.   I humbly thank you.
To sue to live, I find I seek to die,
And seeking death, find life: let it come on.

Enter Isabella.

Isabella. What, ho! Peace here; grace and good com-
    pany!

Provost. Who's there? Come in, the wish deserves a
45 welcome.

18 **provok'st** invokest   23 **certain** invariable   24–25 **For ... moon**
your temperament (desire?) moves to numerous things, changeable
as (or "influenced by") the moon   29 **bowels** offspring   30 **The
mere ... loins** the very issue of your own loins   31 **serpigo** a skin
disease   31 **rheum** catarrh   33 **after-dinner** (time after dinner, the
main meal which, in the 17th century, was taken around noon)   35 **as** as
if   36 **palsied eld** old age shaking with palsy   37 **affection** feeling
39 **bears** deserves

Duke. Dear sir, ere long I'll visit you again.

Claudio. Most holy sir, I thank you.

Isabella. My business is a word or two with Claudio.

Provost. And very welcome. Look, signior, here's
　　your sister.

Duke. Provost, a word with you. 　　　　　　　　　　50

Provost. As many as you please.

Duke. Bring me to hear them speak, where I may be
　　concealed. 　　　　　　　　[*Duke and Provost withdraw.*]

Claudio. Now, sister, what's the comfort?

Isabella. Why, 　　　　　　　　　　　　　　　　　55
　　As all comforts are, most good, most good indeed.
　　Lord Angelo, having affairs to heaven,
　　Intends you for his swift ambassador,
　　Where you shall be an everlasting leiger:°
　　Therefore your best appointment° make with speed; 　60
　　Tomorrow you set on.

Claudio. 　　　　　　　　Is there no remedy?

Isabella. None, but such remedy as, to save a head,
　　To cleave a heart in twain.

Claudio. 　　　　　　　　　But is there any?

Isabella. Yes, brother, you may live;
　　There is a devilish mercy in the judge, 　　　　　　65
　　If you'll implore it, that will free your life,
　　But fetter you till death.

Claudio. 　　　　　　　Perpetual durance?°

Isabella. Ay, just; perpetual durance, a restraint,
　　Though all the world's vastidity° you had,
　　To a determined scope.°

59 **leiger** resident ambassador　60 **appointment** preparation　67 **durance** imprisonment　69 **vastidity** vast spaces　70 **determined scope** fixed
limit (i.e., the reprieve may win him the world, but will cost him his
soul)

70 *Claudio.*   But in what nature?

Isabella. In such a one as, you consenting to't,
    Would bark your honor from that trunk you bear,
    And leave you naked.

Claudio.   Let me know the point.

Isabella. O, I do fear thee, Claudio, and I quake,
75   Lest thou a feverous life shouldst entertain,
    And six or seven winters more respect
    Than a perpetual honor. Dar'st thou die?
    The sense° of death is most in apprehension,°
    And the poor beetle that we tread upon
80   In corporal sufferance finds a pang as great
    As when a giant dies.

Claudio.   Why give you me this shame?
    Think you I can a resolution fetch
    From flow'ry tenderness? If I must die,
    I will encounter darkness as a bride,
85   And hug it in mine arms.

Isabella. There spake my brother, there my father's
        grave
    Did utter forth a voice. Yes, thou must die,
    Thou art too noble to conserve a life
    In base appliances.° This outward-sainted deputy,
90   Whose settled° visage and deliberate word
    Nips youth i' th' head, and follies doth enmew°
    As falcon doth the fowl, is yet a devil;
    His filth within being cast,° he would appear
    A pond as deep as hell.

Claudio.   The prenzie° Angelo!

95 *Isabella.* O, 'tis the cunning livery of hell,
    The damned'st body to invest and cover
    In prenzie guards.° Dost thou think, Claudio,
    If I would yield him my virginity,

78 **sense** feeling   78 **apprehension** imagination   89 **appliances** devices
90 **settled** composed   91 **enmew** drive into the water (as a hawk drives
a fowl)   93 **cast** vomited up   94 **prenzie** (meaning uncertain; often
emended to "princely," or "precise")   97 **guards** trimmings

Thou mightst be freed?

Claudio.   O heavens, it cannot be.

Isabella. Yes, he would give't thee, from this rank
    offense,   *100*
So to offend him still. This night's the time
That I should do what I abhor to name,
Or else thou diest tomorrow.

Claudio.   Thou shalt not do't.

Isabella. O, were it but my life,
    I'd throw it down for your deliverance   *105*
As frankly as a pin.

Claudio.   Thanks, dear Isabel.

Isabella. Be ready, Claudio, for your death tomorrow.

Claudio. Yes. Has he affections° in him,
That thus can make him bite the law by th' nose,
When he would force° it? Sure, it is no sin,   *110*
Or of the deadly seven° it is the least.

Isabella. Which is the least?

Claudio. If it were damnable, he being so wise,
Why would he for the momentary trick
Be perdurably fined?° O Isabel!   *115*

Isabella. What says my brother?

Claudio.   Death is a fearful thing.

Isabella. And shamèd life a hateful.

Claudio. Ay, but to die, and go we know not where,
To lie in cold obstruction° and to rot,
This sensible° warm motion° to become   *120*
A kneaded clod; and the delighted° spirit
To bathe in fiery floods, or to reside

108 **affections** sensual appetites 110 **force** enforce 111 **deadly
seven** (pride, envy, wrath, sloth, avarice, gluttony, lechery) 114–15
Why ... fined i.e., why for the momentary trifle (of sexual intercourse) would he be eternally damned 119 **obstruction** motionless-
ness 120 **sensible** feeling 120 **motion** organism 121 **delighted**
capable of delight

In thrilling region of thick-ribbèd ice;
To be imprisoned in the viewless winds,
125   And blown with restless violence round about
The pendent° world; or to be·worse than worst
Of those that lawless and incertain thought
Imagine howling—'tis too horrible!
The weariest and most loathèd worldly life
130   That age, ache, penury, and imprisonment
Can lay on nature is a paradise
To what we fear of death.

Isabella. Alas, alas.

Claudio.   Sweet sister, let me live:
What sin you do to save a brother's life,
135   Nature dispenses with° the deed so far
That it becomes a virtue.

Isabella.   O you beast,°
O faithless coward, O dishonest wretch!
Wilt thou be made a man out of my vice?°
Is't not a kind of incest, to take life
From thine own sister's shame? What should I
140   think?
Heaven shield° my mother played my father fair,
For such a warpèd slip of wilderness°
Ne'er issued from his blood. Take my defiance,
Die, perish! Might but my bending down
145   Reprieve thee from thy fate, it should proceed.
I'll pray a thousand prayers for thy death,
No word to save thee.

Claudio. Nay, hear me, Isabel.

Isabella.   O, fie, fie, fie!
Thy sin's not accidental, but a trade.
150   Mercy to thee would prove itself a bawd,
'Tis best that thou diest quickly.

Claudio.   O, hear me, Isabella!

126 **pendent** hanging in space   135 **dispenses with** grants a dispensa-
tion for   136 **beast** (which lacks a rational soul)   138 **vice** (there may
be an anatomical pun here)   141 **shield** grant that   142 **wilderness**
wild nature without nurture

[*The Duke comes forward.*]

Duke. Vouchsafe a word, young sister, but one word.

Isabella. What is your will?

Duke. Might you dispense with your leisure, I would
by and by have some speech with you: the satis-   155
faction I would require is likewise your own benefit.

Isabella. I have no superfluous leisure; my stay must
be stolen out of other affairs, but I will attend you
awhile.

Duke. [*Aside to Claudio*] Son, I have overheard what   160
hath passed between you and your sister. Angelo
had never the purpose to corrupt her; only he hath
made an assay° of her virtue to practice his judgment with the disposition of natures. She, having
the truth of honor in her, hath made him that   165
gracious denial which he is most glad to receive. I am
confessor to Angelo, and I know this to be true;
therefore prepare yourself to death. Do not satisfy
your resolution with hopes that are fallible. Tomorrow you must die; go to your knees, and make   170
ready.

Claudio. Let me ask my sister pardon. I am so out
of love with life, that I will sue to be rid of it.

Duke. Hold you there; farewell. [*Exit Claudio.*] Provost, a word with you.   175

[*Enter Provost.*]

Provost. What's your will, father?

Duke. That now you are come, you will be gone.
Leave me awhile with the maid. My mind promises
with my habit° no loss shall touch her by my company.   180

Provost. In good time.°   *Exit.*

Duke. The hand that hath made you fair hath made

163 **assay** test   179 **habit** religious dress   181 **In good time** very
well

185

190

you good. The goodness that is cheap in beauty
makes beauty brief in goodness; but grace, being
the soul of your complexion, shall keep the body
of it ever fair.° The assault that Angelo hath made
to you, fortune hath conveyed to my understanding, and, but that frailty hath examples for his falling, I should wonder at Angelo. How will you do
to content this substitute, and to save your brother?

Isabella. I am now going to resolve° him. I had rather
my brother die by the law than my son should be
unlawfully born. But O, how much is the good
Duke deceived in Angelo! If ever he return and I
can speak to him, I will open my lips in vain, or
discover his government.°

195

Duke. That shall not be much amiss. Yet, as the matter now stands, he will avoid your accusation: he
made trial of you only. Therefore fasten your ear
on my advisings; to the love I have in doing good
a remedy presents itself. I do make myself believe
that you may most uprighteously do a poor
wronged lady a merited benefit; redeem your
brother from the angry law; do no stain to your
own gracious person; and much please the absent
Duke, if peradventure he shall ever return to have
hearing of this business.

200

205

Isabella. Let me hear you speak farther. I have spirit
to do anything that appears not foul in the truth
of my spirit.

210

Duke. Virtue is bold, and goodness never fearful.
Have you not heard speak of Mariana, the sister
of Frederick, the great soldier who miscarried at
sea?

215   *Isabella.* I have heard of the lady, and good words
went with her name.

183–86 **The goodness . . . fair** (The general sense is that beauty will dis-
card that virtue which is not beautiful, but grace being the soul of
Isabella's character [**complexion**] she will always remain both beautiful
and virtuous)   191 **resolve** convey my resolution to   196 **discover his
government** expose his rule

Duke. She should this Angelo have married; was affianced to her by oath,° and the nuptial appointed:
between which time of the contract and limit of the
solemnity,° her brother Frederick was wracked at   220
sea, having in that perished vessel the dowry of his
sister. But mark how heavily this befell to the poor
gentlewoman: there she lost a noble and renowned
brother, in his love toward her ever most kind and
natural; with him, the portion and sinew° of her for-   225
tune, her marriage dowry; with both, her com-
binate° husband, this well-seeming Angelo.

Isabella. Can this be so? Did Angelo so leave her?

Duke. Left her in her tears, and dried not one of them
with his comfort; swallowed his vows whole, pre-   230
tending in her discoveries of dishonor: in few, bestowed her on her own lamentation, which she yet
wears for his sake; and he, a marble to her tears,
is washed with them, but relents not.

Isabella. What a merit were it in death to take this   235
poor maid from the world! What corruption in this
life, that it will let this man live! But how out of
this can she avail?°

Duke. It is a rupture that you may easily heal, and
the cure of it not only saves your brother, but   240
keeps you from dishonor in doing it.

Isabella. Show me how, good father.

Duke. This forenamed maid hath yet in her the continuance of her first affection; his unjust unkindness, that in all reason should have quenched her   245
love, hath, like an impediment in the current, made
it more violent and unruly. Go you to Angelo;
answer his requiring with a plausible obedience;
agree with his demands to the point; only refer
yourself to this advantage: first, that your stay with   250
him may not be long; that the time may have all

217–18 **affianced ... oath** (it was a betrothal that allowed conjugal
rights, although without the approval of the church. If the rights were
exercised, marriage became compulsory.)   219–20 **limit of the solemnity**
date set for the wedding ceremony   225 **sinew** substance   226–27
combinate betrothed   238 **avail** benefit

shadow and silence in it; and the place answer to
convenience. This being granted in course—and
now follows all—we shall advise this wronged maid
255   to stead up° your appointment, go in your place.
If the encounter° acknowledge itself hereafter, it
may compel him to her recompense: and here, by
this, is your brother saved, your honor untainted,
the poor Mariana advantaged, and the corrupt dep-
260   uty scaled.° The maid will I frame° and make fit
for his attempt. If you think well to carry this, as
you may, the doubleness of the benefit defends the
deceit from reproof. What think you of it?

Isabella. The image of it gives me content already,
265   and I trust it will grow to a most prosperous perfection.

Duke. It lies much in your holding up. Haste you
speedily to Angelo: if for this night he entreat you
to his bed, give him promise of satisfaction. I will
270   presently to Saint Luke's;° there at the moated
grange° resides this dejected Mariana. At that
place call upon me, and dispatch with Angelo, that
it may be quickly.

Isabella. I thank you for this comfort. Fare you well,
275   good father.   *Exit.*

[Scene 2. *Before the prison.*]

Enter, [*to the Duke,*] *Elbow, Clown*
[*Pompey, and*] *Officers.*

Elbow. Nay, if there be no remedy for it, but that
you will needs buy and sell men and women like

---

255 **stead up** keep   256 **encounter** i.e. sexual union   260 **scaled**
weighed   260 **frame** prepare   270 **St. Luke's** (St. Luke's day, 18th
October, was considered auspicious for choosing a husband [C. W. Whit-
worth, *SQ* 1985: 214])   271 **grange** farm

beasts, we shall have all the world drink brown and
white bastard.°

Duke. O heavens! What stuff is here?   5

Pompey. 'Twas never merry world since, of two
usuries,° the merriest was put down, and the worser
allowed by order of law a furred gown to keep him
warm; and furred with fox and lamb skins too, to
signify that craft, being richer than innocency,   10
stands for the facing.°

Elbow. Come your way, sir. 'Bless you, good father
friar.

Duke. And you, good brother father. What offense
hath this man made you, sir?   15

Elbow. Marry, sir, he hath offended the law; and, sir,
we take him to be a thief too, sir; for we have found
upon him, sir, a strange picklock, which we have sent
to the deputy.°

Duke. Fie, sirrah, a bawd, a wicked bawd!   20
The evil that thou causest to be done,
That is thy means to live. Do thou but think
What 'tis to cram a maw° or clothe a back
From such a filthy vice; say to thyself,
From their abominable and beastly touches°   25
I drink, I eat, array myself, and live.
Canst thou believe thy living is a life,
So stinkingly depending? Go mend, go mend.

Pompey. Indeed, it does stink in some sort, sir; but
yet, sir, I would prove—   30

Duke. Nay, if the devil have given thee proofs for sin,
Thou wilt prove his. Take him to prison, officer.
Correction° and instruction must both work
Ere this rude beast will profit.

Elbow. He must before the deputy, sir; he has given   35
him warning. The deputy cannot abide a whore-

3.2.4 **bastard** (1) a sweet Spanish wine (2) produce brown and white bastard children 6–7 **two usuries** lending money at interest (a way of
breeding barren metal) and fornication 11 **stands for the facing** represents the trimming 23 **maw** belly 25 **touches** sexual contacts 33
Correction punishment

master; if he be a whoremonger, and comes before
him, he were as good go a mile on his errand.°

Duke. That we were all, as some would seem to be,
40   From our faults, as faults from seeming, free!

Enter Lucio.

Elbow. His neck will come to your waist—a cord,° sir.

Pompey. I spy comfort; I cry bail. Here's a gentleman
and a friend of mine.

Lucio. How now, noble Pompey! What, at the wheels
45   of Caesar? Art thou led in triumph? What, is there
none of Pygmalion's images,° newly made woman,
to be had now, for putting the hand in the pocket
and extracting it clutched? What reply, ha? What
say'st thou to this tune, matter and method? Is't not
50   drowned i' th' last rain, ha? What say'st thou, Trot?
Is the world as it was, man? Which is the way? Is
it sad, and few words? Or how? The trick of it?

Duke. Still thus, and thus; still worse.

Lucio. How doth my dear morsel, thy mistress? Pro-
55   cures she still, ha?

Pompey. Troth, sir, she hath eaten up all her beef,°
and she is herself in the tub.°

Lucio. Why, 'tis good. It is the right of it; it must be
so: ever your fresh whore and your powdered bawd,
60   an unshunned consequence; it must be so. Art going
to prison, Pompey?

Pompey. Yes, faith, sir.

Lucio. Why, 'tis not amiss, Pompey. Farewell; go, say

---

38 **he were ... errand** i.e., he has a hard (or fruitless?) journey
ahead   41 **cord** i.e., the cord around the Friar's waist   46 **Pygmalion's
images** i.e., prostitutes (Pompey is compared to Pygmalion, sculptor of
a female statue that came to life)   56 **beef** prostitutes (who serve as
flesh-food)   57 **in the tub** taking the cure for venereal disease (a tub
was also used for corning beef, hence the reference to powdering—
pickling—in Lucio's next speech)

I sent thee thither. For debt, Pompey? Or how?

Elbow. For being a bawd, for being a bawd.   65

Lucio. Well, then, imprison him. If imprisonment be
the due of a bawd, why, 'tis his right. Bawd is he
doubtless, and of antiquity too, bawd-born. Farewell, good Pompey. Commend me to the prison,
Pompey, you will turn good husband° now, Pom-   70
pey, you will keep the house.

Pompey. I hope, sir, your good worship will be my
bail.

Lucio. No, indeed, will I not, Pompey, it is not the
wear.° I will pray, Pompey, to increase your bond-   75
age. If you take it not patiently, why, your mettle°
is the more. Adieu, trusty Pompey. 'Bless you, friar.

Duke. And you.

Lucio. Does Bridget paint still, Pompey, ha?

Elbow. Come your ways, sir, come.   80

Pompey. You will not bail me then, sir?

Lucio. Then, Pompey, nor now. What news abroad,
friar, what news?

Elbow. Come your ways, sir, come.

Lucio. Go to kennel, Pompey, go. [*Exeunt Elbow,*   85
Pompey, and Officers.] What news, friar, of the
Duke?

Duke. I know none. Can you tell me of any?

Lucio. Some say he is with the Emperor of Russia;
other some, he is in Rome: but where is he, think   90
you?

Duke. I know not where; but wheresoever, I wish him
well.

Lucio. It was a mad fantastical trick of him to steal

70 **husband** housekeeper, manager   75 **wear** fashion   76 **mettle** spirit
(pun on metal of chains)

95   from the state, and usurp the beggary he was never
       born to. Lord Angelo dukes it well in his absence;
       he puts transgression to't.°

Duke. He does well in't.

Lucio. A little more lenity to lechery would do no
100   harm in him; something too crabbed that way, friar.

Duke. It is too general a vice, and severity must
       cure it.

Lucio. Yes, in good sooth, the vice is of a great
       kindred, it is well allied; but it is impossible to
105   extirp it quite, friar, till eating and drinking be
       put down. They say this Angelo was not made by
       man and woman after this downright way of cre-
       ation. Is it true, think you?

Duke. How should he be made, then?

110 *Lucio.* Some report a sea maid° spawned him; some,
       that he was begot between two stockfishes.° But it
       is certain that when he makes water his urine is
       congealed ice; that I know to be true. And he is a
       motion generative;° that's infallible.

115 *Duke.* You are pleasant, sir, and speak apace.

Lucio. Why, what a ruthless thing is this in him, for
       the rebellion of a codpiece to take away the life of
       a man! Would the Duke that is absent have done
       this? Ere he would have hanged a man for the get-
120   ting a hundred bastards, he would have paid for
       the nursing a thousand. He had some feeling of the
       sport; he knew the service, and that instructed him
       to mercy.

Duke. I never heard the absent Duke much detected
125   for° women; he was not inclined that way.

Lucio. O, sir, you are deceived.

97 puts transgression to't vigorously prosecutes law-breaking   **110
sea maid** (to explain his piscatory coldness)   **111 stockfishes** dried
cod   **114 motion generative** masculine puppet   **124–25 detected for**
accused of

Duke. 'Tis not possible.

Lucio. Who, not the Duke? Yes, your beggar of fifty,
and his use was to put a ducat in her clack-dish;°
the Duke had crotchets° in him. He would be drunk   *130*
too; that let me inform you.

Duke. You do him wrong, surely.

Lucio. Sir, I was an inward° of his. A shy fellow was
the Duke, and I believe I know the cause of his
withdrawing.   *135*

Duke. What, I prithee, might be the cause?

Lucio. No, pardon; 'tis a secret must be locked within
the teeth and the lips; but this I can let you understand, the greater file° of the subject held the Duke
to be wise.   *140*

Duke. Wise! Why, no question but he was.

Lucio. A very superficial, ignorant, unweighing fellow.

Duke. Either this is envy in you, folly, or mistaking.
The very stream of his life and the business he hath
helmed° must, upon a warranted need,° give him a   *145*
better proclamation. Let him be but testimonied in
his own bringings-forth,° and he shall appear to the
envious a scholar, a statesman, and a soldier. Therefore you speak unskillfully; or if your knowledge
be more, it is much dark'ned in your malice.   *150*

Lucio. Sir, I know him, and I love him.

Duke. Love talks with better knowledge, and knowledge with dearer love.

Lucio. Come, sir, I know what I know.

Duke. I can hardly believe that, since you know not   *155*
what you speak. But, if ever the Duke return, as
our prayers are he may, let me desire you to make

129 **clack-dish** beggar's bowl (metaphorical here) 130 **crotchets**
whims 133 **inward** intimate companion 139 **greater file** majority
145 **helmed** guided 145 **upon a warranted need** if proof be demanded 147 **bringings-forth** actions

your answer before him. If it be honest you have
spoke, you have courage to maintain it. I am bound
160   to call upon you, and I pray you, your name?

Lucio. Sir, my name is Lucio, well known to the Duke.

Duke. He shall know you better, sir, if I may live to
report you.

Lucio. I fear you not.

165 *Duke.* O, you hope the Duke will return no more, or
you imagine me too unhurtful an opposite. But,
indeed, I can do you little harm: you'll forswear this
again.

Lucio. I'll be hanged first; thou art deceived in me,
170   friar. But no more of this. Canst thou tell if Claudio
die tomorrow or no?

Duke. Why should he die, sir?

Lucio. Why? For filling a bottle with a tundish.° I
would the Duke we talk of were returned again;
175   this ungenitured° agent will unpeople the province
with continency; sparrows must not build in his
house-eaves, because they are lecherous. The Duke
yet would have dark deeds darkly answered; he
would never bring them to light. Would he were
180   returned! Marry, this Claudio is condemned for untrussing.° Farewell, good friar; I prithee, pray for
me. The Duke, I say to thee again, would eat mutton on Fridays.° He's not past it, yet, and I say
to thee, he would mouth with a beggar, though she
185   smelled brown bread and garlic. Say that I said so.
Farewell.   *Exit.*

Duke. No might nor greatness in mortality
Can censure 'scape; back-wounding calumny
The whitest virtue strikes. What kind so strong

173 **tundish** funnel   175 **ungenitured** sexless   180–81 **untrussing**
undressing   182–83 **eat mutton on Fridays** (the Duke allegedly
ate mutton on a Friday, which was a fast day, and also practiced
venery; "mutton" also means "harlot," and Friday is the day of the
planet Venus)

Can tie the gall up in the slanderous tongue?
But who comes here?

Enter Escalus, Provost, and [Officers with]
Bawd [Mistress Overdone].

Escalus. Go, away with her to prison!

Mistress Overdone. Good my lord, be good to me. Your honor is accounted a merciful man, good my lord.

Escalus. Double and treble admonition, and still forfeit in the same kind! This would make mercy swear, and play the tyrant.

Provost. A bawd of eleven years' continuance, may it please your honor.

Mistress Overdone. My lord, this is one Lucio's information against me. Mistress Kate Keepdown was with child by him in the Duke's time; he promised her marriage; his child is a year and a quarter old, come Philip and Jacob;° I have kept it myself, and see how he goes about to abuse me.

Escalus. That fellow is a fellow of much license; let him be called before us. Away with her to prison. Go to, no more words. [*Exeunt Officers with Mistress Overdone.*] Provost, my brother Angelo will not be altered; Claudio must die tomorrow. Let him be furnished with divines, and have all charitable preparation. If my brother wrought by my pity, it should not be so with him.

Provost. So please you, this friar hath been with him, and advised him for th' entertainment° of death.

Escalus. Good even, good father.

Duke. Bliss and goodness on you!

Escalus. Of whence are you?

205 **Philip and Jacob** May 1 (Feast of Saints Philip and James)
216 **entertainment** reception

220 *Duke.* Not of this country, though my chance is now
         To use it for my time; I am a brother
         Of gracious order, late come from the See°
         In special business from his Holiness.

    Escalus. What news abroad i' th' world?

225 *Duke.* None, but that there is so great a fever on good-
         ness, that the dissolution of it must cure it,° novelty
         is only in request,° and it is as dangerous to be
         aged° in any kind of course as it is virtuous to be
         constant in any undertaking. There is scarce truth
230   enough alive to make societies secure, but security°
         enough to make fellowships° accursed. Much upon
         this riddle runs the wisdom of the world. This news
         is old enough, yet it is every day's news. I pray
         you, sir, of what disposition was the Duke?

235 *Escalus.* One that, above all other strifes, contended
         especially to know himself.

    Duke. What pleasure was he given to?

    Escalus. Rather rejoicing to see another merry, than
         merry at anything which professed to make him
240   rejoice: a gentleman of all temperance. But leave
         we him to his events, with a prayer they may prove
         prosperous, and let me desire to know how you
         find Claudio prepared. I am made to understand
         that you have lent him visitation.

245 *Duke.* He professes to have received no sinister meas-
         ure from his judge, but most willingly humbles him-
         self to the determination of justice; yet had he
         framed to himself, by the instruction of his frailty,
         many deceiving promises of life; which I, by my
250   good leisure, have discredited to him, and now is
         he resolved to die.

    Escalus. You have paid the heavens your function,

    222 **the See** the Vatican in Rome   225–26 **fever … cure it** i.e., the
    dissolution of the fever alone can now restore goodness to its pristine
    health   226–27 **novelty is only in request** change is urgently
    needed   228 **aged** old and worn out   230 **security** heedlessness
    231 **fellowships** human societies

and the prisoner the very debt of your calling. I
have labored for the poor gentleman to the extremest shore of my modesty,° but my brother   255
justice have I found so severe, that he hath forced
me to tell him he is indeed Justice.

Duke. If his own life answer the straitness of his pro-
ceeding, it shall become him well; wherein if he
chance to fail, he hath sentenced himself.   260

Escalus. I am going to visit the prisoner. Fare you
well.

Duke. Peace be with you!
                    [*Exeunt Escalus and Provost.*]
He who the sword of heaven will bear
Should be as holy as severe;   265
Pattern in himself to know
Grace to stand, and virtue go;°
More nor less to others paying
Than by self-offenses weighing.
Shame to him whose cruel striking   270
Kills for faults of his own liking.
Twice treble shame on Angelo,
To weed my° vice and let his grow.
O, what may man within him hide,
Though angel on the outward side!   275
How may likeness made in crimes,
Making practice° on the times,
To draw with idle spiders' strings
Most ponderous and substantial things?
Craft against vice I must apply: 280
With Angelo tonight shall lie
His old betrothèd but despisèd;
So disguise shall, by th' disguisèd,
Pay with falsehood false exacting,
And perform an old contracting.   285
                    Exit.

254–55 **extremest shore of my modesty** i.e., as far as is proper
266–67 **Pattern ... go** i.e., he should have a model in himself of
grace which will stand if virtue elsewhere ebbs   273 **my** (used imper-
sonally)   277 **Making practice** practicing deception

ACT 4

Scene 1. [*The moated grange.*]

Enter Mariana and Boy singing.

SONG
Take, O, take those lips away,
    That so sweetly were forsworn;
And those eyes, the break of day,
    Lights that do mislead the morn;
5   But my kisses bring again, bring again;
    Seals of love, but sealed in vain, sealed in vain.

Enter Duke [disguised as before].

Mariana. Break off thy song, and haste thee quick
    away.
Here comes a man of comfort, whose advice
Hath often stilled my brawling° discontent.
                            [Exit Boy.]
10 I cry you mercy, sir; and well could wish
You had not found me here so musical.
Let me excuse me, and believe me so,
My mirth it much displeased, but pleased my woe.

Duke. 'Tis good; though music oft hath such a charm

4.1.9 **brawling** discordant

To make bad good, and good provoke to harm.　　*15*
I pray you, tell me, hath anybody inquired for me
here today? Much upon this time have I promised
here to meet.

Mariana. You have not been inquired after; I have
sat here all day.　　*20*

Enter Isabella.

Duke. I do constantly believe you. The time is come
even now. I shall crave your forbearance° a little;
may be I will call upon you anon, for some advantage to yourself.

Mariana. I am always bound to you.　　　　*Exit. 25*

Duke. Very well met, and well come.
What is the news from this good deputy?

Isabella. He hath a garden circummured° with brick,
Whose western side is with a vineyard backed;
And to that vineyard is a planchèd° gate,　　*30*
That makes his opening with this bigger key.
This other doth command a little door
Which from the vineyard to the garden leads.
There have I made my promise
Upon the heavy° middle of the night　　*35*
To call upon him.

Duke. But shall you on your knowledge find this way?

Isabella. I have ta'en a due and wary note upon't.
With whispering and most guilty diligence,
In action all of precept,° he did show me　　*40*
The way twice o'er.

Duke.　　　　　　Are there no other tokens
Between you 'greed concerning her observance?°

Isabella. No, none, but only a repair i' th' dark,
And that I have possessed° him my most stay

22 **crave your forbearance** request you to withdraw for a while　28
circummured walled around　30 **planchèd** planked　35 **heavy** (when
sleep tends to be heavy)　40 **In . . . precept** teaching by gestures　42
her observance what she must do　44 **possessed** informed

45   Can be but brief; for I have made him know
        I have a servant comes with me along,
        That stays upon° me, whose persuasion° is
        I come about my brother.

Duke.   'Tis well borne up.
        I have not yet made known to Mariana
50   A word of this. What, ho, within! Come forth.

                Enter Mariana.

        I pray you, be acquainted with this maid;
        She comes to do you good.

Isabella.   I do desire the like.

Duke. Do you persuade yourself that I respect you?

Mariana. Good friar, I know you do, and have found
        it.

55 *Duke.* Take, then, this your companion by the hand,
        Who hath a story ready for your ear.
        I shall attend your leisure, but make haste;
        The vaporous night approaches.

Mariana. Will't please you walk aside?
                        Exit [*with Isabella*].

60 *Duke.* O place and greatness, millions of false eyes
        Are stuck upon thee; volumes of report
        Run with these false and most contrarious quests°
        Upon thy doings; thousand escapes° of wit
        Make thee the father of their idle dreams,
        And rack thee in their fancies.

                Enter Mariana and Isabella.

65   Welcome, how agreed?

Isabella. She'll take the enterprise upon her, father,
        If you advise it.

Duke.   It is not my consent

47 **stays upon** waits for   47 **persuasion** conviction   62 **quests** cry
of the hound on the scent   63 **escapes** sallies

But my entreaty too.

Isabella.   Little have you to say
When you depart from him, but, soft and low,
"Remember now my brother."

Mariana.   Fear me not.   70

Duke. Nor, gentle daughter, fear you not at all.
He is your husband on a precontract;°
To bring you thus together, 'tis no sin,
Sith that the justice of your title to him
Doth flourish° the deceit. Come, let us go: 75
Our corn's to reap, for yet our tithe's° to sow.
                                   Exeunt.

Scene 2. [*The prison.*]

Enter Provost and Clown [Pompey].

Provost. Come hither, sirrah. Can you cut off a man's
head?

Pompey. If the man be a bachelor, sir, I can; but if he
be a married man, he's his wife's head,° and I can
never cut off a woman's head.

Provost. Come, sir, leave me your snatches,° and yield
me a direct answer. Tomorrow morning are to die
Claudio and Barnardine. Here is in our prison a
common executioner, who in his office lacks a
helper. If you will take it on you to assist him, it   10
shall redeem you from your gyves;° if not, you
shall have your full time of imprisonment, and your

72 **precontract** legally binding betrothal agreement   75 **flourish** embellish   76 **tithe** tithe corn   4.2.4 **he's his wife's head** (see Ephesians 5:23: "For the husband is the head of the wife")   6 **snatches** quibbles
11 **gyves** shackles

deliverance with an unpitied whipping, for you
have been a notorious bawd.

15 *Pompey.* Sir, I have been an unlawful bawd time out
of mind, but yet I will be content to be a lawful
hangman. I would be glad to receive some instruction from my fellow partner.

Provost. What, ho, Abhorson!° Where's Abhorson,
20   there?

Enter Abhorson.

Abhorson. Do you call, sir?

Provost. Sirrah, here's a fellow will help you tomorrow in your execution. If you think it meet, com-
pound° with him by the year, and let him abide
25   here with you; if not, use him for the present, and
dismiss him. He cannot plead his estimation° with
you; he hath been a bawd.

Abhorson. A bawd, sir? Fie upon him! He will dis-
credit our mystery.°

30 *Provost.* Go to, sir; you weigh equally; a feather will
turn the scale.   *Exit.*

Pompey. Pray, sir, by your good favor—for surely,
sir, a good favor° you have, but that you have a
hanging look—do you call, sir, your occupation
35   a mystery?

Abhorson. Ay, sir; a mystery.

Pompey. Painting, sir, I have heard say, is a mystery;
and your whores, sir, being members of my occupation, using painting, do prove my occupation a
40   mystery; but what mystery there should be in hanging, if I should be hanged, I cannot imagine.

Abhorson. Sir, it is a mystery.

19 **Abhorson** (pun on "ab, whore, son," son from a whore) 23–24
compound settle 26 **estimation** reputation 29 **mystery** craft 33
favor countenance

Pompey. Proof?

Abhorson. Every true man's apparel fits your thief: if
it be too little for your thief, your true man thinks it   45
big enough; if it be too big for your thief, your thief
thinks it little enough: so every true man's apparel
fits your thief.°

Enter Provost.

Provost. Are you agreed?

Pompey. Sir, I will serve him; for I do find your hang-   50
man is a more penitent trade than your bawd; he
doth oft'ner ask forgiveness.°

Provost. You, sirrah, provide your block and your ax
tomorrow four o'clock.

Abhorson. Come on, bawd. I will instruct thee in my   55
trade; follow.

Pompey. I do desire to learn, sir; and I hope, if you
have occasion to use me for your own turn,°
you shall find me yare;° for, truly, sir, for your
kindness I owe you a good turn.   60

Provost. Call hither Barnardine and Claudio.

Exit [Pompey with Abhorson].

Th' one has my pity; not a jot the other,
Being a murderer, though he were my brother.

Enter Claudio.

Look, here's the warrant, Claudio, for thy death.
'Tis now dead midnight, and by eight tomorrow   65
Thou must be made immortal. Where's Barnardine?

Claudio. As fast locked up in sleep as guiltless labor
When it lies starkly° in the traveler's bones;
He will not wake.

44–48 **Every ... thief** (interpretation uncertain)   52 **ask forgiveness**
(the executioner always asked the condemned man to forgive him)
58 **turn** execution (pun)   59 **yare** ready   68 **starkly** stiffly

Provost.   Who can do good on him?
     Well, go, prepare yourself. [*Knocking within.*] But,
70   hark, what noise?—
     Heaven give your spirits comfort. [*Exit Claudio.*]
        By and by.
     I hope it is some pardon or reprieve
     For the most gentle Claudio. Welcome, father.

          Enter Duke [*disguised as before*].

Duke. The best and wholesom'st spirits of the night
     Envelop you, good provost! Who called here of
75   late?

Provost. None since the curfew rung.

Duke. Not Isabel?

Provost.   No.

Duke.   They will, then, ere't be long.

Provost. What comfort is for Claudio?

Duke. There's some in hope.

80 *Provost.* It is a bitter deputy.

Duke. Not so, not so; his life is paralleled
     Even with the stroke and line of his great justice.
     He doth with holy abstinence subdue
     That in himself which he spurs on his pow'r
85   To qualify° in others; were he mealed° with that
     Which he corrects, then were he tyrannous;
     But this being so, he's just.   [*Knocking within.*]
                     Now are they come.
                          [*Exit Provost.*]
     This is a gentle provost—seldom when
     The steelèd° jailer is the friend of men.
                          [*Knocking within.*]
     How now, what noise? That spirit's possessed with
90   haste

85 **qualify** moderate   85 **mealed** stained   89 **steelèd** hardened

That wounds th' unsisting° postern° with these
   strokes.

                [*Enter Provost.*]

Provost. There he must stay until the officer
   Arise to let him in; he is called up.

Duke. Have you no countermand for Claudio yet,
   But he must die tomorrow?

Provost.   None, sir, none.   95

Duke. As near the dawning, provost, as it is,
   You shall hear more ere morning.

Provost.   Happily
   You something know; yet I believe there comes
   No countermand; no such example have we.
   Besides, upon the very siege° of justice   100
   Lord Angelo hath to the public ear
   Professed the contrary.

                Enter a Messenger.

                        This is his lord's man.

Duke. And here comes Claudio's pardon.

Messenger. My lord hath sent you this note, and by
   me this further charge, that you swerve not from   105
   the smallest article of it, neither in time, matter,
   or other circumstance. Good morrow; for, as I
   take it, it is almost day.

Provost. I shall obey him.

                [*Exit Messenger.*]

Duke. [*Aside*] This is his pardon, purchased by such
   sin   110
   For which the pardoner himself is in.
   Hence hath offense his quick celerity,

---

91 **unsisting** (perhaps "unassisting," perhaps a printer's slip for "resist-
ing") 91 **postern** small door 100 **siege** seat

When it is borne in high authority.
When vice makes mercy, mercy's so extended,°
115 That for the fault's love is th' offender friended.
Now, sir, what news?

Provost. I told you. Lord Angelo, belike° thinking
me remiss in mine office, awakens me with this un-
wonted putting-on;° methinks strangely, for he hath
120 not used it before.

Duke. Pray you, let's hear.

Provost. [*Reads*] *the letter.* "Whatsoever you may hear
to the contrary, let Claudio be executed by four
of the clock; and in the afternoon Barnardine. For
125 my better satisfaction, let me have Claudio's head
sent me by five. Let this be duly performed with a
thought that more depends on it than we must yet
deliver. Thus fail not to do your office, as you will
answer it at your peril."
130 What say you to this, sir?

Duke. What is that Barnardine who is to be executed
in th' afternoon?

Provost. A Bohemian born, but here nursed up and
bred; one that is a prisoner nine years old.

135 *Duke.* How came it that the absent Duke had not
either delivered him to his liberty or executed him?
I have heard it was ever his manner to do so.

Provost. His friends still wrought reprieves for him;
and, indeed, his fact,° till now in the government
140 of Lord Angelo, came not to an undoubtful proof.

Duke. It is now apparent?

Provost. Most manifest, and not denied by himself.

Duke. Hath he borne himself penitently in prison?
How seems he to be touched?

145 *Provost.* A man that apprehends death no more dread-
fully but as a drunken sleep; careless, reckless, and

114 **extended** stretched   117 **belike** perhaps   119 **putting-on** urging
139 **fact** evil deed

fearless of what's past, present, or to come; insensible of mortality, and desperately mortal.°

Duke. He wants° advice.

Provost. He will hear none. He hath evermore had the   150
liberty of the prison; give him leave to escape hence,
he would not: drunk many times a day, if not many
days entirely drunk. We have very oft awaked him,
as if to carry him to execution, and showed him a
seeming warrant for it; it hath not moved him at all.   155

Duke. More of him anon. There is written in your
brow, provost, honesty and constancy: if I read it
not truly, my ancient skill beguiles me; but, in the
boldness of my cunning,° I will lay myself in hazard.° Claudio, whom here you have warrant to exe-   160
cute, is no greater forfeit to the law than Angelo who
hath sentenced him. To make you understand this
in a manifested effect,° I crave but four days' res-
pite, for the which you are to do me both a
present° and a dangerous courtesy.   165

Provost. Pray, sir, in what?

Duke. In the delaying death.

Provost. Alack, how may I do it, having the hour limited,° and an express command, under penalty, to
deliver his head in the view of Angelo? I may make   170
my case as Claudio's, to cross this in the smallest.

Duke. By the vow of mine Order I warrant you, if my
instructions may be your guide. Let this Barnardine
be this morning executed, and his head borne to
Angelo.   175

Provost. Angelo hath seen them both, and will discover the favor.°

Duke. O, death's a great disguiser; and you may add

148 **desperately mortal** about to die without hope of the future
149 **wants** needs   159 **cunning** knowledge   159–60 **lay myself in
hazard** take a risk   163 **in a manifested effect** by open proof
165 **present** immediate   168–69 **limited** determined   176–77 **discover the favor** recognize the face

to it. Shave the head, and tie the beard; and say it
180 was the desire of the penitent to be so bared° before his death; you know the course is common.
If anything fall to you upon this, more than thanks
and good fortune, by the saint whom I profess, I
will plead against it with my life.

185 *Provost.* Pardon me, good father; it is against my oath.

Duke. Were you sworn to the Duke, or to the deputy?

Provost. To him, and to his substitutes.

Duke. You will think you have made no offense, if the
Duke avouch the justice of your dealing?

190 *Provost.* But what likelihood is in that?

Duke. Not a resemblance, but a certainty. Yet since
I see you fearful,° that neither my coat, integrity,
nor persuasion can with ease attempt° you, I will
go further than I meant, to pluck all fears out of
195 you. Look you, sir, here is the hand and seal of the
Duke. You know the character,° I doubt not, and
the signet is not strange to you.

Provost. I know them both.

Duke. The contents of this is the return of the Duke.
200 You shall anon overread it at your pleasure, where
you shall find, within these two days he will be
here. This is a thing that Angelo knows not; for he
this very day receives letters of strange tenor, perchance of the Duke's death, perchance entering into
205 some monastery, but by chance nothing of what is
writ. Look, th' unfolding star° calls up the shepherd. Put not yourself into amazement how these
things should be: all difficulties are but easy when
they are known. Call your executioner, and off with
210 Barnardine's head; I will give him a present shrift,°

180 **bared** shaved   192 **fearful** full of fear   193 **attempt** move   196
character handwriting   206 **unfolding star** morning star (signaling the
shepherd to lead the sheep from the fold)   210 **shrift** absolution

and advise him for a better place. Yet you are
amazed; but this shall absolutely resolve° you.
Come away; it is almost clear dawn.

                              Exit [with Provost].

Scene 3. [*The prison.*]

Enter Clown [Pompey].

Pompey. I am as well acquainted here as I was in our
house of profession: one would think it were Mistress Overdone's own house, for here be many of
her old customers. First, here's young Master Rash;
he's in for a commodity° of brown paper and old   5
ginger, ninescore and seventeen pounds, of which
he made five marks,° ready money; marry, then
ginger was not much in request, for the old women
were all dead. Then is there here one Master Caper,
at the suit of Master Three-pile the mercer, for   10
some four suits of peach-colored satin, which now
peaches° him a beggar. Then have we here young
Dizzy, and young Master Deep-vow, and Master
Copper-spur,° and Master Starve-lackey, the rapier
and dagger man, and young Drop-heir that killed   15
lusty Pudding, and Master Forthright the tilter,°
and brave Master Shoe-tie° the great traveler, and
wild Half-can° that stabbed Pots, and, I think,
forty more; all great doers° in our trade, and are
now "for the Lord's sake."°   20

212 **resolve** convince   4.3.5 **commodity** (worthless goods whose
purchase at a heavy price was forced on a debtor in dire need by
a usurious creditor, who thus circumvented the contemporary laws
against usury)   7 **marks** (a mark was about two-thirds of a pound)
12 **peaches** betrays   14 **Copper-spur** i.e., Master Pretentious (cop-
per was a bogus substitute for gold)   16 **tilter** fighter   17 **Shoe-tie**
rosette (worn by gallants)   18 **Half-can** (a larger vessel than a pot)
19 **doers** fornicators   20 **"for the Lord's sake"** (the cry of prisoners
begging alms from passers-by)

Enter Abhorson.

Abhorson. Sirrah, bring Barnardine hither.

Pompey. Master Barnardine! You must rise and be hanged, Master Barnardine!

Abhorson. What, ho, Barnardine!

25 *Barnardine.* (*Within*) A pox o' your throats! Who makes that noise there? What are you?

Pompey. Your friends, sir; the hangman. You must be so good, sir, to rise and be put to death.

Barnardine. [*Within*] Away, you rogue, away! I am
30 sleepy.

Abhorson. Tell him he must awake, and that quickly too.

Pompey. Pray, Master Barnardine, awake till you are executed, and sleep afterwards.

35 *Abhorson.* Go into him, and fetch him out.

Pompey. He is coming, sir, he is coming; I hear his straw rustle.

Enter Barnardine.

Abhorson. Is the ax upon the block, sirrah?

Pompey. Very ready, sir.

40 *Barnardine.* How now, Abhorson? What's the news with you?

Abhorson. Truly, sir, I would desire you to clap into your prayers; for, look you, the warrant's come.

Barnardine. You rogue, I have been drinking all night;
45 I am not fitted for't.

Pompey. O, the better, sir: for he that drinks all night, and is hanged betimes° in the morning, may sleep the sounder all the next day.

47 **betimes** early

Enter Duke [disguised as before].

Abhorson. Look you, sir; here comes your ghostly°
  father. Do we jest now, think you?   50

Duke. Sir, induced by my charity, and hearing how
  hastily you are to depart, I am come to advise you,
  comfort you, and pray with you.

Barnardine. Friar, not I: I have been drinking hard
  all night, and I will have more time to prepare me,   55
  or they shall beat out my brains with billets.° I will
  not consent to die this day, that's certain.

Duke. O, sir, you must; and therefore I beseech you
  Look forward on the journey you shall go.

Barnardine. I swear I will not die today for any man's   60
  persuasion.

Duke. But hear you—

Barnardine. Not a word. If you have anything to say
  to me, come to my ward, for thence will not I today.
                                                    Exit.

Enter Provost.

Duke. Unfit to live or die. O gravel heart!   65
  After him, fellows; bring him to the block.
                        [*Exeunt Abhorson and Pompey.*]

Provost. Now, sir, how do you find the prisoner?

Duke. A creature unprepared, unmeet for death;
  And to transport him in the mind he is
  Were damnable.

Provost.   Here in the prison, father,   70
  There died this morning of a cruel fever
  One Ragozine, a most notorious pirate,
  A man of Claudio's years, his beard and head
  Just of his color. What if we do omit
  This reprobate till he were well inclined,°   75
  And satisfy the deputy with the visage

49 **ghostly** spiritual   56 **billets** cudgels   75 **well inclined** agreeable
to being executed, mentally prepared

Of Ragozine, more like to Claudio?

Duke. O, 'tis an accident that heaven provides.
Dispatch it presently;° the hour draws on
80   Prefixed° by Angelo. See this be done,
And sent according to command, whiles I
Persuade this rude wretch willingly to die.

Provost. This shall be done, good father, presently;
But Barnardine must die this afternoon,
85   And how shall we continue Claudio,
To save me from the danger that might come
If he were known alive?

Duke.   Let this be done:
Put them in secret holds,° both Barnardine and
     Claudio.
Ere twice the sun hath made his journal° greeting
90   To yonder generation, you shall find
Your safety manifested.

Provost. I am your free dependant.°

Duke. Quick, dispatch, and send the head to Angelo.
                              Exit [Provost].
Now will I write letters to Angelo—
95   The provost, he shall bear them—whose contents
Shall witness to him I am near at home,
And that by great injunctions I am bound
To enter publicly. Him I'll desire
To meet me at the consecrated fount,
100   A league below the city; and from thence,
By cold gradation° and well-balanced form,
We shall proceed with Angelo.

                    Enter Provost.

Provost. Here is the head; I'll carry it myself.

Duke. Convenient is it. Make a swift return,

---

79 **presently** at once   80 **Prefixed** predetermined   88 **holds** cells
89 **journal** daily   92 **your free dependant** freely at your service
101 **cold gradation** deliberate steps

For I would commune with you of such things   *105*
That want° no ear but yours.

Provost.   I'll make all speed.

                                        Exit.

Isabella. (Within) Peace, ho, be here!

Duke. The tongue of Isabel. She's come to know
If yet her brother's pardon be come hither.
But I will keep her ignorant of her good,   *110*
To make her heavenly comforts of despair
When it is least expected.

                    Enter Isabella.

Isabella.   Ho, by your leave!

Duke. Good morning to you, fair and gracious daughter.

Isabella. The better, given me by so holy a man.
Hath yet the deputy sent my brother's pardon?   *115*

Duke. He hath released him, Isabel, from the world;
His head is off, and sent to Angelo.

Isabella. Nay, but it is not so.

Duke. It is no other. Show your wisdom, daughter,
In your close° patience.   *120*

Isabella. O, I will to him and pluck out his eyes!

Duke. You shall not be admitted to his sight.

Isabella. Unhappy Claudio, wretched Isabel,
Injurious world, most damnèd Angelo!

Duke. This nor hurts him nor profits you a jot;   *125*
Forbear it therefore, give your cause to heaven.
Mark what I say, which you shall find
By every syllable a faithful verity.
The Duke comes home tomorrow——nay, dry your
eyes——
One of our covent,° and his confessor,   *130*

106 **want** need   120 **close** deep, secret   130 **covent** convent

Gives me this instance:° already he hath carried
Notice to Escalus and Angelo,
Who do prepare to meet him at the gates,
There to give up their pow'r. If you can, pace°
     your wisdom
135   In that good path that I would wish it go,
And you shall have your bosom° on this wretch,
Grace of the Duke, revenges to your heart,
And general honor.

Isabella.   I am directed by you.

Duke. This letter, then, to Friar Peter give;
140   'Tis that he sent me of the Duke's return.
Say, by this token, I desire his company
At Mariana's house tonight. Her cause and yours
I'll perfect him withal, and he shall bring you
Before the Duke; and to the head of Angelo
145   Accuse him home and home. For my poor self,
I am combinèd° by a sacred vow,
And shall be absent. Wend you with this letter;
Command these fretting waters from your eyes
With a light heart; trust not my holy Order,
150   If I pervert your course. Who's here?

                    Enter Lucio.

Lucio. Good even. Friar, where's the provost?

Duke. Not within, sir.

Lucio. O pretty Isabella, I am pale at mine heart to
     see thine eyes so red; thou must be patient. I am
155   fain to dine and sup with water and bran; I dare
     not for my head fill my belly; one fruitful meal
     would set me to't. But they say the Duke will be
     here tomorrow. By my troth, Isabel, I loved thy
     brother. If the old fantastical Duke of dark cor-
160   ners had been at home, he had lived.

                         [*Exit Isabella.*]

131 **instance** proof   134 **pace** conduct   136 **bosom** desire   146 **com-
binèd** bound

Duke. Sir, the Duke is marvelous little beholding to
your reports; but the best is, he lives not in them.

Lucio. Friar, thou knowest not the Duke so well as I
do; he's a better woodman° than thou tak'st him
for.   *165*

Duke. Well, you'll answer this one day. Fare ye well.

Lucio. Nay, tarry, I'll go along with thee: I can tell
thee pretty tales of the Duke.

Duke. You have told me too many of him already,
sir, if they be true; if not true, none were enough.   *170*

Lucio. I was once before him for getting a wench
with child.

Duke. Did you such a thing?

Lucio. Yes, marry, did I; but I was fain to forswear
it: they would else have married me to the rotten   *175*
medlar.°

Duke. Sir, your company is fairer than honest. Rest
you well.

Lucio. By my troth, I'll go with thee to the lane's end.
If bawdy talk offend you, we'll have very little of   *180*
it. Nay, friar, I am a kind of burr; I shall stick.

                                              Exeunt.

Scene 4. [*A room.*]

Enter Angelo and Escalus.

Escalus. Every letter he hath writ hath disvouched°
other.

---

164 **woodman** hunter (here, of women)   176 **medlar** applelike fruit
edible only when partly decayed (here, a prostitute)   4.4.1. **disvouched**
contradicted

Angelo. In most uneven and distracted manner. His
   actions show much like to madness; pray heaven
5 his wisdom be not tainted. And why meet him at
   the gates, and redeliver our authorities there?

Escalus. I guess not.

Angelo. And why should we proclaim it in an hour
   before his ent'ring, that if any crave redress of in-
10 justice, they should exhibit their petitions in the
   street?

Escalus. He shows his reason for that: to have a dispatch of complaints, and to deliver us from devices°
   hereafter which shall then have no power to stand
15 against us.

Angelo. Well, I beseech you, let it be proclaimed.
   Betimes i' th' morn I'll call you at your house. Give
   notice to such men of sort and suit° as are to meet
   him.

20 *Escalus.* I shall, sir. Fare you well.   *Exit.*

Angelo. Good night.
   This deed unshapes me quite, makes me unpreg-
      nant,°
   And dull to all proceedings. A deflow'red maid,
   And by an eminent body that enforced
25 The law against it! But that her tender shame
   Will not proclaim against her maiden loss,°
   How might she tongue me! Yet reason dares her no;
   For my authority bears of a credent bulk,°
   That no particular scandal once can touch
   But it confounds the breather. He should have
30   lived,
   Save that his riotous youth, with dangerous sense,°
   Might in the times to come have ta'en revenge,
   By so receiving a dishonored life

13 **devices** false complaints, plots   18 **men of sort and suit** noblemen
22 **unpregnant** unreceptive   26 **maiden laws** laws of maidenhood
28 **bears of a credent bulk** is derived from a trusted personage   31
sense feeling

With ransom of such shame. Would yet he had
    lived!
Alack, when once our grace we have forgot,   *35*
Nothing goes right; we would, and we would not.

                                     Exit.

Scene 5. [*Outside the town.*]

Enter Duke [*in his own habit*] *and Friar Peter.*

Duke. These letters at fit time deliver me.°
The provost knows our purpose and our plot.
The matter being afoot, keep your instruction,
And hold you ever to our special drift,
Though sometimes you do blench° from this to that,   *5*
As cause doth minister. Go call at Flavius' house,
And tell him where I stay; give the like notice
To Valencius, Rowland, and to Crassus,
And bid them bring the trumpets to the gate;
But send me Flavius first.

Friar Peter.   It shall be speeded well.   *10*
                                   [*Exit.*]

Enter Varrius.

Duke. I thank thee, Varrius; thou hast made good
    haste.
Come, we will walk. There's other of our friends
Will greet us here anon, my gentle Varrius.   *Exeunt.*

4.5.1 **me** for me   5 **blench** deviate

Scene 6. [*Near the city gate.*]

Enter Isabella and Mariana.

Isabella. To speak so indirectly I am loath:
I would say the truth; but to accuse him so,
That is your part. Yet I am advised to do it,
He says, to veil full purpose.

Mariana.   Be ruled by him.

5   *Isabella.* Besides, he tells me that, if peradventure
He speak against me on the adverse side,
I should not think it strange; for 'tis a physic
That's bitter to sweet end.

Mariana. I would Friar Peter—

Enter Friar Peter.

Isabella.   O peace! The friar is come.

Friar Peter. Come, I have found you out a stand most
10   fit
Where you may have such vantage° on the Duke,
He shall not pass you. Twice have the trumpets
sounded.
The generous° and gravest citizens
Have hent° the gates, and very near upon
15   The Duke is ent'ring: therefore, hence, away!

                                   Exeunt.

4.6.11 **vantage** advantageous position 13 **generous** highborn 14
hent gathered at

ACT 5

Scene 1. [*The city gate.*]

Enter Duke, Varrius, Lords, Angelo, Escalus,
Lucio, [Provost, Officers, and] Citizens, at
several doors.

Duke. My very worthy cousin,° fairly met.
  Our old and faithful friend, we are glad to see you.

Angelo, Escalus. Happy return be to your royal
  Grace.

Duke. Many and hearty thankings to you both.
  We have made inquiry of you, and we hear   5
  Such goodness of your justice, that our soul
  Cannot but yield you forth to public thanks,
  Forerunning more requital.°

Angelo.   You make my bonds still greater.

Duke. O, your desert speaks loud, and I should wrong
    it
  To lock it in the wards of covert bosom,°   10

5.1.1 **cousin** (a sovereign's address to a nobleman) 8 **Forerunning
more requital** preceding additional reward 10 **To ... bosom** i.e.,
to keep it locked hidden in my heart

When it deserves, with characters of brass,
A forted residence 'gainst the tooth of time
And razure° of oblivion. Give me your hand,
And let the subject see, to make them know
15   That outward courtesies would fain proclaim
Favors that keep° within. Come, Escalus,
You must walk by us on our other hand—
And good supporters are you.

Enter [Friar] Peter and Isabella.

Friar Peter. Now is your time: speak loud, and kneel
before him.

20   *Isabella.* Justice, O royal Duke! Vail your regard°
Upon a wronged—I would fain have said, a maid.
O worthy prince, dishonor not your eye
By throwing it on any other object
Till you have heard me in my true complaint
25   And given me justice, justice, justice, justice!

Duke. Relate your wrongs. In what? By whom? Be
brief.
Here is Lord Angelo shall give you justice;
Reveal yourself to him.

Isabella.   O worthy Duke,
You bid me seek redemption of the devil.
30   Hear me yourself, for that which I must speak
Must either punish me, not being believed,
Or wring redress from you. Hear me, O hear me,
here!

Angelo. My lord, her wits, I fear me, are not firm.
She hath been a suitor to me for her brother
Cut off by course of justice—

35   *Isabella.*   By course of justice!

Angelo. And she will speak most bitterly and strange.

Isabella. Most strange, but yet most truly, will I speak.

13 **razure** erasure   16 **keep** dwell   20 **Vail your regard** cast your
attention

That Angelo's forsworn, is it not strange?
That Angelo's a murderer, is't not strange?
That Angelo is an adulterous thief,   40
An hypocrite, a virgin-violator;
Is it not strange, and strange?

Duke.   Nay, it is ten times strange.

Isabella. It is not truer he is Angelo
Than this is all as true as it is strange.
Nay, it is ten times true, for truth is truth   45
To th' end of reck'ning.

Duke.   Away with her! Poor soul,
She speaks this in th' infirmity of sense.

Isabella. O prince, I conjure thee, as thou believ'st
There is another comfort than this world,
That thou neglect me not, with that opinion   50
That I am touched with madness. Make not impossible
That which but seems unlike.° 'Tis not impossible
But one, the wicked'st caitiff on the ground,
May seem as shy, as grave, as just, as absolute°
As Angelo; even so may Angelo,   55
In all his dressings, caracts,° titles, forms,
Be an arch-villain. Believe it, royal prince;
If he be less, he's nothing; but he's more,
Had I more name for badness.

Duke.   By mine honesty,
If she be mad, as I believe no other,   60
Her madness hath the oddest frame of sense,
Such a dependency of thing on thing,
As e'er I heard in madness.

Isabella.   O gracious Duke,
Harp not on that; nor do not banish reason
For inequality,° but let your reason serve   65
To make the truth appear where it seems hid,
And hide the false seems° true.

52 **unlike** unlikely 54 **absolute** perfect 56 **caracts** symbols of
office 65 **inequality** injustice 67 **seems** which seems

Duke.   Many that are not mad
   Have, sure, more lack of reason. What would you
   say?

Isabella. I am the sister of one Claudio,
70   Condemned upon the act of fornication
   To lose his head, condemned by Angelo.
   I, in probation° of a sisterhood,
   Was sent to by my brother, one Lucio
   As then the messenger—

Lucio.   That's I, and't like° your Grace.
75   I came to her from Claudio, and desired her
   To try her gracious fortune with Lord Angelo
   For her poor brother's pardon.

Isabella.   That's he indeed.

Duke. You were not bid to speak.

Lucio.   No, my good lord,
   Nor wished to hold my peace.

Duke.   I wish you now, then;
80   Pray you, take note of it, and when you have
   A business for yourself, pray heaven you then
   Be perfect.°

Lucio.   I warrant your honor.

Duke. The warrant's° for yourself; take heed to't.

Isabella. This gentleman told somewhat of my tale—

85 *Lucio.* Right.

Duke. It may be right; but you are i' the wrong
   To speak before your time. Proceed.

Isabella.   I went
   To this pernicious caitiff deputy—

Duke. That's somewhat madly spoken.

---

72 **probation** novitiate   74 **and't like** if it please   82 **perfect** thoroughly prepared   83 **warrant** warning

Isabella.　　　　　　　　　　　　　Pardon it;
　　The phrase is to the matter.° 　　　　　　　　　90

Duke. Mended again. The matter: proceed.

Isabella. In brief, to set the needless process by,
　　How I persuaded, how I prayed, and kneeled,
　　How he refelled° me, and how I replied—
　　For this was of much length—the vild° conclusion 　　95
　　I now begin with grief and shame to utter.
　　He would not, but by gift of my chaste body
　　To his concupiscible intemperate lust,
　　Release my brother; and after much debatement,
　　My sisterly remorse° confutes mine honor, 　　　　100
　　And I did yield to him; but the next morn betimes,
　　His purpose surfeiting,° he sends a warrant
　　For my poor brother's head.

Duke. 　　　　　　　　　　This is most likely!

Isabella. O, that it were as like as it is true!

Duke. By heaven, fond wretch, thou know'st not what
　　　　thou speak'st, 　　　　　　　　　　　　　105
　　Or else thou art suborned against his honor
　　In hateful practice.° First, his integrity
　　Stands without blemish. Next, it imports no reason°
　　That with such vehemency he should pursue
　　Faults proper° to himself; if he had so offended, 　　110
　　He would have weighed thy brother by himself,
　　And not have cut him off. Someone hath set you on;
　　Confess the truth, and say by whose advice
　　Thou cam'st here to complain.

Isabella. 　　　　　　　　　　And is this all?
　　Then, O you blessèd ministers above, 　　　　　　115
　　Keep me in patience, and with ripened time
　　Unfold the evil which is here wrapped up
　　In countenance.° Heaven shield your Grace from
　　　　woe,

90 **to the matter** appropriate　94 **refelled** repelled　95 **vild** vile　100
remorse pity　102 **surfeiting** satiating　107 **practice** plot　108 **imports no reason** does not stand to reason　110 **proper** belonging　118
countenance confident expression

As I, thus wrongèd, hence unbelievèd go!

120 *Duke.* I know you'd fain be gone. An officer,
To prison with her! Shall we thus permit
A blasting and a scandalous breath to fall
On him so near us? This needs must be a practice.
Who knew of your intent and coming hither?

125 *Isabella.* One that I would were here, Friar Lodowick.

Duke. A ghostly° father, belike. Who knows that
Lodowick?

Lucio. My lord, I know him; 'tis a meddling friar,
I do not like the man. Had he been lay,° my lord,
For certain words he spake against your Grace
130 In your retirement, I had swingèd° him soundly.

Duke. Words against me! This's a good friar, belike!
And to set on this wretched woman here
Against our substitute! Let this friar be found.

Lucio. But yesternight, my lord, she and that friar,
135 I saw them at the prison; a saucy friar,
A very scurvy° fellow.

Friar Peter. Blessed be your royal Grace!
I have stood by, my lord, and I have heard
Your royal ear abused. First, hath this woman
140 Most wrongfully accused your substitute,
Who is as free from touch or soil with her
As she from one ungot.°

Duke.   We did believe no less.
Know you that Friar Lodowick that she speaks of?

Friar Peter. I know him for a man divine and holy;
145 Not scurvy, nor a temporary meddler,°
As he's reported by this gentleman;
And, on my trust, a man that never yet
Did, as he vouches, misreport your Grace.

Lucio. My lord, most villainously; believe it.

126 **ghostly** spiritual, incorporeal 128 **lay** layman 130 **swinged**
thrashed 136 **scurvy** worthless 142 **ungot** unbegotten 145 **tem-**
porary meddler meddler in temporal affairs

Friar Peter. Well, he in time may come to clear him-
     self,   *150*
But at this instant he is sick, my lord,
Of a strange fever. Upon his mere° request,
Being come to knowledge that there was complaint
Intended 'gainst Lord Angelo, came I hither,
To speak, as from his mouth, what he doth know   *155*
Is true and false; and what he with his oath
And all probation° will make up full clear,
Whensoever he's convented.° First, for this woman,
To justify this worthy nobleman,
So vulgarly and personally accused,   *160*
Her shall you hear disprovèd to her eyes,
Till she herself confess it.

Duke.   Good friar, let's hear it.
               [*Isabella is carried off guarded.*]

         Enter Mariana [*veiled*].

Do you not smile at this, Lord Angelo?
O heaven, the vanity of wretched fools!
Give us some seats. Come, cousin Angelo,   *165*
In this I'll be impartial; be you judge
Of your own cause. Is this the witness, friar?
First, let her show her face, and after speak.

Mariana. Pardon, my lord; I will not show my face
   Until my husband bid me.   *170*

Duke. What, are you married?

Mariana. No, my lord.

Duke. Are you a maid?

Mariana. No, my lord.

Duke. A widow, then?   *175*

Mariana. Neither, my lord.

Duke. Why, you are nothing, then: neither maid,
   widow, nor wife?

152 **mere** special   157 **probation** proof   158 **convented** sent for

Lucio. My lord, she may be a punk;° for many of
180   them are neither maid, widow, nor wife.

Duke. Silence that fellow. I would he had some cause
To prattle for himself.

Lucio. Well, my lord.

Mariana. My lord, I do confess I ne'er was married,
185   And I confess, besides, I am no maid.
I have known° my husband; yet my husband
Knows not that ever he knew me.

Lucio. He was drunk, then, my lord; it can be no
better.

190   *Duke.* For the benefit of silence, would thou wert so
too!

Lucio. Well, my lord.

Duke. This is no witness for Lord Angelo.

Mariana. Now I come to't, my lord:
195   She that accuses him of fornication,
In selfsame manner doth accuse my husband,
And charges him, my lord, with such a time
When I'll depose I had him in mine arms
With all th' effect of love.

Angelo. Charges she moe than me?

200   *Mariana.*   Not that I know.

Duke. No? You say your husband?

Mariana. Why, just, my lord, and that is Angelo,
Who thinks he knows that he ne'er knew my body,
But knows he thinks that he knows Isabel's.

205   *Angelo.* This is a strange abuse. Let's see thy face.

Mariana. My husband bids me; now I will unmask.
                                    [*Unveiling.*]
This is that face, thou cruel Angelo,

179 **punk** harlot   186 **known** had intercourse with

Which once thou swor'st was worth the looking on;
This is the hand which, with a vowed contract,
Was fast belocked in thine; this is the body   *210*
That took away the match° from Isabel,
And did supply thee at thy garden house
In her imagined person.

Duke.   Know you this woman?

Lucio. Carnally, she says.

Duke.   Sirrah, no more!

Lucio. Enough, my lord.   *215*

Angelo. My lord, I must confess I know this woman:
    And five years since there was some speech of mar-
        riage
    Betwixt myself and her, which was broke off,
    Partly for that her promisèd proportions°
    Came short of composition,° but in chief,   *220*
    For that her reputation was disvalued
    In levity;° since which time of five years
    I never spake with her, saw her, nor heard from her,
    Upon my faith and honor.

Mariana.   Noble prince,
    As there comes light from heaven and words from
        breath,   *225*
    As there is sense in truth and truth in virtue,
    I am affianced this man's wife as strongly
    As words could make up vows; and, my good lord,
    But Tuesday night last gone in's garden house
    He knew me as a wife. As this is true,   *230*
    Let me in safety raise me from my knees,
    Or else forever be confixèd° here,
    A marble monument.

Angelo.   I did but smile till now;
    Now, good my lord, give me the scope of justice;
    My patience here is touched. I do perceive   *235*

211 **match** meeting   219 **proportions** dowry   220 **composition** previous agreement   221–22 **disvalued/In levity** discredited for lightness   232 **confixèd** fixed firmly

These poor informal° women are no more
But instruments of some more mightier member
That sets them on. Let me have way, my lord,
To find this practice out.

Duke.   Ay, with my heart,
240   And punish them to your height of pleasure.
Thou foolish friar and thou pernicious woman,
Compact° with her that's gone, think'st thou thy
      oaths,
Though they would swear down each particular
      saint,
Were testimonies against his worth and credit,
245   That's sealed in approbation?° You, Lord Escalus,
Sit with my cousin; lend him your kind pains
To find out this abuse, whence 'tis derived.
There is another friar that set them on;
Let him be sent for.

Friar Peter. Would he were here, my lord, for he, in-
250   deed,
Hath set the women on to this complaint:
Your provost knows the place where he abides,
And he may fetch him.

Duke.   Go, do it instantly. [*Exit Provost.*]
And you, my noble and well-warranted cousin,
255   Whom it concerns to hear this matter forth,
Do with your injuries as seems you best,
In any chastisement. I for a while
Will leave you, but stir not you till you have
Well determined upon these slanderers.

260   *Escalus.* My lord, we'll do it throughly. *Exit* [*Duke*].
Signior Lucio, did not you say you knew that Friar
Lodowick to be a dishonest person?

Lucio. Cucullus non facit monachum;° honest in
nothing but in his clothes, and one that hath spoke
265   most villainous speeches of the Duke.

236 **informal** (1) crazy (2) informing   242 **Compact** in collu-
sion   245 **approbation** attested integrity   263 **Cucullus non facit
monachum** the cowl does not make the monk (Latin)

Escalus. We shall entreat you to abide here till he
　come, and enforce° them against him; we shall find
　this friar a notable° fellow.

Lucio. As any in Vienna, on my word.

Escalus. Call that same Isabel here once again; I　270
　would speak with her. [*Exit an Attendant.*] Pray
　you, my lord, give me leave to question; you shall
　see how I'll handle her.

Lucio. Not better than he, by her own report.

Escalus. Say you?　275

Lucio. Marry, sir, I think, if you handled her pri-
　vately, she would sooner confess; perchance, pub-
　licly, she'll be ashamed.

　　　Enter Duke [*as friar*], *Provost, Isabella,*
　　　　[*and Officers*].

Escalus. I will go darkly° to work with her.

Lucio. That's the way; for women are light at mid-　280
　night.

Escalus. Come on, mistress, here's a gentlewoman
　denies all that you have said.

Lucio. My lord, here comes the rascal I spoke of—
　here with the provost.　285

Escalus. In very good time. Speak not you to him till
　we call upon you.

Lucio. Mum.

Escalus. Come, sir, did you set these women on to
　slander Lord Angelo? They have confessed you did.　290

Duke. 'Tis false.

Escalus. How! Know you where you are?

Duke. Respect to your great place; and let the devil

267 **enforce** urge　268 **notable** notorious　279 **darkly** subtly

  Be sometime honored for his burning throne.
295 Where is the Duke? 'Tis he should hear me speak.

Escalus. The Duke's in us, and we will hear you speak.
  Look you speak justly.

Duke. Boldly, at least. But, O poor souls,
  Come you to seek the lamb here of the fox?
300 Good night to your redress. Is the Duke gone?
  Then is your cause gone too. The Duke's unjust,
  Thus to retort° your manifest° appeal,
  And put your trial in the villain's mouth
  Which here you come to accuse.

305 *Lucio.* This is the rascal; this is he I spoke of.

Escalus. Why, thou unreverend and unhallowed friar,
  Is't not enough thou hast suborned these women
  To accuse this worthy man, but in foul mouth,
  And in the witness of his proper° ear,
310 To call him villain? And then to glance from him
  To th' Duke himself, to tax him with injustice?
  Take him hence; to th' rack with him. We'll touse°
   you
  Joint by joint, but we will know his purpose.
  What, "unjust"!

Duke.   Be not so hot. The Duke
315 Dare no more stretch this finger of mine than he
  Dare rack his own: his subject am I not,
  Nor here provincial.° My business in this state
  Made me a looker-on here in Vienna,
  Where I have seen corruption boil and bubble
320 Till it o'errun the stew. Laws for all faults,
  But faults so countenanced, that the strong statutes
  Stand like the forfeits° in a barber's shop,
  As much in mock as mark.°

Escalus. Slander to th' state! Away with him to prison!

302 **retort** refer back 302 **manifest** clear 309 **proper** very 312
touse pull 317 **provincial** belonging to the ecclesiastical province of
this state 322 **forfeits** extracted teeth (barbers acted as dentists) 323
as much . . . mark to be mocked at as much as to be seen

Angelo. What can you vouch against him, Signior 325
Lucio? Is this the man that you did tell us of?

Lucio. 'Tis he, my lord. Come hither, goodman bald-
pate; do you know me?

Duke. I remember you, sir, by the sound of your
voice. I met you at the prison, in the absence of 330
the Duke.

Lucio. O, did you so? And do you remember what
you said of the Duke?

Duke. Most notedly, sir.

Lucio. Do you so, sir? And was the Duke a flesh- 335
monger, a fool, and a coward, as you then reported
him to be?

Duke. You must, sir, change persons with me, ere you
make that my report. You, indeed, spoke so of
him; and much more, much worse. 340

Lucio. O thou damnable fellow! Did not I pluck thee
by the nose for thy speeches?

Duke. I protest I love the Duke as I love myself.

Angelo. Hark, how the villain would close° now, after
his treasonable abuses. 345

Escalus. Such a fellow is not to be talked withal.
Away with him to prison! Where is the provost?
Away with him to prison, lay bolts enough upon
him, let him speak no more. Away with those gig-
lets° too, and with the other confederate compan- 350
ion.

Duke. [*To the Provost*] Stay, sir; stay awhile.

Angelo. What, resists he? Help him, Lucio.

Lucio. Come, sir; come, sir; come, sir; foh, sir! Why,
you bald-pated, lying rascal, you must be hooded, 355
must you? Show your knave's visage, with a pox

344 **close** conclude   349–50 **giglets** wanton women

to you. Show your sheep-biting° face, and be
hanged an hour. Will't not off?
[*Pulls off the friar's hood, and discovers the Duke.*]

Duke. Thou art the first knave that e'er mad'st a
Duke.
360   First, provost, let me bail these gentle three.
[*To Lucio*] Sneak not away, sir; for the friar and
you
Must have a word anon. Lay hold on him.

Lucio. This may prove worse than hanging.

Duke. [*To Escalus*] What you have spoke I pardon.
Sit you down.
We'll borrow place of him. [*To Angelo*] Sir, by
365   your leave.
Hast thou or word, or wit, or impudence,
That yet can do thee office?° If thou hast,
Rely upon it till my tale be heard,
And hold no longer out.

Angelo.   O my dread lord,
370   I should be guiltier than my guiltiness,
To think I can be undiscernible,
When I perceive your Grace, like pow'r divine,
Hath looked upon my passes.° Then, good prince,
No longer session° hold upon my shame,
375   But let my trial be mine own confession.
Immediate sentence then, and sequent death,
Is all the grace I beg.

Duke.   Come hither, Mariana.
Say, wast thou e'er contracted to this woman?

Angelo. I was, my lord.

380 *Duke.* Go take her hence, and marry her instantly.
Do you the office, friar, which consummate,
Return him here again. Go with him, provost.

Exit [*Angelo with Mariana, Friar Peter, and Provost*].

357 **sheep-biting** currish   367 **office** service   373 **passes** trespasses   374
session trial

Escalus. My lord, I am more amazed at his dishonor
  Than at the strangeness of it.

Duke.   Come hither, Isabel.
  Your friar is now your prince. As I was then   385
  Advertising and holy° to your business,
  Not changing heart with habit, I am still
  Attorneyed at your service.

Isabella.   O, give me pardon,
  That I, your vassal, have employed and pained
  Your unknown sovereignty!

Duke.   You are pardoned, Isabel: 390
  And now, dear maid, be you as free to us.
  Your brother's death, I know, sits at your heart,
  And you may marvel why I obscured myself,
  Laboring to save his life, and would not rather
  Make rash remonstrance of my hidden pow'r   395
  Than let him so be lost. O most kind maid,
  It was the swift celerity of his death,
  Which I did think with slower foot came on,
  That brained° my purpose. But, peace be with him.
  That life is better life, past fearing death,   400
  Than that which lives to fear. Make it your comfort,
  So happy is your brother.

      Enter Angelo, Mariana, [Friar] Peter, Provost.

Isabella.   I do, my lord.

Duke. For this new-married man, approaching here,
  Whose salt° imagination yet hath wronged
  Your well-defended honor, you must pardon   405
  For Mariana's sake. But as he adjudged your
      brother,
  Being criminal, in double violation,
  Of sacred chastity, and of promise-breach,
  Thereon dependent, for your brother's life,
  The very mercy of the law cries out   410

386 **Advertising and holy** attentive and devoted   399 **brained** knocked
on the head   404 **salt** lecherous

Most audible, even from his proper tongue,
"An Angelo for Claudio, death for death!"
Haste still pays haste, and leisure answers leisure;
Like doth quit like, and Measuré still for Measure.°
415   Then, Angelo, thy fault's thus manifested;
Which, though thou wouldst deny, denies thee vantage.
We do condemn thee to the very block
Where Claudio stooped to death, and with like haste.
Away with him.

Mariana.   O my most gracious lord,
420   I hope you will not mock me with a husband.

Duke. It is your husband mocked you with a husband.
Consenting to the safeguard of your honor,
I thought your marriage fit; else imputation,°
For that he knew you, might reproach your life,
425   And choke your good to come. For his possessions,
Although by confiscation they are ours,
We do instate and widow you withal,
To buy you a better husband.

Mariana.   O my dear lord,
I crave no other, nor no better man.

430   *Duke.* Never crave him; we are definitive.°

Mariana. Gentle my liege—   [*Kneeling.*]

Duke.   You do but lose your labor.
Away with him to death! [*To Lucio*] Now, sir, to you.

Mariana. O my good lord! Sweet Isabel, take my part,
Lend me your knees, and all my life to come
435   I'll lend you all my life to do you service.

Duke. Against all sense° you do importune her;

414 **Measure still for Measure** (see Matthew 7:1–2: "Judge not, that ye be not judged. For with what judgment ye judge, ye shall be judged: and with what measure ye mete, it shall be measured to you again") 423 **imputation** accusation 430 **definitive** determined 436 **sense** natural feeling and reason

Should she kneel down in mercy of this fact,°
Her brother's ghost his pavèd° bed would break,
And take her hence in horror.

Mariana.   Isabel,
Sweet Isabel, do yet but kneel by me,   440
Hold up your hands, say nothing, I'll speak all.
They say, best men are molded out of faults;
And, for the most, become much more the better
For being a little bad; so may my husband.
O Isabel, will you not lend a knee?   445

Duke. He dies for Claudio's death.

Isabella. [*Kneeling*]   Most bounteous sir,
Look, if it please you, on this man condemned,
As if my brother lived. I partly think
A due sincerity governèd his deeds,
Till he did look on me. Since it is so,   450
Let him not die. My brother had but justice,
In that he did the thing for which he died.
For Angelo,
His act did not o'ertake his bad intent,
And must be buried but as an intent   455
That perished by the way. Thoughts are no sub-
    jects,°
Intents but merely thoughts.

Mariana.   Merely, my lord.

Duke. Your suit's unprofitable; stand up, I say.
I have bethought me of another fault.
Provost, how came it Claudio was beheaded   460
At an unusual hour?

Provost.   It was commanded so.

Duke. Had you a special warrant for the deed?

Provost. No, my good lord; it was by private message.

Duke. For which I do discharge you of your office;
Give up your keys.

437 **fact** crime 438 **pavèd** slab-covered 456 **no subjects** i.e., not
subject to law

465 *Provost.*   Pardon me, noble lord.
   I thought it was a fault, but knew it not;°
   Yet did repent me, after more advice;°
   For testimony whereof, one in the prison,
   That should by private order else have died,
   I have reserved alive.

   Duke.   What's he?

470 *Provost.*   His name is Barnardine.

   Duke. I would thou hadst done so by Claudio.
   Go fetch him hither; let me look upon him.
                    [*Exit Provost.*]

   Escalus. I am sorry, one so learnèd and so wise
      As you, Lord Angelo, have still° appeared,
475   Should slip so grossly, both in the heat of blood,
      And lack of tempered judgment afterward.

   Angelo. I am sorry that such sorrow I procure,
      And so deep sticks it in my penitent heart,
      That I crave death more willingly than mercy;
480   'Tis my deserving, and I do entreat it.

         Enter Barnardine and Provost,
            Claudio [*muffled*], *Juliet.*

   Duke. Which is that Barnardine?

   Provost.   This, my lord.

   Duke. There was a friar told me of this man.
      Sirrah, thou art said to have a stubborn soul,
      That apprehends no further than this world,
      And squar'st° thy life according. Thou'rt con-
485   demned;
      But, for those earthly faults, I quit° them all,
      And pray thee take this mercy to provide
      For better times to come. Friar, advise him;
      I leave him to your hand. What muffled fellow's
         that?

466 **knew it not** was not sure   467 **advice** thought   474 **still** ever
485 **squar'st** regulate   486 **quit** pardon

Provost. This is another prisoner that I saved,   490
　　Who should have died when Claudio lost his head;
　　As like almost to Claudio as himself.
　　　　　　　　　　　　[*Unmuffles Claudio.*]

Duke. [*To Isabella*] If he be like your brother, for his
　　sake
　　Is he pardoned; and, for your lovely sake,
　　Give me your hand, and say you will be mine,   495
　　He is my brother too; but fitter time for that.
　　By this Lord Angelo perceives he's safe;
　　Methinks I see a quick'ning° in his eye.
　　Well, Angelo, your evil quits you well;
　　Look that you love your wife; her worth, worth
　　　　yours.   500
　　I find an apt remission° in myself,
　　And yet here's one in place I cannot pardon.
　　[*To Lucio*] You, sirrah, that knew me for a fool, a
　　　coward,
　　One all of luxury,° an ass, a madman;
　　Wherein have I so deserved of you,   505
　　That you extol me thus?

Lucio. 'Faith, my lord, I spoke it but according to the
　　trick.° If you will hang me for it, you may; but I
　　had rather it would please you I might be whipped.

Duke. Whipped first, sir, and hanged after.   510
　　Proclaim it, provost, round about the city,
　　If any woman wronged by this lewd fellow—
　　As I have heard him swear himself there's one
　　Whom he begot with child—let her appear,
　　And he shall marry her. The nuptial finished,   515
　　Let him be whipped and hanged.

Lucio. I beseech your highness, do not marry me to a
　　whore. Your highness said even now, I made you a
　　duke: good my lord, do not recompense me in
　　making me a cuckold.   520

---

498 **quick'ning** animation   501 **remission** wish to forgive   504 **lux-ury** lust   508 **trick** fashion

Duke. Upon mine honor, thou shalt marry her.
   Thy slanders I forgive; and therewithal
   Remit thy other forfeits. Take him to prison,
   And see our pleasure herein executed.°

525 *Lucio.* Marrying a punk, my lord, is pressing to death,
   whipping, and hanging.

Duke. Slandering a prince deserves it.
                [Exeunt Officers with Lucio.]
   She, Claudio, that you wronged,° look you restore.°
   Joy to you, Mariana. Love her, Angelo;
530 I have confessed her, and I know her virtue.
   Thanks, good friend Escalus, for thy much goodness;
   There's more behind° that is more gratulate.°
   Thanks, provost, for thy care and secrecy;
   We shall employ thee in a worthier place.
535 Forgive him, Angelo, that brought you home
   The head of Ragozine for Claudio's;
   Th' offense pardons itself. Dear Isabel,
   I have a motion° much imports your good,
   Whereto if you'll a willing ear incline,
540 What's mine is yours, and what is yours is mine.
   So, bring us to our palace, where we'll show
   What's yet behind, that's meet° you all should
     know.   *[Exeunt.]*

FINIS.

524 **executed** carried out   528 **wronged** (because his type of betrothal did not give conjugal rights to him according to the church)   528
restore i.e., by marriage   532 **behind** to come   532 **gratulate** gratifying   538 **motion** proposal   542 **meet** fitting

Textual Note

Our only authority for the text of *Measure for Measure* is the First Folio, whose text is on the whole a good one, probably based on a transcript (not extant) of Shakespeare's manuscripts made by Ralph Crane, the scrivener of the King's Players. He may have had access to the fair copy made for theater use and may have interfered with the text when it was not clear to him. The compositors who set up the text may have imposed their idiosyncracies, of spelling, for example, on the text. It seems a little disturbed in Act 1; the Duke's speech on "place and greatness" in this act would be more appropriate preceding his lines in 3.2, after the exit of Lucio. In the present text the act and scene divisions are translated from Latin and in two places depart from the Folio in order to correspond to the Globe text (the Globe's divisions are used in most books on Shakespeare): Globe 1.2 is split in the Folio into a new scene after the exit of Pompey, and Globe 3.2 is not marked in the Folio. The present edition corrects obvious typographical errors, modernizes spelling and punctuation, expands and regularizes speech prefixes, adjusts the lineation of a few passages, transfers the indication of locale ("The Scene: Vienna") and the *dramatis personae* ("The names of all the actors.") from the end to the beginning, and slightly alters the position of a few stage directions. Other substantial departures from the Folio are listed below, the present reading in italics and then the Folio reading in roman.

1.3.27 *Becomes more* More   43 *it* in

1.4.54 *givings-out* giuing-out

2 1.12 *your* our   39 *breaks* brakes (see Judith Rosenheim, *SQ* 35 [1984]: 87–91)

2.2.96 *new* now   111 *ne'er* neuer

2.4.9 *seared* feard   53 *or, to* and to   76 *Let me be* Let be   94 *all-binding* all-building

3.1.31 *serpigo* Sapego   52 *Bring me to hear them* Bring them to heare me   69 *Though* Through   130 *penury* periury   218 *by oath* oath

3.2.26 *eat, array* eate away   48 *extracting it* extracting   153 *dearer* deare   227 *and it* and as it   278 *strings* stings

4.1.62 *quests* Quest   64 *dreams* dreame

4.2.44–48 *If it be too little . . fits your thief* [F gives to Pompey]

4.3 16 *Forthright* Forthlight   90 *yonder* yond

4.4.6 *redeliver* reliuer

5.1.13 *me* we   168 *her face* your face   426 *confiscation* confutation   542 *that's* that

A Note on the Sources
of *Measure for Measure*

The principal sources of *Measure for Measure* are George Whetstone's play of *Promos and Cassandra* (1578) and its prose redaction in the same author's *Heptameron of Civil Discourses* (1582). Whetstone's own source was Giraldi Cinthio's *Hecatommithi* (1565); and Shakespeare almost certainly knew this work, which contains the story of Othello. He may, in addition, have also known Cinthio's posthumously published play of *Epitia* (1583). Brief summaries of these sources are given here for comparison with Shakespeare's treatment of the story.

CINTHIO'S *Hecatommithi*, DECADE 8, NOVELLA 5

The Emperor Maximian appoints one of his trusted men, Juriste, to rule over the city of Innsbruck. He charges him particularly to observe justice scrupulously. Juriste, who lacks all self-knowledge, accepts the grave responsibility with alacrity and for a while he is a model ruler.

A young man called Vico is brought before Juriste for violating a virgin, and is condemned to death according to the laws of the city. Vico's sister, Epitia, who is a student of philosophy and has a sweet way of speaking, pleads for her brother. Her brother is very young; he was moved by the impulse of love; the ravished maiden is unmarried and Vico is willing to marry her. The law was made so severe only to deter would-be offenders, not really to be enforced. Captivated by Epitia's beauty and eloquence, Juriste promises to reconsider the case. When she meets him again, he proposes that she should lie with him if she wants her brother's sentence to be mitigated. Epitia refuses unless Juriste is willing to marry her afterward. Juriste does not promise to do this, though he hints at the possibility. When Epitia goes to the prison to prepare her brother for his fate, Vico pleads passionately with her and appeals to her sisterly affection to save him. So Epitia reluctantly consents to Juriste's proposal. Juriste, however, orders the execution of Vico before lying with her.

In the morning Epitia goes home to find that Juriste has indeed kept his promise to release her brother—dead. She thinks of revenge, but instead appeals to the Emperor. The Emperor sends for Juriste and finds that the complaint is true. He first forces Juriste to marry Epitia, who is quite unwilling, and then he orders that Juriste be put to death. Now that Juriste is her husband, Epitia is in a cruel dilemma. She discourses to the Emperor on the superiority of clemency to justice. The Emperor is impressed with her forgiving nature and pardons Juriste. Epitia and her husband live happily ever after.

CINTHIO'S *Epitia*

The story is much the same as that in the *Hecatommithi*, but there are some new characters and the brother is secretly saved by the captain of the prison. The latter announces this fact at the end of the play, to the astonishment of the other characters and also the reader, who is not given a hint of it in the prefatory "argument."

Principal among the new characters are Angela, Juriste's sister, who conveys an offer of marriage from him to Epitia and testifies against him before the Emperor when Juriste breaks his word; a secretary and a podesta who argue respectively for and against forgiving Vico; a messenger who reports how Vico was put to death on special commission from the podesta, who had Juriste's authority to do so; and the captain of the prison, who brings the supposed head of Vico to Epitia.

Epitia refuses to plead for Juriste until she learns that her brother is alive. Believing that Juriste should be punished for evil intent, the Emperor is at first unwilling to pardon him even after Vico reappears, but he finally grants Epitia's suit in order that she may have "complete contentment."

WHETSTONE'S *Promos and Cassandra* AND *Heptameron*

In the play, Promos is appointed to rule over the city of Julio, and declares his resolve to render justice impartially. Reviving a defunct law, he sentences Andrugio to death for incontinence. The law will not accept marriage as sufficient recompense for the wrong. Andrugio's sister, Cassandra, weeps over the hard fate of her young brother, who appeals to her to plead with Promos. She therefore meets Promos and obtains a postponement of the execution. After she has left, Promos reveals in a soliloquy that he has fallen in love with her but is determined to overcome the temptation. However, having been encouraged by his corrupt servant, Phallax, to believe that Cassandra might be overcome, he is unable to subdue his desire for her. When she meets him again to know his final decision, he first defends the law and then, when she pleads for mercy, makes his infamous proposal.

Amazed and horrified, Cassandra refuses. Promos promises to make her his wife and gives her two days in which to think it over. She goes to her brother's cell to inform him of Promos' vile condition and to prepare him for death. Andrugio, taken aback that a judge of Promos' supposed integrity has been corrupted by the same lust for which he would condemn another, appeals to his sister to accept the proposed terms and thereby save his life. Brother and sister argue, but finally Cassandra is won over.

After satisfying his desire, Promos decides to break his word, since no one knows of his promise and Cassandra cannot reveal her own shame. He orders that Andrugio should be executed secretly and his head sent to Cassandra. While the girl is eagerly looking forward to welcoming her brother, the jailer brings her the severed head. She conceals her grief, pretending to be quite satisfied. She thinks of suicide, but later decides to appeal to the King. The jailer has in fact brought her the head of an executed criminal and released Andrugio, who goes into hiding. Promos is secretly troubled at what he has done.

In the second part of the play, the King comes to Julio. He hears Cassandra's story and promises to see that justice is done. Upon examination, Promos at once confesses, and the King orders that he first be married to Cassandra and then put to death. Promos pleads for mercy, but in vain. In the meantime, Andrugio, hiding in the woods, comes to know what is happening. Cassandra bewails her hard fate. Duty commands that she should love the husband for whose sentence she has been responsible. She appeals to the King to pardon him, but the ruler is adamant. Andrugio, now in the city under a disguise, sees his sister's unhappiness and resolves to surrender himself to the King at the risk of being put to death. Promos makes a sincere confession of his misdeeds and is led out to execution. Andrugio's boy enters with the news that his master is alive. The King pardons Andrugio, and then pardons Promos for the sake of Cassandra, exhorting Promos always to measure grace with justice. He restores him to the governorship of the city. "The lost sheep found, for joy the feast was made."

Whetstone's play has also a comic underplot, involving a courtesan, unscrupulous officers, informers, and bawds. With the corruption of the magistrates, all the city becomes corrupt.

The version in the *Heptameron* is substantially the same as that of the play. Andrugio is disguised as a hermit, and reveals himself after hearing the King say that Promos might be pardoned if Andrugio were alive. The entire story is narrated by one Isabella.

Summary

Measure for Measure is generally closer to Whetstone's versions than to *Epitia*; but it does show significant correspondences with Cinthio's play at certain points where Whetstone differs markedly. "The relation of *Measure for Measure* to Giraldi's *novella* is ambiguous, since some of the correspondences to that might have come through Whetstone, some through *Epitia*."[1] Among the similarities be-

[1]Madeleine Doran, *Endeavors of Art: A Study of Form in Elizabethan Drama.* Madison, Wisconsin: University of Wisconsin Press, 1954, pp. 386–87

tween *Measure for Measure* and *Epitia* may be mentioned the following: the secretary in *Epitia* protests to the podesta of the harshness of the law and the severity of its enforcement; in a soliloquy he comments on the rigor of those in power (compare Escalus' protests to Angelo in 2.1); the criminal whose head is substituted for that of Vico is hopelessly evil (compare Ragozine, described as a notorious pirate); like Isabella, Epitia also distinguishes between act and intention. Some close verbal parallels have been noted by Kenneth Muir.[2]

[2]*Shakespeare's Sources.* London. Methuen & Co., Ltd., 1957, I, pp 104–5.

Commentaries

G. WILSON KNIGHT

Measure for Measure and the Gospels

In *Measure for Measure* we have a careful dramatic pattern, a studied explication of a central theme: the moral nature of man in relation to the crudity of man's justice, especially in the matter of sexual vice. There is, too, a clear relation existing between the play and the Gospels, for the play's theme is this:

> Judge not, that ye be not judged. For with what judgment ye judge, ye shall be judged: and with what measure ye mete, it shall be measured to you again.   (Matthew 7:1–2)

The ethical standards of the Gospels are rooted in the thought of *Measure for Measure*. Therefore, in this analysis we shall, while fixing attention primarily on the play, yet inevitably find a reference to the New Testament continually helpful, and sometimes essential.

Measure for Measure is a carefully constructed work. Not until we view it as a deliberate artistic pattern of certain pivot ideas determining the play's action throughout shall we understand its peculiar nature. Though there is consummate psychological insight here and at least one person of most vivid and poignant human interest, we must first have

From *The Wheel of Fire* by G. Wilson Knight. 4th ed. rev. (London: Methuen & Co., Ltd., New York: British Book Centre, 1949). Reprinted by permission of Methuen & Co., Ltd.

regard to the central theme, and only second look for exact verisimilitude to ordinary processes of behavior. We must be careful not to let our human interest in any one person distort our single vision of the whole pattern. The play tends towards allegory or symbolism. The poet elects to risk a certain stiffness, or arbitrariness, in the directing of his plot rather than fail to express dramatically, with variety and precision, the full content of his basic thought. Any stiffness in the matter of human probability is, however, more than balanced by its extreme fecundity and compacted significance of dramatic symbolism. The persons of the play tend to illustrate certain human qualities chosen with careful reference to the main theme. Thus Isabella stands for sainted purity, Angelo for Pharisaical righteousness, the Duke for a psychologically sound and enlightened ethic. Lucio represents indecent wit, Pompey and Mistress Overdone professional immorality. Barnardine is hardheaded, criminal insensitiveness. Each person illumines some facet of the central theme: man's moral nature. The play's attention is confined chiefly to sexual ethics: which in isolation is naturally the most pregnant of analysis and the most universal of all themes. No other subject provides so clear a contrast between human consciousness and human instinct; so rigid a distinction between the civilized and the natural qualities of man; so amazing, yet so slight, a boundary set in the public mind between the foully bestial and the ideally divine in humanity. The atmosphere, purpose, and meaning of the play are throughout ethical. The Duke, lord of this play in the exact sense that Prospero is lord of *The Tempest*, is the prophet of an enlightened ethic. He controls the action from start to finish, he allots, as it were, praise and blame, he is lit at moments with divine suggestion comparable with his almost divine power of foreknowledge, and control, and wisdom. There is an enigmatic, otherworldly mystery suffusing his figure and the meaning of his acts: their results, however, in each case justify their initiation; wherein we see the allegorical nature of the play, since the plot is so arranged that each person receives his deserts in the light of the Duke's—which is really the Gospel—ethic.

The poetic atmosphere is one of religion and critical

morality. The religious coloring is orthodox, as in *Hamlet*. Isabella is a novice among "the votarists of St. Clare" (1.4.5); the Duke disguises himself as a Friar, exercising the divine privileges of his office towards Juliet, Barnardine, Claudio, Pompey. We hear of "the consecrated fount, a league below the city" (4.3.99). The thought of death's eternal damnation, which is prominent in *Hamlet*, recurs in Claudio's speech:

> Ay, but to die, and go we know not where,
> To lie in cold obstruction and to rot,
> This sensible warm motion to become
> A kneaded clod; and the delighted spirit
> To bathe in fiery floods, or to reside
> In thrilling region of thick-ribbèd ice;
> To be imprisoned in the viewless winds,
> And blown with restless violence round about
> The pendant world; or to be worse than worst
> Of those that lawless and incertain thoughts
> Imagine howling—'tis too horrible!
> The weariest and most loathèd worldly life
> That age, ache, penury, and imprisonment
> Can lay on nature is a paradise
> To what we fear in death.   (3.1.118–32)

So powerful can orthodox eschatology be in *Measure for Measure*: it is not, as I shall show, all-powerful. Nor is the play primarily a play of death philosophy: its theme is rather that of the Gospel ethic. And there is no more beautiful passage in all Shakespeare on the Christian redemption than Isabella's lines to Angelo:

>   Alas! Alas!
> Why, all the souls that were were forfeit once;
> And He that might the vantage best have took
> Found out the remedy. How would you be,
> If He which is the top of judgment, should
> But judge you as you are? O, think on that,
> And mercy then will breathe within your lips,
> Like man new made.   (2.2.72–79)

This is the natural sequence to Isabella's earlier lines:

> Well, believe this:
> No ceremony that to great ones 'longs,
> Not the king's crown, nor the deputed sword,
> The marshal's truncheon, nor the judge's robe,
> Become them with one half so good a grace
> As mercy does.   (58–63)

These thoughts are a repetition of those in Portia's famous "mercy" speech. There they come as a sudden, gleaming, almost irrelevant beam of the ethical imagination. But here they are not irrelevant: they are intrinsic with the thought of the whole play, the pivot of its movement. In *The Merchant of Venice* the Gospel reference is explicit:

> . . . We do pray for mercy,
> And that same prayer doth teach us all to render
> The deeds of mercy.   (4.1.199–201)

And the central idea of *Measure for Measure* is this:

> And forgive us our debts as we forgive our debtors.
>   (Matthew 6:12)

Thus "justice" is a mockery: man, himself a sinner, cannot presume to judge. That is the lesson driven home in *Measure for Measure*.

The atmosphere of Christianity pervading the play merges into the purely ethical suggestion implicit in the inter-criticism of all the persons. Though the Christian ethic be the central theme, there is a wider setting of varied ethical thought, voiced by each person in turn, high or low. The Duke, Angelo, and Isabella are clearly obsessed with such ideas and criticize freely in their different fashions. So also Elbow and the officers bring in Froth and Pompey, accusing them. Abhorson is severely critical of Pompey:

> A bawd? Fie upon him! He will discredit our mystery.
>   (4.2.28–29)

Lucio traduces the Duke's character, Mistress Overdone informs against Lucio. Barnardine is universally despised. All, that is, react to each other in an essentially ethical mode: which mode is the peculiar and particular vision of this play. Even music is brought to the bar of the ethical judgment:

> . . . music oft hath such a charm
> To make bad good, and good provoke to harm.
>
> (4.1.14–15)

Such is the dominating atmosphere of this play. Out of it grow the main themes, the problem and the lesson of *Measure for Measure*. There is thus a pervading atmosphere of orthodoxy and ethical criticism, in which is centered the mysterious holiness, the profound death-philosophy, the enlightened human insight and Christian ethic of the protagonist, the Duke of Vienna.

The satire of the play is directed primarily against self-conscious, self-protected righteousness. The Duke starts the action by resigning his power to Angelo. He addresses Angelo, outspoken in praise of his virtues, thus:

> Angelo,
> There is a kind of character in thy life,
> That to th' observer doth thy history
> Fully unfold. Thyself and thy belongings
> Are not thine own so proper, as to waste
> Thyself upon thy virtues, they on thee.
> Heaven doth with us as we with torches do,
> Not light them for themselves; for if our virtues
> Did not go forth of us, 'twere all alike
> As if we had them not. Spirits are not finely touched,
> But to fine issues, nor Nature never lends
> The smallest scruple of her excellence
> But like a thrifty goddess she determines
> Herself the glory of a creditor,
> Both thanks and use.   (1.1.26–40)

The thought is similar to that of the Sermon on the Mount:

Ye are the light of the world. A city that is set on an hill cannot
be hid. Neither do men light a candle, and put it under a bushel, but
on a candlestick; and it giveth light unto all that are in the house.

(Matthew 5:14–15)

Not only does the Duke's "torch" metaphor clearly recall
this passage, but his development of it is vividly paralleled
by other of Jesus' words. The Duke compares "Nature" to "a
creditor," lending qualities and demanding both "thanks and
use." Compare:

For the Kingdom of Heaven is as a man traveling into a far
country, who called his own servants, and delivered unto them his
goods.
And unto one he gave five talents, to another two, and to another
one; to every man according to his several ability; and straightway
took his journey.

(Matthew 25:14–15)

The sequel needs no quotation. Now, though Angelo modestly refuses the honor, the Duke insists, forcing it on him.
Later, in conversation with Friar Thomas, himself disguised
as a Friar now, he gives us reason for his strange act:

> We have strict statutes and most biting laws,
> The needful bits and curbs to headstrong steeds,
> Which for this fourteen years we have let slip;
> Even like an o'ergrown lion in a cave,
> That goes not out to prey. Now, as fond fathers,
> Having bound up the threat'ning twigs of birch,
> Only to stick it in their children's sight
> For terror, not to use; in time the rod
> Becomes more mocked than feared; so our decrees,
> Dead to infliction, to themselves are dead,
> And Liberty plucks Justice by the nose;
> The baby beats the nurse, and quite athwart
> Goes all decorum.   (1.3.19–31)

Therefore he has given Angelo power and command to
"strike home." Himself he will not exact justice, since he has

already, by his laxity, as good as bade the people sin by his
"permissive pass": the people could not readily understand
such a change in himself—with a new governor it would be
different. But these are not his only reasons. He ends:

> Moe reasons for this action
> At our more leisure shall I render you;
> Only, this one: Lord Angelo is precise,
> Stands at a guard with envy; scarce confesses
> That his blood flows, or that his appetite
> Is more to bread than stone. Hence shall we see,
> If power change purpose, what our seemers be.   (48–54)

The rest of the play slowly unfolds the rich content of the
Duke's plan, and the secret, too, of his lax rule.

Escalus tells us that the Duke was

> One that, above all other strifes, contended especially to know
> himself.   (3.2.235–36)

But he has studied others, besides himself. He prides himself
on his knowledge:

> There is written in your brow, provost, honesty and constancy: if
> I read it not truly, my ancient skill beguiles me.   (4.2.156–58)

Herein are the causes of his leniency. His government has
been inefficient, not through an inherent weakness or laxity
in him, but rather because meditation and self-analysis,
together with profound study of human nature, have shown
him that all passions and sins from other men have reflected
images in his own soul. He is no weakling: he has been "a
scholar, a statesman, and a soldier" (3.2.148). But to such
a philosopher government and justice may begin to appear a
mockery, and become abhorrent. His judicial method has
been original: all criminals were either executed promptly or
else freely released (4.2.135–37). Nowhere is the peculiar
modernity of the Duke in point of advanced psychology
more vividly apparent. It seems, too, if we are to judge by his
treatment of Barnardine (4.3.65–82), that he could not tol-

erate an execution without the criminal's own approval! The
case of Barnadine troubles him intensely:

> A creature unprepared, unmeet for death;
> And to transport him in the mind he is
> Were damnable.   (68–70)

The Duke's sense of human responsibility is delightful
throughout: he is like a kindly father, and all the rest are his
children. Thus he now performs the experiment of handing
the reins of government to a man of ascetic purity who has
an hitherto invulnerable faith in the rightness and justice
of his own ideals—a man of spotless reputation and self-
conscious integrity, who will have no fears as to the "justice" of enforcing precise obedience. The scheme is a plot,
or trap: a scientific experiment to see if extreme ascetic
righteousness can stand the test of power.

The Duke, disguised as the Friar, moves through the play,
a dark figure, directing, watching, moralizing on the actions
of the other persons. As the play progresses and his plot on
Angelo works he assumes an ever-increasing mysterious
dignity, his original purpose seems to become more and
more profound in human insight, the action marches with
measured pace to its appointed and logical end. We have
ceased altogether to think of the Duke as merely a studious
and unpractical governor, incapable of office. Rather he
holds, within the dramatic universe, the dignity and power
of a Prospero, to whom he is strangely similar. With both,
their plot and plan is the plot and plan of the play: they make
and forge the play, and thus are automatically to be equated
in a unique sense with the poet himself—since both are symbols of the poet's controlling, purposeful, combined movement of the chessmen of the drama. Like Prospero, the Duke
tends to assume proportions evidently divine. Once he is
actually compared to the Supreme Power:

> O my dread lord,
> I should be guiltier than my guiltiness,
> To think I can be undiscernible,
> When I perceive your Grace, like pow'r divine,
> Hath looked upon my passes.   (5.1.369–73)

So speaks Angelo at the end. We are prepared for it long before. In the rhymed octosyllabic couplets of the Duke's soliloquy in 3.2 there is a distinct note of supernatural authority, forecasting the rhymed mystic utterances of divine beings in the Final Plays. He has been talking with Escalus and the Provost, and dismisses them with the words:

> Peace be with you!

They leave him and he soliloquizes:

> He who the sword of heaven will bear
> Should be as holy as severe;
> Pattern in himself to know
> Grace to stand, and virtue go;
> More nor less to other paying
> Than by self-offenses weighing.
> Shame to him whose cruel striking
> Kills for faults of his own liking!
> Twice treble shame on Angelo,
> To weed my vice and let his grow!
> O, what may man within him hide,
> Though angel on the outward side!
> How may likeness made in crimes,
> Making practice on the times,
> To draw with idle spiders' strings
> Most ponderous and substantial things?
> Craft against vice I must apply:
> With Angelo tonight shall lie
> His old betrothed but despisèd;
> So disguise shall, by th' disguisèd,
> Pay with falsehood false exacting,
> And perform an old contracting.   (264–85)

This fine soliloquy gives us the Duke's philosophy: the philosophy that prompted his original plan. And it is important to notice the mystical, prophetic tone of the speech.

The Duke, like Jesus, is the prophet of a new order of ethics. This aspect of the Duke as teacher and prophet is also illustrated by his cryptic utterance to Escalus just before this soliloquy:

Escalus. Good even, good father.

Duke. Bliss and goodness on you.

Escalus. Of whence are you?

Duke. Not of this country, though my chance is now
To use it for my time; I am a brother
Of gracious order, late come from the See
In special business from his Holiness.

Escalus. What news abroad i' th' world?

Duke. None, but that there is so great a fever on goodness, that the
dissolution of it must cure it, novelty is only in request, and it is
as dangerous to be aged in any kind of course as it is virtuous to
be constant in any undertaking. There is scarce truth enough
alive to make societies secure, but security enough to make fel-
lowships accursed. Much upon this riddle runs the wisdom of
the world. This news is old enough, yet it is every day's news.
I pray you, sir, of what disposition was the Duke?

Escalus. One that, above all other strifes, contended especially to
know himself.   (2.17–36)

This remarkable speech, with its deliberate, incisive, cryptic sentences, has a profound quality and purpose which
reaches the very heart of the play. It deserves exact attention.
Its expanded paraphrase runs thus:

No news, but that goodness is suffering such a disease that a
complete dissolution of it (goodness) is needed to cure it. That is,
our whole system of conventional ethics should be destroyed and
rebuilt. A change (novelty) never gets beyond request, that is, is
never actually put in practice. And it is as dangerous to continue
indefinitely a worn-out system or order of government, as it is
praiseworthy to be constant in any individual undertaking. There
is scarcely enough knowledge of human nature current in the
world to make societies safe; but ignorant self-confidence (i.e., in
matters of justice) enough to make human intercourse within a

society a miserable thing. This riddle holds the key to the wisdom
of the world (probably, both the false wisdom of the unenlight-
ened, and the true wisdom of great teachers). This news is old
enough, and yet the need for its understanding sees daily proof.

I paraphrase freely, admittedly interpreting difficulties in the
light of the recurring philosophy of this play on the blindness of men's moral judgments, and especially in the light of
the Duke's personal moral attitude as read from his other
words and actions. This speech holds the poetry of ethics. Its
content, too, is very close to the Gospel teaching, the insistence on the blindness of the world, its habitual disregard of
the truth exposed by prophet and teacher:

> And this is the condemnation, that light is come into the world,
> and men loved darkness rather than light, because their deeds were
> evil.   (John 3:19)

The same almost divine suggestion rings in many of the
Duke's measured prose utterances. There are his supremely
beautiful words to Escalus (4.2.206–9):

> Look, th' unfolding star calls up the shepherd. Put not yourself
> into amazement how these things should be: all difficulties are but
> easy when they are known.

The first lovely sentence—a unique beauty of Shakespearean prose, in a style peculiar to this play—derives part of its
appeal from New Testament associations, and the second
sentence holds the mystic assurance of Matthew 10:26:

> . . . for there is nothing covered, that shall not be revealed; and hid,
> that shall not be known.

The Duke exercises the authority of a teacher throughout his
disguise as a friar. He speaks authoritatively on repentance
to Juliet:

> *Duke.*   . . . . But lest you do repent
>   As that the sin hath brought you to this shame—
>   Which sorrow is always toward ourselves, not heaven,

> Showing we would not spare Heaven as we love it,
> But as we stand in fear——
>
> *Juliet.* I do repent me, as it is an evil,
>   And take the shame with joy.
>
> *Duke.* There rest.   (2.3.30–36)

After rebuking Pompey the bawd very sternly but not unkindly, he concludes:

> Go mend, go mend.   (3.2.28)

His attitude is that of Jesus to the woman taken in adultery:

> Neither do I condemn thee: go, and sin no more.   (John 8:11)

Both are more kindly disposed towards honest impurity than light and frivolous scandalmongers, such as Lucio, or Pharisaic self-righteousness such as Angelo's.

The Duke's ethical attitude is exactly correspondent with Jesus': the play must be read in the light of the Gospel teaching, if its full significance is to be apparent. So he, like Jesus, moves among men suffering grief at their sins and deriving joy from an unexpected flower of simple goodness in the deserts of impurity and hardness. He finds softness of heart where he least expects it—in the Provost of the prison:

> *Duke.* This is a gentle provost—seldom when
>   The steelèd jailer is the friend of men.   (4.2.88–89)

So, too, Jesus finds in the centurion,

> a man under authority, having soldiers under me.
>   (Matthew 8:9)

a simple faith where he least expects it:

> . . . I say unto you, I have not found so great faith, no, not in Israel.

The two incidents are very similar in quality. Now, in that he represents a perfected ethical philosophy joined to supreme

authority, the Duke is, within the dramatic universe, automatically comparable with Divinity; or we may suggest that
he progresses by successive modes, from worldly power
through the prophecy and moralizing of the middle scenes,
to the supreme judgment at the end, where he exactly reflects the universal judgment as suggested by many Gospel
passages. There is the same apparent injustice, the same
tolerance and mercy. The Duke is, in fact, a symbol of the
same kind as the Father in the Parable of the Prodigal Son
(Luke 15) or the Lord in that of the Unmerciful Servant
(Matthew 18). The simplest way to focus correctly the quality and unity of *Measure for Measure* is to read it on the
analogy of Jesus' parables.

Though his ethical philosophy is so closely related to the
Gospel teaching, yet the Duke's thoughts on death are
devoid of any explicit belief in immortality. He addresses
Claudio, who is to die, and his words at first appear vague,
agnostic: but a deeper acquaintance renders their profundity
and truth. Claudio fears death. The Duke comforts him by
concentrating not on death, but on life. In a series of pregnant sentences he asserts the negative nature of any single
life-joy. First, life is slave to death and may fail at any
chance moment; however much you run from death, yet you
cannot but run still towards it; nobility in man is inextricably
twined with "baseness" (this is, indeed, the moral of *Measure for Measure*), and courage is ever subject to fear; sleep
is man's "best rest," yet he fears death which is but sleep;
man is not a single independent unit, he has no solitary self
to lose, but rather is compounded of universal "dust"; he is
always discontent, striving for what he has not, forgetful of
that which he succeeds in winning; man is a changing,
wavering substance; his riches he wearily carries till death
unloads him; he is tortured by disease and old age. The cata-
logue is strong in unremittent condemnation of life:

> Thou hast nor youth nor age,
> But, as it were, an after-dinner's sleep,
> Dreaming on both; for all thy blessèd youth
> Becomes as agèd, and doth beg the alms
> Of palsied eld, and when thou art old and rich,
> Thou hast neither heat, affection, limb, nor beauty,

To make thy riches pleasant. What's yet in this
That bears the name of life? Yet in this life
Lie hid moe thousand deaths; yet death we fear,
That makes these odds all even.   (3.1.32–41)

Life is therefore a sequence of unrealities, strung together in
a time succession. Everything it can give is in turn killed.
Regarded thus, it is unreal, a delusion, a living death. The
thought is profound. True, the Duke has concentrated especially on the temporal aspect of life's appearances, regarding
only the shell of life and neglecting the inner vital principle
of joy and hope; he has left deeper things untouched. He
neglects love and all immediate transcendent intuitions. But
since it is only this temporal aspect of decayed appearances
which death is known to end, since it is only the closing of
this very time-succession which Claudio fears, it is enough
to prove this succession valueless. Claudio is thus com-
forted. The death of such a life is indeed not death, but rather
itself a kind of life:

I humbly thank you.
To sue to live, I find I seek to die,
And seeking death, find life: let it come on.   (41–43)

Now he "will encounter darkness as a bride," like Antony
(84). The Duke's death philosophy is thus the philosophy of
the great tragedies to follow—of *Timon of Athens*, of *Antony
and Cleopatra*. So, too, his ethic is the ethic of *King Lear*. In
this problem play we find the profound thought of the
supreme tragedies already emergent and given careful and
exact form, the Duke in this respect being analogous to
Agamemnon in *Troilus and Cressida*. Both his ethical and
his death thinking are profoundly modern. But Claudio soon
reverts to the crude time-thinking (and fine poetry) of his
famous death speech, in which he regards the afterlife in
terms of orthodox eschatology, thinking of it as a temporal
process, like Hamlet:

Ay, but to die, and go we know not where.   (118)

In the Shakespearean mode of progressive thought it is essential first to feel death's reality strongly as the ender of what we call "life": only then do we begin to feel the tremendous pressure of an immortality not known in terms of time. We then begin to attach a different meaning to the words "life" and "death." The thought of this scene thus wavers between the old and the new death philosophies.

The Duke's plot pivots on the testing of Angelo. Angelo is a man of spotless reputation, generally respected. Escalus says

> If any in Vienna be of worth
> To undergo such ample grace and honor,
> It is Lord Angelo. (1.1.22–24)

Angelo, hearing the Duke's praise, and his proposed trust, modestly declines, as though he recognizes that his virtue is too purely idealistic for the rough practice of state affairs:

> Now, good my lord,
> Let there be some more test made of my mettle,
> Before so noble and so great a figure
> Be stamped upon it. (47–50)

Angelo is not a conscious hypocrite: rather a man whose chief faults are self-deception and pride in his own righteousness—an unused and delicate instrument quite useless under the test of active trial. This he half-recognizes, and would first refuse the proffered honor. The Duke insists: Angelo's fall is thus entirely the Duke's responsibility. So this man of ascetic life is forced into authority. He is

> . . . a man whose blood
> Is very snow-broth; one who never feels
> The wanton stings and motions of the sense,
> But doth rebate and blunt his natural edge
> With profits of the mind, study and fast. (1.4.57–61)

Angelo, indeed, does not know himself: no one receives so great a shock as he himself when temptation overthrows his virtue. He is no hypocrite. He cannot, however, be acquitted

of Pharisaical pride: his reputation means much to him, he
"stands at a guard with envy" (1.3.51). He "takes pride" in
his "gravity" (2.4.10). Now, when he is first faced with the
problem of Claudio's guilt of adultery—and commanded,
we must presume, by the Duke's sealed orders to execute
stern punishment wholesale, for this is the Duke's ostensible
purpose—Angelo pursues his course without any sense of
wrongdoing. Escalus hints that surely all men must know
sexual desire—how then is Angelo's procedure just? Escalus
thus adopts the Duke's ethical point of view, exactly:

> Let but your honor know,
> Whom I believe to be most strait in virtue,
> That, in the working of your own affections,
> Had time cohered with place or place with wishing,
> Or that the resolute acting of your blood
> Could have attained the effect of your own purpose,
> Whether you had not some time in your life,
> Err'd in this point which now you censure him,
> And pulled the law upon you.   (2.1.8–16)

Which reflects the Gospel message:

> Ye have heard that it was said by them of old time, Thou shalt
> not commit adultery:
> But I say unto you, that whosoever looketh on a woman to lust
> after her hath committed adultery with her already in his heart.
> (Matthew 5:27–28)

Angelo's reply, however, is sound sense:

> 'Tis one thing to be tempted, Escalus,
> Another thing to fall.   (17–18)

Isabella later uses the same argument as Escalus:

> . . . go to your bosom,
> Knock there, and ask your heart what it doth know
> That's like my brother's fault; if it confess
> A natural guiltiness such as is his,

> Let it not sound a thought upon your tongue
> Against my brother's life.   (2.2.136–41)

We are reminded of Jesus' words to the Scribes and Pharisees concerning the woman "taken in adultery":

> He that is without sın among you, let him first cast a stone at her.
> (John 8:7)

Angelo is, however, sincere: terribly sincere. He feels no personal responsibility, since he is certain that he does right. We believe him when he tells Isabella:

> It is the law, not I, condemn your brother:
> Were he my kinsman, brother, or my son,
> It should be thus with him.   (80–82)

To execute justice, he says, is kindness, not cruelty, in the long run.

Angelo's arguments are rationally conclusive. A thing irrational breaks them, however: his passion for Isabella. Her purity, her idealism, her sanctity enslave him—she who speaks to him of

>   true prayers
> That shall be up at heaven and enter there
> Ere sunrise, prayers from preservèd souls,
> From fasting maids whose minds are dedicate
> To nothing temporal.   (151–55)

Angelo is swiftly enwrapped in desire. He is finely shown as falling a prey to his own love of purity and asceticism:

>   What is't I dream on?
> O cunning enemy, that, to catch a saint,
> With saints dost bait thy hook!   (178–80)

He "sins in loving virtue"; no strumpet could ever allure him; Isabella subdues him utterly. Now he who built so strongly on a rational righteousness, understands for the first time the sweet unreason of love:

> Ever till now,
> When men were fond, I smiled, and wond'red how.
>
> (185–86)

Angelo struggles hard: he prays to Heaven, but his thoughts
"anchor" on Isabel (2.4.4). His gravity and learning—all are
suddenly as nothing. He admits to himself that he has taken
"pride" in his well-known austerity, adding "let no man hear
me"—a pathetic touch which casts a revealing light both on
his shallow ethic and his honest desire at this moment to
understand himself. The violent struggle is short. He surren-
ders, his ideals all toppled over like ninepins:

> Blood, thou are blood.
> Let's write "good angel" on the devil's horn,
> 'Tis not the devil's crest.   (15–17)

Angelo is now quite adrift: all his old contacts are irrevo-
cably severed. Sexual desire has long been anathema to him,
so his warped idealism forbids any healthy love. Good and
evil change places in his mind, since this passion is immediately recognized as good, yet, by every one of his stock judgments, condemned as evil. The devil becomes a "good
angel." And this wholesale reversion leaves Angelo in sorry
plight now: he has no moral values left. Since sex has been
synonymous with foulness in his mind, this new love, reft
from the start of moral sanction in a man who "scarce confesses that his blood flows," becomes swiftly a devouring
and curbless lust:

> I have begun,
> And now I give my sensual race the rein.   (159–60)

So he addresses Isabella. He imposes the vile condition of
Claudio's life. All this is profoundly true: he is at a loss with
this new reality—embarrassed as it were, incapable of pursuing a normal course of love. In proportion as his moral
reason formerly denied his instincts, so now his instincts
assert themselves in utter callousness of his moral reason.

He swiftly becomes an utter scoundrel. He threatens to have
Claudio tortured. Next, thinking to have had his way with
Isabella, he is so conscience-stricken and tortured by fear
that he madly resolves not to keep faith with her: he orders
Claudio's instant execution. For, in proportion as he is nau-
seated at his own crimes, he is terror-struck at exposure. He
is mad with fear, his story exactly pursues the Macbeth
rhythm:

> This deed unshapes me quite, makes me unpregnant,
> And dull to all proceedings. A deflow'red maid!
> And by an eminent body that enforced
> The law against it! But that her tender shame
> Will not proclaim against her maiden loss,
> How might she tongue me! Yet reason dares her no;
> For my authority bears of a credent bulk,
> That no particular scandal once can touch
> But it confounds the breather. He should have lived,
> Save that his riotous youth, with dangerous sense,
> Might in the times to come have ta'en revenge,
> By so receiving a dishonored life
> With ransom of such shame. Would yet he had lived!
> Alack, when once our grace we have forgot,
> Nothing goes right; we would, and we would not.
>
> (4.4.22–36)

This is the reward of self-deception, of Pharisaical pride, of
an idealism not harmonized with instinct—of trying, to use
the Duke's pregnant phrase:

> To draw with idle spiders' strings
> Most ponderous and substantial things. (3.2.278–79)

Angelo has not been overcome with evil. He has been
ensnared by good, by his own love of sanctity, exquisitely
symbolized in his love of Isabella: the hook is baited with a
saint, and the saint is caught. The cause of his fall is this and
this only. The coin of his moral purity, which flashed so bril-
liantly, when tested does not ring true. Angelo is the symbol

of a false intellectualized ethic divorced from the deeper springs of human instinct.

The varied close-inwoven themes of *Measure for Measure* are finally knit in the exquisite final act. To that point the action—reflected image always of the Ducal plot—marches

> By cold gradation and well-balanced form.   (4.3.101)

The last act of judgment is heralded by trumpet calls:

> Twice have the trumpets sounded.
> The generous and gravest citizens
> Have hent the gates, and very near upon
> The Duke is ent'ring.   (4.6.12–15)

So all are, as it were, summoned to the final judgment. Now Angelo, Isabella, Lucio—all are understood most clearly in the light of this scene. The last act is the key to the play's meaning, and all difficulties are here resolved. I shall observe the judgment measured to each, noting retrospectively the especial significance in the play of Lucio and Isabella.

Lucio is a typical loose-minded, vulgar wit. He is the product of a society that has gone too far in condemnation of human sexual desires. He keeps up a running comment on sexual matters. His very existence is a condemnation of the society which makes him a possibility. Not that there is anything of premeditated villainy in him: he is merely superficial, enjoying the unnatural ban on sex which civilization imposes, because that very ban adds point and spice to sexual gratification. He is, however, sincerely concerned about Claudio, and urges Isabella to plead for him. He can be serious—for a while. He can speak sound sense, too, in the full flow of his vulgar wit:

> Yes, in good sooth, the vice is of a great kindred; it is well allied: but it is impossible to extirp it quite, friar, till eating and drinking be put down. They say this Angelo was not made by man and woman after this downright way of creation. Is it true, think you?
> (3.2.103–8)

This goes to the root of our problem here. Pompey has voiced the same thought (2.1.238–54). This is, indeed, what the Duke has known too well: what Angelo and Isabella do not know. Thus Pompey and Lucio here at least tell down-right facts—Angelo and Isabella pursue impossible and valueless ideals. Only the Duke holds the balance exact throughout. Lucio's running wit, however, pays no consis-tent regard to truth. To him the Duke's leniency was a sign of hidden immorality:

> Ere he would have hanged a man for the getting a hundred bas-tards, he would have paid for the nursing a thousand. He had some feeling of the sport; he knew the service, and that instructed him to mercy. (3.2.119–23)

He traduces the Duke's character wholesale. He does not pause to consider the truth of his words. Again, there is no intent to harm—merely a careless, shallow, truthless wit-philosophy which enjoys its own sex chatter. The type is common. Lucio is refined and vulgar, and the more vulgar because of his refinement; whereas Pompey, because of his natural coarseness, is less vulgar. Lucio can only exist in a society of smug propriety and self-deception: for his mind's life is entirely parasitical on those insincerities. His false—because fantastic and shallow—pursuit of sex is the result of a false, fantastic denial of sex in his world. Like so much in *Measure for Measure* he is eminently modern. Now Lucio is the one person the Duke finds it all but impossible to forgive:

> I find an apt remission in myself,
> And yet here's one in place I cannot pardon.
> (5.1.501–2)

All the rest have been serious in their faults. Lucio's con-demnation of his triviality, his insincerity, his profligate idleness, his thoughtless detraction of others' characters:

> You, sirrah, that knew me for a fool, a coward,
> One all of luxury, an ass, a madman;

> Wherein have I so deserved of you,
> That you extol me thus?   (503–6)

Lucio's treatment at the close is eminently, and fittingly, undignified. He is threatened thus: first he is to marry the mother of his child, about whose wrong he formerly boasted; then to be whipped and hanged. Lucio deserves some credit, however: he preserves his nature and answers with his characteristic wit. He cannot be serious. The Duke, his sense of humor touched, retracts the sentence:

> *Duke.* Upon mine honor, thou shalt marry her.
>   Thy slanders I forgive; and therewithal
>   Remit thy other forfeits. Take him to prison,
>   And see our pleasure herein executed.
>
> *Lucio.* Marrying a punk, my lord, is pressing to death,
>   whipping, and hanging.
>
> *Duke.* Slandering a prince deserves it.   (521–27)

Idleness, triviality, thoughtlessness receive the Duke's strongest condemnation. The thought is this:

> But I say unto you, That every idle word that men shall speak, they shall give account thereof in the day of judgment.
>
> (Matthew 12:36)

Exactly what happens to Lucio. His wit is often illuminating, often amusing, sometimes rather disgusting. He is never wicked, sometimes almost lovable, but terribly dangerous.[1]

Isabella is the opposite extreme. She is more saintly than Angelo, and her saintliness goes deeper, is more potent than his. When we first meet her, she is about to enter the secluded life of a nun. She welcomes such a life. She even wishes

> a more strict restraint
> Upon the sisterhood, the votarists of Saint Clare.
>
> (1.4.4–5)

---

[1]For Lucio, see also *The Imperial Theme*, p. 20.

Even Lucio respects her. She calls forth something deeper than his usual wit:

> I would not, though 'tis my familiar sin
> With maids to seem the lapwing, and to jest,
> Tongue far from heart, play with all virgins so.
> I hold you as a thing enskied and sainted,
> By your renouncement, an immortal spirit;
> And to be talked with in sincerity,
> As with a saint.   (31–37)

Which contains a fine and exact statement of his shallow behavior, his habitual wit for wit's sake. Lucio is throughout a loyal friend to Claudio: truer to his cause, in fact, than Isabella. A pointed contrast. He urges her to help. She shows a distressing lack of warmth. It is Lucio that talks of "your poor brother." She is cold:

> *Lucio.*   Assay the pow'r you have.
>
> *Isabella.* My power? Alas, I doubt——
>
> *Lucio.*   Our doubts are traitors,
> And makes us lose the good we oft might win,
> By fearing to attempt.   (76–79)

Isabella's self-centered saintliness is thrown here into strong contrast with Lucio's manly anxiety for his friend. So, contrasted with Isabella's ice-cold sanctity, there are the beautiful lines with which Lucio introduces the matter to her:

> Your brother and his lover have embraced;
> As those that feed grow full, as blossoming time
> That from the seedness the bare fallow brings
> To teeming foison, even so her plenteous womb
> Expresseth his full tilth and husbandry.   (40–44)

Compare the pregnant beauty of this with the chastity of Isabella's recent lisping line:

Upon the sisterhood, the votarists of Saint Clare.   (5)

Isabella lacks human feeling. She starts her suit to Angelo
poorly enough. She is lukewarm:

> There is a vice that most I do abhor,
> And most desire should meet the blow of justice,
> For which I would not plead, but that I must,
> For which I must not plead, but that I am
> At war 'twixt will and will not.   (2.2.29–33)

Lucio has to urge her on continually. We begin to feel that
Isabella has no real affection for Claudio; has stifled all
human love in the pursuit of sanctity. When Angelo at last
proposes his dishonorable condition she quickly comes to
her decision:

> Then, Isabel, live chaste, and, brother, die.
> More than our brother is our chastity.   (2.4.184–85)

When Shakespeare chooses to load his dice like this—which
is seldom indeed—he does it mercilessly. The Shakespearean satire here strikes once, and deep: there is no need to
point it further. But now we know our Isabel. We are not surprised that she behaves to Claudio, who hints for her sacrifice, like a fiend:

> Take my defiance,
> Die, perish! Might but my bending down
> Reprieve thee from thy fate, it should proceed.
> I'll pray a thousand prayers for thy death,
> No word to save thee.   (3.1.143–47)

Is her fall any less than Angelo's? Deeper, I think. With
whom is Isabel angry? Not only with her brother. She has
feared this choice—terribly: "O, I do fear thee, Claudio,"
she said (74). Even since Angelo's suggestion she has been
afraid. Now Claudio has forced the responsibility of choice
on her. She cannot sacrifice herself. Her sex inhibitions have
been horribly shown her as they are, naked. She has been

stung—lanced on a sore spot of her soul. She knows now that it is not all saintliness, she sees her own soul and sees it as something small, frightened, despicable, too frail to dream of such a sacrifice. Though she does not admit it, she is infuriated not with Claudio, but with herself. "Saints" should not speak like this. Again, the comment of this play is terribly illuminating. It is significant that she readily involves Mariana in illicit love: it is only her own chastity which assumes, in her heart, universal importance.[2]

Isabella, however, was no hypocrite, any more than Angelo. She is a spirit of purity, grace, maiden charm: but all these virtues the action of the play turns remorselessly against herself. In a way, it is not her fault. Chastity is hardly a sin—but neither, as the play emphasizes, is it the whole of virtue. And she, like the rest, has to find a new wisdom. Mariana in the last act prays for Angelo's life. Confronted by that warm, potent, forgiving, human love, Isabella herself suddenly shows a softening, a sweet humanity. Asked to intercede, she does so—she, who was at the start slow to intercede for a brother's life, now implores the Duke to save Angelo, her wronger:

> I partly think
> A due sincerity governèd his deeds,
> Till he did look on me.   (5.1.448–50)

There is a suggestion that Angelo's strong passion has itself moved her, thawing her ice-cold pride. This is the moment of her trial: the Duke is watching her keenly, to see if she has learnt her lesson—nor does he give her any help, but deliberately puts obstacles in her way. But she stands the test: she bows to a love greater than her own saintliness. Isabella, like Angelo, has progressed far during the play's action: from sanctity to humanity.

Angelo, at the beginning of this final scene, remains firm in denial of the accusations leveled against him. Not till the Duke's disguise as a friar is made known and he understands that deception is no longer possible, does he show outward

---

[2] I now doubt if Isabella's attitude to Mariana should be held against her (1955).

repentance. We know, however, that his inward thoughts must have been terrible enough. His earlier agonized soliloquies put this beyond doubt. Now, his failings exposed, he seems to welcome punishment:

> Immediate sentence then, and sequent death,
> Is all the grace I beg.   (376–77)

Escalus expresses sorrow and surprise at his actions. He answers:

> I am sorry that such sorrow I procure,
> And so deep sticks it in my penitent heart,
> That I crave death more willingly than mercy;
> 'Tis my deserving, and I do entreat it.   (477–80)

To Angelo, exposure seems to come as a relief: the horror of self-deception is at an end. For the first time in his life he is both quite honest with himself and with the world. So he takes Mariana as his wife. This is just: he threw her over because he thought she was not good enough for him,

> Partly for that her promisèd proportions
> Came short of composition, but in chief,
> For that her reputation was disvalued
> In levity.   (219–22)

He aimed too high when he cast his eyes on the sainted Isabel: now, knowing himself, he will find his true level in the love of Mariana. He has become human. The union is symbolical. Just as his supposed love-contact with Isabel was a delusion, when Mariana, his true mate, was taking her place, so Angelo throughout has deluded himself. Now his acceptance of Mariana symbolizes his new self-knowledge. So, too, Lucio is to find his proper level in marrying Mistress Kate Keepdown, of whose child he is the father. Horrified as he is at the thought, he has to meet the responsibilities of his profligate behavior. The punishment of both is this only: to know, and to be, themselves. This is both their punishment and at the same time their highest reward for their sufferings:

self-knowledge being the supreme, perhaps the only, good.
We remember the parable of the Pharisee and the Publican
(Luke 18).

So the Duke draws his plan to its appointed end. All,
including Barnardine, are forgiven, and left, in the usual
sense, unpunished. This is inevitable. The Duke's original
leniency has been shown by his successful plot to have been
right, not wrong. Though he sees "corruption boil and
bubble" (319) in Vienna, he has found, too, that man's
sainted virtue is a delusion: "judge not that ye be not
judged." He has seen an Angelo to fall from grace at the first
breath of power's temptation, he has seen Isabella's purity
scarring, defacing her humanity. He has found more gentle-
ness in "the steeled jailer" than in either of these. He has
found more natural honesty in Pompey the bawd than in
Angelo the ascetic; more humanity in the charity of Mistress
Overdone than in Isabella condemning her brother to death
with venomed words in order to preserve her own chastity.
Mistress Overdone has looked after Lucio's illegitimate
child:

> . . . Mistress Kate Keepdown was with child by him in the Duke's
> time; he promised her marriage; his child is a year and a quarter
> old, come Philip and Jacob; I have kept it myself.   (3.2.202–5)

Human virtue does not flower only in high places: nor is it
the monopoly of the pure in body. In reading *Measure for
Measure* one feels that Pompey with his rough humor and
honest professional indecency is the only one of the major
persons, save the Duke, who can be called "pure in heart."
Therefore, knowing all this, the Duke knows his tolerance to
be now a moral imperative: he sees too far into the nature of
man to pronounce judgment according to the appearances
of human behavior. But we are not told what will become of
Vienna. There is, however, a hint, for the Duke is to marry
Isabel, and this marriage, like the others, may be understood
symbolically. It is to be the marriage of understanding with
purity; of tolerance with moral fervor. The Duke, who alone
has no delusions as to the virtues of man, who is incapable
of executing justice on vice since he finds forgiveness
implicit in his wide and sympathetic understanding—he

alone wins the "enskied and sainted" Isabel. More, we are
not told. And we may expect her in future to learn from him
wisdom, human tenderness, and love:

> What's mine is yours, and what is yours is mine
>
> (5.1.540)

If we still find this universal forgiveness strange—and many
have done so—we might observe Mariana, who loves
Angelo with a warm and realistically human love. She sees
no fault in him, or none of any consequence:

> O my dear lord,
> I crave no other, nor no better man.   (428–29)

She knows that

> best men are molded out of faults;
> And, for the most, become much more the better
> For being a little bad.   (442–44)

The incident is profoundly true. Love asks no questions, sees
no evil, transfiguring the just and unjust alike. This is one of
the surest and finest ethical touches in this masterpiece of
ethical drama. Its moral of love is, too, the ultimate splendor
of Jesus' teaching.

Measure for Measure is indeed based firmly on that
teaching. The lesson of the play is that of Matthew 5:20:

> For I say unto you, That except your righteousness shall exceed
> the righteousness of the scribes and Pharisees, ye shall in no case
> enter into the Kingdom of Heaven.

The play must be read, not as a picture of normal human
affairs, but as a parable, like the parables of Jesus. The plot
is, in fact, an inversion of one of those parables—that of the
Unmerciful Servant (Matthew 18); and the universal and
level forgiveness at the end, where all alike meet pardon, is
one with the forgiveness of the Parable of the Two Debtors
(Luke 7). Much has been said about the difficulties of
Measure for Measure. But, in truth, no play of Shakespeare

shows more thoughtful care, more deliberate purpose, more consummate skill in structural technique, and, finally, more penetrating ethical and psychological insight. None shows a more exquisitely inwoven pattern. And, if ever the thought at first sight seems strange, or the action unreasonable, it will be found to reflect the sublime strangeness and unreason of Jesus' teaching.

MARY LASCELLES

From Shakespeare's *Measure for Measure*

. . . The Duke himself does not engage our concern by
what he does, or suffers. How, we may fairly ask, does he—
or should he—engage it? Criticism has for some while
inclined towards the opinion that here is one of those persons in Shakespearean drama who should be regarded as
important in respect rather of function than of character, and
are to be interpreted as we should interpret the principal persons in allegory.[1] Now, the language of allegory is at least
approximately translatable. These persons, therefore, must
stand for something that can be expressed in other than allegorical terms, and the concept for which the Duke stands be
capable of formulation in such terms as criticism may
employ. What is this concept?

This is not an easy question to answer, nor are the answers
so far proposed easy to discuss. Since those that suggest a
religious allegory, and hint at a divine analogy, are shocking
to me, and cannot be anything of the sort to those who have
framed them, it must follow that my objections are all too
likely to shock in their turn. This offense is apt to be mutual;
for, where reverence is concerned, there is even less hope
of reaching agreement by argument than in matters of taste.
I would not willingly offend; but there is not room for
compromise.

Let me recall the burden of the popular tale of the monstrous ransom: the situation in which the woman, the judge,

From *Shakespeare's "Measure for Measure"* by Mary Lascelles (London.
The Athlone Press, University of London, 1953; New York John De Graff,
Inc., 1954). Reprinted by permission of the Athlone Press.

[1] This opinion is shared by those who find in the play an explicitly Christian
meaning. See p 41 above [The number refers to Miss Lascelles' earlier allusion to G Wilson Knight and R. W. Chambers.]

and the ruler confronted one another signified power, exerted to its full capacity against weakness, and weakness
(reduced to uttermost misery) gathering itself up to appeal
beyond power to authority. Expressed thus, in simple and
general terms, it seems indeed analogous with that allegory
of divine might invoked to redress abuse of human inequality which is shadowed in Browning's *Instans Tyrannus*. But
it should be remembered that such simplification obliterates
one particular which, if fairly reckoned with, might for-
bid religious analogy: in the old tale, the ruler was distant,
ignorant, brought to intervene only by uncommon exertion
on the part of those whom his absence had exposed to
oppression;[2] and none of the amplifications designed to
make the tale more acceptable had done anything to shift or
reduce this untoward circumstance. Indeed, by magnifying
the whole, they made the part more obvious.

Lupton's *Siuqila* beyond the rest develops that element in
the story which draws us to think about the maintenance of
justice, not merely in the version it gives of this tale but also
in the similar tales surrounding it. And it is notable that,
whereas this one tale is told by the wretched Siuqila to show
that even in his own country one who has no longer anything
to lose will tell all and thus bring about retribution, Omen's
tales are told to illustrate the happier state of Mauqsun. The
theme of three of them is the success of the good ruler who
goes about his domain incognito to discover and redress
wrong. In one, a judge who waylays and interrogates suitors
is able to rescue a woman from oppression. In both of the
others, the king himself is shown using disguise and similar
subterfuge, not only to obtain truth but also to make it publicly apparent. In one, he learns by means of his "privie
Espials," who ride about the country at his command in the
character of private gentlemen, the plight of a woman who
has been ill used by her stepson. He hides her at court and
lets it be rumored that she is dead; and, after much handling
of witnesses, confronts the offender with his victim, and
delivers sentence. The other tells how he "changed his
apparell, making himselfe like a Servingmā, and went out at

a privie Posterngate, and so enquired in the prisons, what prisoners were there," and was able to confute the cunning oppressor by bringing him face to face with the oppressed.

Now, in all these variations on a single theme, the activity of some magistrate or ruler—going about or sending out his agents, in disguise—*assists* in bringing smothered truth to light. Reflecting on opportune intervention in one,[3] Siuqila sums up the moral of all: "It was only the Lords working, that putte it into his heart" to speak with the woman who was secretly oppressed, and into hers to tell this stranger what she has hitherto forborne to utter; for "God works al this by marvellous means, if we would consider it, for the helping of the innocent and godly." Even under an ideal system of justice, that is, the discovery of wrong might well be impossible were it not for the intervention of divine providence, which, on some particular occasion, puts it into the heart of this or that human agent to make a pertinent inquiry. Now, this is in keeping with popular thought, which comes very near to supposing an element of caprice in divine government,[4] because it does not look ahead, but complacently descries pieces of pattern in particular events, without considering the ugly unreason of the total design which such parts much compose. But, how fearfully the distance between this false start and its logical conclusion diminishes, if the ruler is regarded not as agent but as emblem of divine providence! It is difficult to believe that those who would have us interpret the Duke's part so can have followed the implied train of thought all the way.

The center of gravity for this interpretation is the passage in which Angelo capitulates to the alliance of knowledge and power in the reinstated Duke:

> Oh, my dread lord,
> I should be guiltier than my guiltiness,
> To think I can be undiscernible,
> When I perceive your Grace, like pow'r divine,
> Hath looked upon my passes.[5]

[3]The story of the ill-used stepmother.
[4]This is well exemplified by the speech of Whetstone's compassionate jailer, after he has released Andrugio (in *Promos and Cassandra,* 4.5).
[5]5.1.369–73.

On this Professor Wilson Knight comments:

> Like Prospero, the Duke tends to assume proportions evidently divine. Once he is actually compared to the Supreme Power.[6]

So to argue is surely to misunderstand the nature and usage of imagery—which does not liken a thing to itself. Yet this argument has been widely accepted; if not unreservedly, yet with reservations which do not reach the real difficulty. To suggest that the comparison may have been made "unconsciously" by Shakespeare, and to admit that "both the Duke in *Measure for Measure*, and Prospero, are endowed with characteristics which make it impossible for us to regard them as direct representatives of the Deity, such as we find in the miracle plays . . . Prospero, at least, [having] human imperfections"[7]—this is not enough. There will, of course, be human imperfections in any human representation, most plentiful where least desired, for what we ourselves are is most evident when we declare what we would be, in the endeavor to represent ideal beings. But observe where the prime fault occurs, in the character of this ruler: he is to blame in respect of the performance of that very function in virtue of which he is supposedly to be identified with Divine Providence. Read the sentence

> . . . I perceive your Grace, like pow'r divine,
> Hath looked upon my passes   (372–73)

as the figurative expression which its syntax proclaims it—that is, as a comparison proposed between distinct, even diverse, subjects in respect of a particular point of resemblance—and it yields nothing at odds with the accepted idea

---

[6]*The Wheel of Fire* (1949), p. 79.
[7]S. L. Bethell, *Shakespeare and the Popular Dramatic Tradition* (1944), pp. 106–7. See also Leavis, "The Greatness of *Measure for Measure*," and Traversi, *"Measure for Measure"* (*Scrutiny*, January and Summer 1942). V. K. Whitaker ("Philosophy and Romance in Shakespeare's 'Problem' Comedies" in *The Seventeenth Century* by R. F. Jones and others, Stanford University Press, 1951, p. 353) suggests that this passage approaches as nearly to a reference to God "as Shakespeare could come under the law of 1605 against stage profanity"—an explanation which raises many more questions than it answers.

of a ruler who, despite the utmost exertion of human good will, must still be indebted to a power beyond his own for any success in performance of that duty which is entailed on him as God's vice-regent, and who, when such success visits his endeavors, will transiently exemplify the significance of that vice-regency. But, exact from that same sentence more than figurative expression has to give, and you are confronted with the notion of a divine being who arrives (like a comic policeman) at the scene of the disaster by an outside chance, and only just in time.

Treat the whole story as fairy tale, and you are not obliged to challenge any of its suppositions. Treat it as moral apologue, expressed in terms proper to its age, and it will answer such challenge as may fairly be offered. The Duke's expedients will then serve to illustrate the energy and resources of a human agent. But, suppose him other than human,[8] and the way leads inescapably to that conclusion which Sir Edmund Chambers reaches, when he reflects on this play: "Surely the treatment of Providence is ironical."[9] Unless *Measure for Measure* is to be accepted, and dismissed, as simple fairy tale—and what fairy tale ever troubled so the imagination?—the clue to this central and enigmatic figure must be sought in representations of the good ruler as subjects of a Tudor sovereign conceived him; above all, in those illustrative anecdotes which writers (popular and learned alike) were glad to employ, and content to draw from common sources.

A number of these are to be found associated with the name and reputation of the Emperor Alexander Severus.[10] Developing on a course similar to that taken by Guevara's Marcus Aurelius romance, this curious legend was for a spell popular in England. Its fullest, most circumstantial, and most influential exemplar I take to be Sir Thomas

---

[8]For the extreme form of this supposition, see Battenhouse, "*Measure for Measure* and Christian Doctrine of the Atonement" (*Publications of the Modern Language Association of America*, December 1946).

[9]*Shakespeare: A Survey* (1925), p 215.

[10]For an account of this legend, its development in England and range of application, see my article: "Sir Thomas Elyot and the Legend of Alexander Severus" (*Review of English Studies*, October 1951).

Elyot's *Image of Governance*.[11] Here the salient features of
the ideal portrait are these: inheriting a legacy of disorder
and corruption, the good emperor is zealous in the reform of
manners by means of social legislation and the careful
appointment and assiduous supervision of his ministers
of justice. To ensure a just outcome he will intervene in a
case by subterfuge, not merely employing spies but acting in
that capacity himself, and, when he has detected wrongdoing, not content merely to bring the accused to trial, he
will handle the witnesses, cause false information to be
put about, and trick the culprit into pronouncing his own
sentence.[12] One after another, Tudor and Stuart sovereigns
were addressed obliquely through anecdotes of Alexander
Severus, congratulated on resemblance to him in respect of
those virtues which the writer most desired in a ruler, and
delicately invited to put to opportune employment those
powers and qualities of which the country stood in need.[13]
These pseudo-historical anecdotes, of which more than
one bears a resemblance to those in Lupton's *Siuqila*, are many
of them commonplaces of popular fiction; but, used by
writers whose main intention was not to tell a story (either
historical or fictitious), they illustrate an idea of the business
of government which could then be seriously canvassed by
men involved in that very business, or eager to advise those
so involved. They chart the tides and currents that a writer
for an Elizabethan audience must have reckoned with, and
remind us how far the direction of these habitual sympathies
and antipathies has since altered: thus removing some of the
obstacles to a fair estimate of the Duke's conduct. . . .

Isabel is the chief of those characters who are themselves
engaged, and engage us, by the opportunity and capacity
they are given for suffering; of whose sentient core we are
keenly aware. And yet our consciousness of it is not con-

---

[11]*The Image of Governance Compiled of the Acts and Sentences notable, of
the moste noble Emperour Alexander Severus* (1541). This purports to be a
translation from a Greek work by the Emperor's secretary, supplemented
from other sources.

[12]See particularly Chapters VIII to XIX, XXIV, XXXVIII, and XXXIX

[13]For an illustration of the adaptability of Elyot's anecdotes, see Whetstone's *Mirour for Magestrates of Cyties*, apparently a free version of those
that Whetstone found congenial to his own times, and temper.

stant. From the moment when she presents herself before Angelo to that of the Duke's intervention between her and Claudio, she holds our imagination subject by her alternations of hope and fear. Then she seems to abdicate. Her reaction to the one subsequent event which should reinstate her, the news of Claudio's death, is, as the text stands, hardly more than squirrel's chatter, "anger insignificantly fierce." From the moment of her submission to the Duke, until that in which she pleads for Angelo against his express injunction, she *is* insignificant. We may usefully recall, here, the comparison afforded by *The Heart of Midlothian*: whereas Jeanie takes matters into her own hands and, at severe cost to herself, wins her sister's pardon, Isabel appears to relinquish initiative and, under another's direction, to follow a course at once easier and less admirable. Out of her seeming subservience the opinion has arisen that Shakespeare wearied of her; had never (perhaps) intended that she should fill so big a place, or else, had designed her to perform a particular task and had now no further use for her. And yet, in the estimation of many, a full tide of significance flows back into her even in that instant of recovered independence. Here is an extreme, if not a singular, instance of a character fluctuating between two and three dimensions.

I believe that the explanation must be sought through scrutiny of a greater anomaly, within the character. Isabel's chief activity in the play springs from the passions generated by a personal relationship—and yet this *source of all she does* is very strangely treated. The conventions of poetic drama bear hard on minor personal relationships; but *this* is of major importance. It is, besides, almost the only such relationship explicit in the play. Escalus' recollection of Claudio's father hardly alters this strangely *un-familied* world; and, though he is seen entering the prison, we do not see him with the prisoner. As for Claudio and Juliet, the extant text leaves me in doubt whether they are ever seen together. More surprising still, Claudio seems never to speak of Juliet, after that single reference in talk with Lucio. Shakespeare's *improvers*, mindful of those proprieties which are rather social than literary, attempt a remedy: Davenant making Claudio commit Juliet to Isabella's care, and introducing a letter to him from Juliet; Gildon adding a scene between these two.[14] Their officiousness is at least understandable: Claudio's silence must appear an oversight, unless we suppose that Shakespeare was deliberately flattening this part of his composition in order to throw into relief another relationship—and what should this be but the relationship between brother and sister? It is as Claudio's sister that Isabel comes into the play: as the woman who is drawn by a personal attachment into a dire predicament. And yet in her pleading on his behalf this personal relationship is faintly expressed. Many times, in her most moving passages, it would be possible to substitute "neighbor" for "brother," and hardly wake a ripple. Not that her pleading is passionless—to suppose so is to fall into Lucio's error. The very incandescence of her fiery compassion transcends the personal occasion, carrying her to a height at which, if she would plead for one man, she must plead for all. By contrast, the sense of personal relationship is sharply, even intolerably, explicit in the scene of her conflict with Claudio—the only scene in which they speak together. It puts an edge on her anger and fear; and it is in terms of their common heritage, and what it entails of participation in shame, that she denounces him. Thus this personal connection, which is the pivot of the play's action, is presented in its full significance only at the instant of its apparent dislocation.

Suppose we should find a single explanation valid for these, and all those other apparent anomalies in this character which have emerged from the foregoing examination of the play: it would surely be a master key. Let me briefly recapitulate the perplexities that have to be taken into account. When Isabel first hears of Claudio's predicament, her thought follows that course taken by Epitia's and Cassandra's: "Oh, let him marry her."[15] But, when she intercedes with Angelo, she does not urge, as they had done, and as all Vienna is ready to do, that the law is at fault if it demands the life of an offender who is able and willing to

[14]Juliet committed to Isabella's care: Davenant, *The Law against Lovers*, p. 161; Gildon, *Measure for Measure, or Beauty the Best Advocate*, p. 24. Juliet's letter, Davenant, *op. cit.*, p. 185; Gildon's scene between Claudio and Juliet, *op. cit.*, pp. 34–36.
[15]I.4.49.

repair the wrong he has done. Nevertheless, when the Duke proposes to her a course of action whose justification is that it will commit Angelo to an act for which he may be compelled to make similar reparation, she acquiesces; and this, although she has reiterated to him her abhorrence of Claudio's act. And, if we explain this compliance in terms of her anxiety on her brother's behalf, we are reminded of strange fluctuations in her relationship with that very brother—and even, in the *density* of her own substance.

To understand what has happened, we must take into consideration something that emerges from a comparison between Giraldi's various developments of this theme, of a woman confronted with an abominable choice. Where this woman is sister to the condemned man and herself unmarried, it is assumed that any wrong done and suffered, in her surrender to his adversary, can be repaired by marriage.[16] But the situation that this assumption yields is fundamentally undramatic: there is no real conflict between characters, nor within any character; merely such a show of opposition as suffices for a slight story. The sister has only to say on her brother's behalf: "Since he can, and will, make good the wrong done, your sentence is too severe." And to say this costs her nothing. Likewise, when her opponent—bearing down this acknowledged right by might—tempts her to obtain what she asks by consenting to an offense the counterpart of her brother's, the two of them agree that she has but to stipulate for the same reparation, marriage. Thus, the whole cause of her distress is the advantage which strength takes of weakness: the double breach of faith by a man whose will is—for the time being—law. It is a piteous tale. It does not yield the stuff of a play. In those other versions of this theme, however, which make the woman wife to the condemned man, dramatic tension is developed through her abhorrence of the act required of her as injurious to that very relationship by force of which she is brought to consent: she must buy his life at the price of an infamy in which he is to be sharer. This is a dilemma such as we

---

[16]Whetstone, despite national and religious differences, is in accord with Giraldi here.

associate with tragedy, because it presents a choice of courses from which there can be no good issue. (Hence, such versions as those of Roilletus, Lupton and Belleforest.) Now, in Giraldi's variations on this theme, still in his favorite mood of tragicomedy, his tales of Dorothea and Gartiosa, romance and comedy are respectively invoked and given power to challenge the assumption that a choice must be made between two bad ways. And, in both, this favorable intervention forestalls any possible distress, and so prevents painful engagement of our sympathies: for, no sooner is the wicked proposal made than something points to the existence of a third door.

Shakespeare accepted the version in which the woman is the condemned man's sister, and unmarried. As an experienced dramatist, however, he could not but recognize the dramatic insufficiency of this situation. It offered him an unhitched rope, one of which the slack would never be taken up; and the only means of making it taut was to give Isabel a motive for reluctance equivalent to that which forbade the wife's surrender. He gave her the convent.[17] So much may be common knowledge; but, like a troublesome debtor, I must still ask more patience of the reader, before I can show any return on what I have already borrowed. In making this one alteration, Shakespeare found himself committed to a number of others. As to plot, he must prevent the violation of her person; or else a happy ending would be repugnant to moral sentiment. As to character, she is marked at the outset by her sense of separateness: she cannot plead in the terms others use; and no shadow of comparison between Juliet or Mariana and herself ever crosses her mind. What, then, has become of her isolation when, with no apparent consciousness of doing anything questionable, she publishes her fictitious shame, and incurs suspicion of which she cannot count on being cleared?

I suggest that the dramatic center of the play, until the Duke intervenes, is an abhorrence of unchastity which carries the force of the original situation in which a wife faces a tragic dilemma. The form is changed, Shakespeare having

[17]By the same means, he fastens guilt upon Angelo's inclination, barring the way to love and marriage

taken (deliberately or no) that one of Giraldi's two channels for carrying the story away from tragedy which necessitates a change of relationship between the woman and the condemned man; but it is the old current which flows between these new banks. The pressure which we feel comes, as in a stream dammed up, from such a reluctance on the woman's part as neither Epitia nor Cassandra had fully known. But this dam does not hold. Once the responsibility for choosing has been lifted from Isabel's shoulders, the obstacle to choice begins to lose its significance. In the situation as it is refashioned by the Duke, it is no longer a factor. Presently it vanishes from recollection. In a world rapidly becoming secular; on a stage which was (by force of tacit agreement as well as censorship) the most secular institution in that world; and in the hands of a dramatist who

> in matters of conscience adhered to two rules,
> To advise with no bigots, and jest with no fools,

it did not offer itself to free and familiar expression. An Elizabethan dramatist of far less than Shakespeare's power could far more easily have conveyed to an Elizabethan audience, within the conventions both understood, the reluctance, say, of Lucrece.

When a storyteller has to devise an equivalent for something in his story, as he originally knew or conceived it, which has proved intractable to his purpose, this new constituent is liable to remain imperfectly substantiated, perhaps because he unconsciously reckons on its retaining the potency which his imagination still associates with that which it replaces. Here it may signify all that he requires, and there, dwindle into insignificance. An echo of this story as it may first have visited Shakespeare's imagination seems to reverberate in that antagonism which develops between brother and sister, when she perceives that he does not participate in her sense of the infamy of consent. But that very sense, and its justification, are so little evident in the part of the play which follows that Isabel's account of herself as one "in probation of a sisterhood,"[18] seems but a

[18] 5.1.72.

reminder of something lost by the way. It is only when she stands alone again, opposed even to the Duke, that her former separateness seems for an instant to recover its importance.

MARCIA RIEFER POULSEN

"Instruments of Some More Mightier Member": The Constriction of Female Power in *Measure for Measure*

Isabella has recently been called *Measure for Measure*'s "greatest problem."[1] She has not always been taken so seriously. Coleridge dismissed her by saying simply that Isabella "of all Shakespeare's female characters, interests me the least."[2] Criticism of her character has been cyclical and paradoxical, in part because critics have tended to focus on one implicit question: is she or is she not an exemplar of rectitude? On the one hand Isabella has been idealized as a paragon of feminine virtue; on the other hand she has been denigrated as an example of frigidity. Over the centuries, Isabella has been labeled either "angel" or "vixen," as if a judgment of her moral nature were the only important statements to be made about her.[3] When not

Reprinted by permission from *Shakespeare Quarterly* 35 (1984): 157–69, where the author's name is given as Marcia Riefer. Copyright © 1984 by Marcia Riefer.

[1]George L. Geckle, "Shakespeare's Isabella," *Shakespeare Quarterly* 22 (1971): 163

[2]Samuel Taylor Coleridge, *Coleridge's Miscellaneous Criticism,* ed. Thomas Middleton Raysor (Cambridge, Mass.: Harvard Univ. Press, 1936), p. 49.

[3]Among those who idealize Isabella are Anna Jameson (*Shakespeare's Heroines: Characteristics of Women, Moral, Poetical, and Historical* [London: G. Bell, 1913], p. 66) and George Geckle, who call her, respectively, an "angel of light" and a "heroine of superior moral qualities." Taking the opposite stance are Sir Arthur Quiller-Couch ("Introduction" to *Measure for Measure,* ed. Quiller-Couch and J. Dover Wilson [Cambridge: Cambridge Univ. Press, 1922], p. xxx), who calls Isabella a "bare procuress" who "is something rancid in her chastity", Charlotte Lennox (*Shakespear Illustrated,* 1 [London, 1753], p 32), who calls her a "Vixen in her Virtue"; and Una Mary Ellis-Fermor (*The Jacobean Drama: An Interpretation* [London: Methuen,

idealizing or denigrating Isabella, critics have generally ignored her.[4]

I

The debate over Isabella's virtue obscures a more important point, namely that through her one can explore the negative effects of patriarchal attitudes on female characters and on the resolution of comedy itself.[5] In the course of the play, Isabella changes from an articulate, compassionate woman during her first encounter with Angelo (2.2), to a stunned, angry, defensive woman in her later confrontations with Angelo and with her imprisoned brother (2.4 and 3.1), to, finally, a shadow of her former articulate self, on her knees before male authority in Act 5. As the last and one of the most problematic of the pre-romance comedies, *Measure for Measure* traces Isabella's gradual loss of autonomy and ultimately demonstrates, among other things, the incompatibility of sexual subjugation with successful comic dramaturgy.

1936], p. 262), who refers to her as "Hard as an icicle." I am grateful to George Geckle for several of these references.

[4]Frank Harris (*Women of Shakespeare* [New York: Mitchell Kennerley, 1912]) ignores Isabella, presumably because he could not identify a correlative for her in Shakespeare's life. A book by "An Actress" (*The True Ophelia and Other Studies of Shakespeare's Women* [New York: Putnam, 1914]) similarly excludes Isabella, as does Helena Faucit, Lady Martin's *On Some of Shakespeare's Female Characters* (Edinburgh and London: William Blackwood, 1887). Even recent feminist critics slight Isabella. In *The Woman's Part: Feminist Criticism of Shakespeare* (eds. Carolyn Ruth Swift Lenz, Gayle Greene, Carol Thomas Neely [Urbana: Univ. of Illinois Press, 1980]), only two articles make significant mention of her, pointing out that Isabella is one of the few female characters in Shakespeare to confront men without benefit of men's garments. (See Paula S. Berggren, "Female Sexuality as Power in Shakespeare's Plays," p. 22, and Clara Claiborne Park, "As We Like It: How a Girl Can Be Smart and Still Popular," p. 109.) Two other recent books written from a feminist perspective—Irene Dash, *Wooing, Wedding, and Power: Women in Shakespeare's Plays* (New York: Columbia Univ. Press, 1981), and Linda Bamber, *Comic Women, Tragic Men: A Study of Gender and Genre in Shakespeare* (Stanford: Stanford Univ. Press, 1982)—have little more to say about Isabella, relegating her to footnotes or oblique references.

[5]For a discussion of patriarchy as a destructive force in Shakespeare's tragedies, see Madelon Gohlke, " 'I wooed thee with my sword'· Shakespeare's Tragic Paradigms" in *The Woman's Part*.

The kind of powerlessness Isabella experiences is an anomaly in Shakespearean comedy.[6] Most of the heroines in whose footsteps Isabella follows have functioned as surrogate dramatist figures who are generally more powerful, in terms of manipulating plot, than the male characters in the same plays. One need only recall the Princess of France and her ladies in *Love's Labor's Lost*, Portia in *The Merchant of Venice*, Mistresses Page and Ford in *The Merry Wives of Windsor*, Beatrice in *Much Ado About Nothing*, Viola in *Twelfth Night*, Helena in *All's Well That Ends Well*, and, of course, Rosalind in *As You Like It*. Those heroines who have not actually been in control of the comic action have at least participated in it more actively than Isabella ever does. In *A Midsummer Night's Dream*, for instance, Helena and Hermia, while admittedly acting within Oberon's master plot, still take the initiative in pursuing their loves, which is certainly not true of Isabella. Even Kate in *The Taming of the Shrew* exercises dramaturgical skills. In her final "tour de force" she employs those very tactics which Petruchio has taught her, reversing them subtly on him and indicating through loving opposites—as he has done in his "taming" of her—that she may have some taming of her own in store for him.[7] Her "obedience" to Petruchio's dramatic manipulation is far more playful and even assertive than Isabella's obedience to Vincentio. Besides, as Richard Wheeler points out, Petruchio's long-range significance is that the model of love by male conquest he embodies very soon drops out of the maturing world of Shakespeare's comedy, to be replaced by such forceful, loving heroines as Portia and Rosalind.[8]

It is hardly incidental that in *Measure for Measure* Shakespeare places dramaturgical control almost exclusively in

---

[6]See Linda Bamber's *Comic Women, Tragic Men* for an articulate recent analysis of the centrality of women in Shakespeare's comedies

[7]Note the similarity between Kate's descriptions of the ideal husband—far from Petruchio's shrewish behavior thus far—(a "prince," a man "that cares for thee and for thy maintenance," someone who is "loving" and "honest," and who "commits his body to painful labor" for his wife's sake, 5 2 147–60) and Petruchio's earlier descriptions of the ideal Kate—far from her behavior at that time—(her "mildness prais'd in every town," her "virtues spoke of," and her "beauty sounded," 2.1 185–94).

[8]Richard Wheeler, *Shakespeare's Development and the Problem Comedies: Turn and Counter-Turn* (Berkeley Univ of California Press, 1981). p. 141.

the hands of a male character—Duke Vincentio—who is, in effect, a parody of his more successful, mostly female, predecessors. An understanding of Vincentio's function in this play is essential background for exploring Isabella's character and dramatic function, so it is to him that we must turn our attention first.

II

As a dramatist figure, the Duke perverts Shakespeare's established comic paradigm in that he lacks certain essential dramaturgical skills and qualities previously associated with comic dramatist figures—qualities necessary for a satisfying resolution of comedy—especially (1) a consistent desire to bring about sexual union, what Northrop Frye calls "comic drive,"[9] and (2) a sensitivity to "audience."[10] The prime victim of the Duke's flawed dramaturgy is, of course, Isabella, who, more than any of Shakespeare's heroines so far, is excluded from the "privileges of comedy," namely the privileges of exercising control over the events of the plot—privileges from which, Linda Bamber claims, it is Shakespeare's men who are typically excluded.[11] Deprived of her potential for leadership, Isabella succumbs to the control of a man she has no choice but to obey—a man whose orders are highly questionable—and as a consequence her character is markedly diminished.

That the Duke's actions are questionable is apparent from the beginning, when he unexpectedly appoints Angelo to rule in his place instead of Escalus, who, as the opening scene establishes, is clearly the logical choice. Throughout the play, the Duke continues to undermine his credibility as

---

[9]Northrop Frye, *A Natural Perspective: The Development of Shakespearean Comedy and Romance* (New York: Harcourt-Brace, 1965). p 73.

[10]The merry wives, for example, must correctly gauge their "audience's"—Falstaff's—vanity in order for their plots to succeed Viola demonstrates a similar sensitivity to audience response when, disguised as Cesario, she explains to Olivia the way a man should present himself if he wants to elicit a woman's love (*Twelfth Night*, 1.5.266–74). In *As You Like It*, the splendidly dramatic Rosalind is not only astute about her own audience, but she teaches Orlando to be more sensitive to *his* as well (see, for example, 4.1.41–46).

[11]Bamber. p 120.

a dramatist figure by making decisions strictly according to his own desires without considering the responses of those he is attempting to manipulate. For instance, his lofty tone in lecturing Claudio on how to make himself "absolute for death" (3.1.5–41)* is far from sensitive to the condemned man's situation. Not surprisingly, his effort fails; within a hundred lines Claudio is begging, "Sweet sister, let me live" (132). Similarly unsympathetic, and similarly unsuccessful, is the Duke's attempt to convince the recalcitrant Barnardine to offer his head in place of Claudio's. This attempt results in the ridiculous appearance of a head whose owner, Ragozine, has no other purpose in the play than to cover for (even while calling attention to) Vincentio's insensitivity to the exigencies of motivation. The Duke's ineptitude as a playwright surrogate lies partly in his failure, in Viola's words, to "observe their mood on whom he jests" (*Twelfth Night*, 3.1.63)—a failure which will prove especially detrimental to Isabella.

Another way in which the Duke perverts the Shakespearean comic paradigm is in his unusual antagonistic relationship to the "normal action" of comedy, which Frye defines as the struggle of the main characters to overcome obstacles in order to achieve sexual union.[12] The Duke *appears* to be possessed by a comic drive toward union when he proposes the bed-trick (dubious as it is) or when he arranges what Anne Barton refers to as the "outbreak of that pairing-off disease"[13] in Act 5. But his explicit denial that he has anything in common with those sinners and weaklings who allow themselves to be struck by the "dribbling dart of love" (1.3.2)—along with his implicit condoning of Angelo's revival of obsolete sexual restrictive policies ("I have on Angelo imposed the office, / Who may, in th' ambush of my name, strike home" [40–41])—sets him apart from earlier comic dramatists, predominantly women,

*All quotations from *Measure for Measure* are from the Signet Classic paperback edition, ed. S. Nagarajan (New York: New American Library, 1964, 2nd rev. ed 1998); all other quotations from Shakespeare are from *The Complete Signet Classic Shakespeare*, ed. Sylvan Barnet (New York: Harcourt, Brace, Jovanovich, 1972).

[12]Frye, *A Natural Perspective*, p. 72.

[13]Anne Barton, Introduction to *Measure for Measure* in *The Riverside Shakespeare*, p. 548

whose desire was to escape, rather than to impose, sexual restriction. As Wheeler says, *"Measure for Measure* is guided to its comic conclusion by a character whose essence is the denial of family ties and sexuality, the denial, that is to say, of the essence of comedy."[14] Vincentio represents not love's facilitator but its "blocking" agent. In this play, the hero and the "alazon" figure—the main obstacle to resolution in a typical comedy[15]—are, ironically, identical. Thus, the Duke, as protagonist, also embodies those traits characteristic of a comic antagonist. The "savior" in *Measure for Measure* turns out to be a villain as well. (Vincentio even allies himself with the play's more obvious antagonist, announcing that Angelo can "my part in him advertise" [1.1.41] and inviting Angelo, in his absence, to be "at full ourself" [43]. The Duke's intent may be to flatter Angelo with these phrases, but by positing this unity of their characters, he leaves himself open to suspicion.)

Part of what is comically "villainous" in the Duke is his excessive self-interest. Thomas Van Laan is among those critics who point out the Duke's egotism, arguing that he "cares about his image above all else." Van Laan describes the Duke as writer/producer/director of his own "carefully devised playlet," a man who is "like some film star more interested in his own virtuosity than ideal film representation of the script." Indeed, the Duke's purpose for relinquishing his public responsibilities—a purpose he himself admits is "grave and wrinkled" (1.3.5)—is reminiscent of Tom Sawyer's reason for playing dead: he wants to find out what people will say about him when he's gone.[16]

While some may argue that such an evaluation of the Duke as selfishly motivated is unduly harsh, there is much in this play to support it, especially in those scenes in which the Duke's actions seem well-intentioned. During the opening scene, for example, Vincentio lavishes praise on Angelo in an unnecessarily long and rhetorically elaborate passage (1.1.26–41), all the while knowing that Angelo has aban-

---

[14]Wheeler, p. 149

[15]Frye, *Anatomy of Criticism: Four Essays* (Princeton Univ. Press, 1957), pp 164–65, 172.

[16]See Thomas F. Van Laan, *Role-Playing in Shakespeare* (Toronto: Univ. of Toronto Press, 1978), pp 98–100. See also Wheeler, pp 130–32

doned Mariana, an act which the Duke later calls "unjust" (3.1.244). Far from having Vienna's best interests in mind as he claims—and as many critics accept—the Duke is actually setting up Angelo for a fall while protecting himself ("my nature never in the fight / To do it slander" [1.3.42–43]), and at the same time betraying the public as well, a public whom he admits he has effectively "bid" to be promiscuous through his permissiveness (36–38). His ultimate intention seems to be setting the stage for his final dramatic saving of the day—a day which would not need saving except for his contrivances in the first place. Vincentio's brand of dramaturgy is not as well-meaning as it first appears, and it should make us apprehensive about the Duke's potential to warp the experiences of those involved in his plots.

III

The female characters in this play, Mariana and Isabella, are the prime victims of the Duke's disturbing manipulativeness—a significant reversal of the roles women have played in earlier comedies. While both male and female characters serve to some extent as the Duke's "puppets,"[17] only the men resist his orders; the women are bound to be "directed" by him (4.3.138), "advised" by him (4.6.3), "ruled" by him (4). As Jean E. Howard points out, Barnardine, Lucio, and Angelo, even though punished in the end, do at times "refuse to be pawns in someone else's tidy playscript": Barnardine refuses to die, Angelo refuses to pardon Claudio, Lucio refuses to shut up.[18] Neither Mariana nor Isabella ever exhibits such defiance. Thus this play creates a disturbing and unusual sense of female powerlessness. But far from prescribing female reticence, *Measure for Measure* serves to reveal contingencies that make it difficult for women, even strong-willed women like Isabella, to assert themselves in a patriarchal society like Vienna—

---

[17] William Empson (*The Structure of Complex Words* [London: Chatto and Windus, 1951], p. 283) sees the Duke as a character who manipulates "his subjects as puppets for the fun of seeing them twitch."

[18] Jean E Howard, "*Measure for Measure* and the Restraints of Convention," *Essays in Literature* 10 (1983): 151–52. Dr. Howard has provided immeasurable support to me in my preparation of this study.

contingencies that do not impinge in the same way on the men. By allowing such contingencies to dominate the action, Shakespeare throws into question both the play's status as a comedy and the legitimacy of the prevailing social standards it portrays.

When we judge Isabella, we must consider, as Wheeler does, that she is surrounded by "the threat of sexual degradation"—a threat which, in this play, is "moved to the very center of the comic action," while in the festive comedies that threat is "deflected by wit and subordinated to the larger movements" of those plays.[19] More than any comic heroine thus far, Isabella has reason to take sexual degradation seriously. Whereas in most Shakespearean comedies the patriarchal world is peripheral to the main action, thereby allowing female characters exceptional latitude, in this play the expansiveness of a "green world" is inconceivable. Isabella has no Arden to retreat to. As Frye suggests, the green world in *Measure for Measure*, if present at all, has shrunk to the size of Mariana's all but inconsequential moated grange.[20]

The constriction of the heroine's power throughout the course of Shakespeare's pre-romance comedies has been noted by Anthony Dawson, but only with regard to Portia, Rosalind, and Helena.[21] Isabella represents the logical extension of this trend. The restrictiveness of Isabella's environment in *Measure for Measure* is evident in her doubts about her effectiveness ("My power? Alas, I doubt—" [1.4.77]) in the world as it must appear to her—a Vienna in which lust is rampant and in which even fiancées and wives are referred to in the same terms as whores. Elbow's speeches, for instance, denigrate, if inadvertently, his own wife: "My wife, sir, whom I detest before Heaven and your honor—" (2.1.68–69), and "Marry, sir, by my wife, who, if she had been a woman cardinally given, might have been accused in fornication, adultery, and all uncleanliness there"

[19]Wheeler, p. 102.
[20]Frye, *A Natural Perspective*, pp. 141–45, and *Anatomy of Criticism*, pp 182–83. See also Bamber, pp. 36–38, on the relationship between the world of "holiday brilliance" (the green world) and that of "political hegemony" (the patriarchal world) in Shakespeare's comedies.
[21]Anthony Dawson, *Indirections. Shakespeare and the Art of Illusion* (Toronto: Univ. of Toronto Press, 1978), p. 87.

(78–80). Of the female characters who appear in this play, none are actually wives, and the one who is betrothed, Juliet, is called a "fornicatress" (2.2.23). Otherwise, one of the women has been wronged (Mariana), one is a nun who has withdrawn from this lust-infected Vienna, one is trying to withdraw (Isabella), and the last is a whore (Mistress Overdone, nicknamed Madam Mitigation) whose customers are all sent to jail, leaving her to fret over her lost income. Sex in this Vienna is to be either punished or belittled. While Claudio, the true lover, sits in prison, the rakish Lucio roams the streets, joking about getting caught at a game of "tick-tack" (1.2.194–95). The word "healthy" could hardly be associated with female sexuality in such an environment, no matter how positively a woman saw herself.

What Isabella is afraid of, synonymous with her loss of virginity, is her loss of respect, both her own self-respect and the respect of the community. Her desire for "a more strict restraint / Upon the sisterhood" (1.4.4–5) must be linked with a strong fear of the consequences of integrating herself into a society dominated by exploitative men. In Irene Dash's terms, "In *Measure for Measure* Shakespeare again raises the question of woman's personal autonomy—her right to control her body."[22] For Isabella, in light of the Vienna facing her, sexuality and self-esteem are mutually exclusive options. She has made her choice before she ever sets foot on stage. A woman in her position would not make such a decision without difficulty, even resentment. Isabella realizes that her "prosperous art," her ability to "play with reason and discourse" (1.2.188–89), would be wasted in the city. So she attempts to withdraw to the protective cloister—an option much missed by women in post-Reformation England.[23] Just as Kate has taken "perverse refuge" behind the role of Shrew,[24] Isabella tries to take refuge behind the role of Nun.

[22]Dash, p. 251.
[23]English convents, offering "a haven and a vocation for gentlewomen," were closed at the Reformation (Ian Watt, *The Rise of the Novel* [Berkeley: Univ. of California Press, 1957], p. 145). According to Watt, "What was most needed, it was generally thought, was a substitute for the convents."
[24]Wheeler, p. 140.

But just as Isabella is on the brink of forswearing the company of men, Lucio arrives to pull her back into it. Reluctantly she returns to Vienna, where, gradually, her character dissolves, her spirit erodes. and she becomes an obedient follower of male guidance: an actress in a male-dominated drama.

IV

If we examine Isabella's development in this play, we can see how her sense of self is undetermined and finally destroyed through her encounters with patriarchal authority represented emphatically, but not exclusively, by the insensitive Duke. Her dilemma initially becomes apparent when she appears, a mere nun, before the Duke's appointed deputy. At first she is hesitant to assert herself against Angelo and is ready, at the slightest resistance, to give up her task of persuading him to free Claudio. But with Lucio's prompting, her "prosperous art" with words becomes evident. More and more masterfully she develops her argument, pleading eloquently for her brother's life:

> go to your bosom,
> Knock there, and ask your heart what it doth know
> That's like my brother's fault; if it confess
> A natural guiltiness such as is his,
> Let it not sound a thought upon your tongue
> Against my brother's life. (2.2.136–41)

Even though at this early point in the play Isabella is already acting according to male direction, namely Lucio's, her integrity, which she so adamantly desires to protect. is still intact. Her voice remains, impressively, her own.

But Angelo assaults that integrity when he forces Isabella to choose between her brother's life and her maidenhood. He commands her, "Be that you are, / That is, a woman," defining a woman's "destined livery" in no uncertain terms (2.4.134 ff.). As hard as she has tried to avoid understanding Angelo earlier in this scene, Isabella can now no longer claim to be ignorant of his "pernicious purpose" (150). When the deputy finally departs, leaving Isabella in the wake of his promise to torture her brother if she doesn't yield up her body to his will ("thy unkindness shall his death draw out / To ling'ring sufferance" [166–67]), she cries out in exasperation, "To whom shall I complain?" Her only hope for compassion lies with Claudio: "I'll to my brother," she declares, assured that there is at least one man in the world possessed of "a mind of honor" (171–79).

Naturally, when Claudio echoes Angelo's demands, arguing that Isabella's surrendering her virginity in this case would be a virtue, her frustration is exacerbated. She reacts the way a woman might if she had been raped and had found those closest to her unsympathetic; she feels isolated, hurt, terrified, enraged. Loss of virginity, after all, is never a light matter for Shakespeare's calumniated, or potentially calumniated, women. In *Much Ado About Nothing*, the perception of Hero as sexually tainted corresponds directly with the illusion of her as dead. For Isabella, too, the prospect of giving herself to Angelo is tantamount to dying: "Better it were a brother died at once, / Than that a sister . . . / Should die for ever" (106–8). If we understand how high the stakes are, we can hardly justify labeling Isabella a "vixen" when her strong will, until now subdued, gets the better of her and she swears,

> O you beast!
> O faithless coward! O dishonest wretch!
> . . . . .
> Take my defiance,
> Die, perish! Might but my bending down
> Reprieve thee from thy fate, it should proceed.
> I'll pray a thousand prayers for thy death,
> No word to save thee.   (3.1.137–47)

Her oaths here are far from endearing. But what they expose is neither rigidity nor coldness but a deeply rooted fear of exploitation, a fear justified by the attitudes toward women prevalent in this Vienna. Claudio's urging Isabella to give up her virginity, understandable as it is from his point of view, compounds her increasing sense of vulnerability and helplessness.

Our experience of Isabella's being "thwarted here, there,

and everywhere"[25] is reinforced by the intervention of the Duke at precisely this troublesome point in the play. Although his intentions appear honorable at first, in his own way he replicates Angelo's and Claudio's indifference to Isabella's desire to remain true to herself. Like Angelo and Claudio before him, Vincentio sees in Isabella a reflection of his own needs. Consider his surprising endorsement of her attack on her brother. Rather than recoil at the harshness of her attack (as most of the play's critics have done), the Duke responds with delight: "The hand that hath made you fair hath made you good; the goodness that is cheap in beauty makes beauty brief in goodness; but grace, being the soul of your complexion, shall keep the body of it ever fair" (182–86). The Duke's perceptions of Isabella here reveal more about his character than about hers. What the Duke sees at this moment is the ideal woman that Hamlet never found: a woman who combines beauty and honesty; a woman who doesn't need to be told to get herself to a nunnery; a woman who represents the opposite of Frailty. Unfortunately for Isabella, the Duke is so taken by his Hamletian fantasies that he fails to see the woman she really is— a woman in distress, who fears the very thing he will eventually require: the sacrifice of her autonomy.

Isabella's willingness to cooperate with the Duke's unscrupulous plot—and so to forfeit her autonomy—is clearly related to his choice of disguises. Vincentio, wearing Friar Francis' robe, has become the very thing he accuses Angelo of being: an "angel on the outward side" (3.2.275).[26] Lucio is right to call him the "Duke of dark corners" (4.3.159).[27] But whatever "crotchets" the Duke has in him (3.2.130), his disguise represents an authority that Isabella, as a nun, can

---

[25]Sarojini Shintri, *Woman In Shakespeare* (Dharwad: Karnatak Univ., 1977), p. 276.

[26]Christopher Marlowe (*The Tragical History of the Life and Death of Doctor Faustus* [Oxford: Clarendon Press, 1950], p. 9, 1.3.25–26) supplies a literary precedent for Vincentio's hypocritical disguise when he has Faustus assert that the "holy shape" of a Franciscan friar "becomes a devil best."

[27]Calvin S. Hall (*A Primer of Freudian Psychology* [New York: New American Library, 1979], p. 92) could be describing Duke Vincentio when he explains "reaction formation" (caused by a repressed wish to possess something). "Romantic notions of chastity and purity may mask crude sexual desires, altruism may hide selfishness, and piety may conceal sinfulness."

hardly repudiate. When he invites her to fasten her ear on his advisings, she agrees to follow his direction. But like the Provost, who protests that the Duke's orders will force him to break an oath (4.2.185), Isabella makes it clear that she does not want to play any part that would require her to violate her personal sense of truth: "I have spirit to do any thing that appears not foul in the truth of my spirit" (3.1.208–10). She does not want to have to sacrifice her own voice.

But by the time the fourth act closes, the Duke has imposed on Isabella a role which goes against her wishes. As she explains to Mariana in the last scene of that act, "To speak so indirectly I am loath: I would say the truth" (4.2.1–2). However, because a supposed religious superior has instructed her to "veil full purpose" (4), she denies her personal inclinations and obeys the Duke without questioning. Neither green world nor cloister is available to Isabella now; she can neither subvert nor avoid the distorted value system which Vienna represents. She has no alternative but to submit to the Duke's authority. The Church, which was originally to function as Isabella's protector, has become her dictator.[28] Even though she was able to resist both Angelo's attempt to ravish her body and Claudio's attempt to change her mind, Isabella is unable, finally, to resist the Duke's demands on her spirit.

V

This negation of Isabella's essentially self-defined character becomes complete upon the Duke's taking control of the action in Act 3. Critics have noted this change variously. Richard Fly, for example, says that Isabella, "formerly an independent and authentic personality with a voice

[28]Church-supported witch hunts were still a reality in Shakespeare's England. The playwright could hardly have been unaware of the sexual oppressiveness, latent and actual, in religious doctrine of his day. For information on the involvement of both Catholic and Protestant churches in the witch hunts, see Barbara Ehrenreich and Deirdre English, *For Her Own Good: 150 Years of the Experts' Advice to Women* (New York: Doubleday, 1978), pp. 35–39, or their booklet *Witches, Midwives, and Nurses: A History of Women Healers* (Old Westbury, N.Y.: The Feminist Press, 1971), pp. 6–15.

of her own," is "suddenly reduced to little more than a willing adjunct to the Duke's purpose."[29] Clara Claiborne Park refers to Isabella as losing center stage.[30] Whatever autonomy Isabella possessed in the beginning of the play, whatever "truth of spirit" she abided by, disintegrates once she agrees to serve in the Duke's plan. As soon as this "friar" takes over, Isabella becomes an actress whose words are no longer her own. There are no more outbursts. In complying with the role Vincentio has created for her, Isabella becomes his creation in a way that the male characters never do. When he presents her with the irreverent idea of the bedtrick, Isabella simply answers, "Show me how, good father" (3.1.242) and "The image of it gives me content already" (264). She cooperates with the Duke throughout the last act, in spite of her preference for "saying truth." When Angelo says that he perceives these "poor informal women" as "instruments of some more mightier member / That sets them on" (5.1.236–38), he doesn't know how truly he speaks.

The Duke claims, of course, to be acting in Isabella's best interest, just as he has claimed to be acting in the best interests of Vienna. He professes to be withholding the news that Claudio is alive in order to make Isabella "heavenly comforts of despair, / When it is least expected" (4.3.111–12). But the relationship between his professed intentions and the scenario he asks Isabella to act out is tenuous. In reward for her cooperation, Isabella has to kneel and swear in public that she, a recognized member of a local convent, "did yield" to the learned deputy (5.1.101)—a humiliating position to be forced into, no matter how cleverly the Duke may be intending to redeem her reputation.[31] In retrospect, the Duke's promise to comfort Isabella—what Frye calls a "brutal lie"[32]—appears to be a veiled justification for perpetuating his control over her. The passage in which the Duke urges Isabella to "pace" her wisdom "In that good path that [he] would wish it go"—a passage densely packed with

[29]Richard Fly, *Shakespeare's Mediated World* (Amherst. Univ of Massachusetts Press, 1976), p. 59.
[30]Claiborne Park, p. 109
[31]See Wheeler, p. 129.
[32]Frye. *A Natural Perspective*, p. 11

imperatives (4.3.119–50)—is followed, significantly, by the entrance of the ego-puncturing Lucio. This juxtaposition of scenes should warn us not to take the Duke's proclaimed altruism at face value—just as the Duke's proclaimed aversion to staging himself to the people's eyes (1.1.68) belies *its* face value. Vincentio's grand opus, Act 5—complete with trumpets to announce his entrance—is so conspicuously dramaturgical that it divides into a five-part structure.[33] Clearly we are not to rest easy with this man's proclamations, nor should we be comfortable with the role he is asking Isabella to play.

Isabella's last words reveal just how far this imposed role diminishes her character. To those who argue that rather than depriving Isabella of autonomy the Duke is actually releasing her from moral rigidity by arranging for her to plead for Angelo's life, I answer that Isabella's final speech, often accepted as representing character growth, in fact represents the opposite.[34] Ostensibly, Isabella is once again displaying her "prosperous art," using rhetoric to reveal a new-found capacity for mercy. But the quality of mercy here is strained:

> Most bounteous sir,
> Look, if it please you, on this man condemned.
> As if my brother lived. I partly think
> A due sincerity governèd his deeds,
> Till he did look on me. Since it is so,
> Let him not die. My brother had but justice,
> In that he did the thing for which he died;
> For Angelo,
> His act did not o'ertake his bad intent,
> And must be buried but as an intent
> That perished by the way. Thoughts are no subjects,
> Intents but merely thoughts.   (5.1.446–57)

This speech lacks the integrity of Isabella's earlier speeches in which she pleaded with Angelo to ask his heart what it

---

[33]See Josephine Bennett, *"Measure for Measure" as Royal Entertainment* (New York. Columbia Univ. Press, 1966), pp. 131–33

[34]See Fly, p. 69. Dawson, p 114. and Geckle, p. 168, for discussions of the problematic nature of this passage.

knew that was like her brother's fault. Logic, used so con-
vincingly in the earlier speeches, has become twisted. For
example, Isabella argues that since Claudio did "the thing
for which he died" but Angelo did not commit the sin he
thought he had, Angelo should not be punished. This argument is illogical because it wrongfully implies that evil
actions, when carried out under mistaken circumstances, are
harmless. If the crime had been misdirected murder, by this
logic Isabella would have claimed that the act was no crime
since the intended victim was still alive. Not only the laws of
logic, but the concept of justice is twisted here. Isabella
claims—as she need not—that her brother's supposed execution was, in fact, just. Her mode of argument is unsettling,
not only because she sounds indifferent to Claudio's death,
but also because she resorts to specious legalism where one
would expect her to appeal to her faith, as she did when
pleading for Claudio's salvation in 2.2.75–77:

> How would you be,
> If He, which is the top of judgment, should
> But judge you as you are?

In comparison with this earlier speech, Isabella's final
appeal represents not an increased but a stunted capacity
for mercy. Her "prosperous art," subjected to the Duke's
perverted dramaturgical efforts, has itself become perverted.
Vincentio's charge—"trust not my holy Order, / If I pervert your course" (4.3.149–50)—becomes retrospectively
ominous.

With the conclusion of her final speech, Isabella is immediately confronted with a series of overwhelming events: a
living Claudio appears, the Duke proposes marriage, and
Angelo is pardoned. All of Isabella's main assumptions—
that Angelo was condemned, that the Duke was a committed
celibate, that her brother was dead, and that she herself
would remain chaste for life—are challenged, if not negated,
in the space of five lines. She remains speechless, a baffled
actress who has run out of lines. The gradual loss of her personal voice during the course of the play has become,
finally, a literal loss of voice. In this sense, *Measure for*

Measure is Isabella's tragedy. Like Lavinia in *Titus Andronicus*, the eloquent Isabella is left with no tongue.

VI

If we see Isabella as a victim of bad playwriting, we can compare her bewilderment at the end of *Measure for Measure* with our own. She has trusted the Duke, as we've trusted our playwright, to pattern events as he has led her to expect events to be patterned—and the Duke, sharing Shakespeare's affinity for surprises in this play, pulls those expectations out from under her.[35] But by using Ragozine's head, for example—*caput ex machina*—to call attention to the ridiculousness of the Duke's machinations, Shakespeare simultaneously calls attention to his own superior skills. With this play Shakespeare has moved from comedy's romantic pole to its opposite, ironic, pole.[36] What he has created in *Measure for Measure* is not a poorly written play, but, to some extent, a model for poor playwriting.[37] (Such a

[35]Surprise is an important element of the plot—both for the characters and for us as audience. Among the bewildered audiences that *Measure for Measure* leaves in its wake are Angelo and Escalus at the end of 1.1, just after the Duke's sudden exit; Mistress Overdone in the following scene ("But shall all our houses of resort in the suburbs be pulled down?" 1.2.105–5); Friar Thomas, not quite grasping the Duke's partial explanation for his abdication ("It rested in your Grace / To unloose this tied-up Justice when you pleased," 1.3.31–32); Isabella, hearing of her brother's imprisonment ("Woe me! For what?" 1.4.26); Escalus and Angelo, confounded by the bumbling protestations of Pompey, Elbow, and Froth (2.1); Angelo, surprised at his awakened lust (2.2.162); Isabella, hearing of Angelo's mistreatment of Mariana ("Can this be so? Did Angelo so leave her?" 3.1.228); the Duke, shocked at Angelo's order for Claudio's immediate execution (4.2.122–29); the Provost, "amazed" when the disguised Duke miraculously produces a letter with the Duke's seal on it (212); the Duke, surprised by Barnardine's resistance and by Ragozine's conveniently appearing head (4.3.77); Escalus and Angelo, confused by the Duke's "uneven and distracted" letters (4.4.1–7); and, of course, Isabella, stupefied at the Duke's proposal of marriage, along with Angelo and Lucio, distressed at their suddenly ordered couplings.
[36]Frye, *Anatomy of Criticism*, pp. 177–79
[37]Those who view the play as exemplifying some lapse on Shakespeare's part include Philip Edwards (*Shakespeare and the Confines of Art* [London: Methuen, 1968], pp. 108–10), who deems the play a "failure" because of its "insistence on a happy ending in spite of the evidence." On the other hand, critics like Howard and Fly credit Shakespeare with having purposefully created a disruptive audience experience—an argument prefigured by Michael Goldman's appendix on *Measure for Measure* in *Shakespeare and the Energies of Drama* (Princeton. Princeton Univ. Press, 1972), p. 164, in which he

model, clearly of abiding interest to Shakespeare, is less
subtly depicted in the rustics' production of "Pyramus and
Thisby" in *A Midsummer Night's Dream*.) By creating in
Duke Vincentio a model third-rate playwright—one whose
mind-set Jean Howard calls "confining, inelastic, danger-
ously reductive," one who has no qualms about "[draining]
the life out of previously vital characters such as Isabella"[38]—
Shakespeare calls into question the ethics of his own craft,
including the ethics involved in handling characters of the
opposite sex. However, the intent to which Shakespeare
transcends the Duke's limitations is not clear, especially
with regard to the treatment of female characters. It is in this
area that the comparison between the playwright and his surrogate becomes most murky.

Vincentio's sexual double standard is hardly subtle. Ever
oblivious to female experience, Vincentio tells Juliet that
because she returns Claudio's affection—because the "most
offenseful act" is "mutually committed"—her sin is therefore "of heavier kind" than Claudio's (2.3.26–28). Such
chauvinism, while present in Shakespeare's previous comedies, has almost always eventually been subverted in favor
of mutuality.[39] It would be tempting to claim that because
the expected subversion of chauvinistic values does not
occur in *Measure for Measure*, therefore Shakespeare must
be consciously critiquing the Duke's double standard, once
again—as in the case of Ragozine's head—showing himself
to be the superior craftsman. But this claim would be ill-
founded, considering that Shakespeare's own treatment of
female characters at this point in his career becomes less
than generous. As Vincentio "drains" life out of Isabella and
Mariana, so Shakespeare drains life out of Gertrude and
Ophelia, giving them scarcely any character at all. Joel
Fineman's well-documented discussion of Shakespeare's
"not uncommon defensive gynophobia," which erupts in

suggests that in *Measure for Measure*, as in *Hamlet* and *Lear*, audience experience is "turned against itself to produce a comment on the action."
    [38]Howard, pp 155 and 151, respectively
    [39]See, for example, Marianne L. Novy, "Giving, Taking, and the Role
of Portia in *The Merchant of Venice*," *Philological Quarterly* 58 (1979)
137–54 for a discussion of mutuality in relationships in Shakespearean
comedy.

certain tragedies, would support such an argument.[40] If Shakespeare can be credited with critiquing Vincentio's treatment of female "characters," which seems unlikely, then he must also be said to be critiquing his treatment of some of his own.

But regardless of the playwright's intention, *Measure for Measure*, more than any of his previous plays, exposes the dehumanizing effect on women of living in a world dominated by powerful men who would like to re-create womanhood according to their fantasies. Duke Vincentio's distorted interpretation of Isabella's outrage in the prison scene is only one example of this kind of dehumanizing mind-set. His tampering with Isabella's character in Act 5— which she must endure, according to religious edict—is no less a violation than Angelo's attempt to possess her body. As Hans Sachs puts it, the Duke succeeds in committing "in a legitimate and honorable way, the crime which Angelo attempted in vain."[41]

This play reveals, among other things, the price women pay in order for male supremacy to be maintained. That price for Isabella is, precisely, a mandatory denial of her personal standards. But Isabella's plight is only one element in a larger pattern. As a whole, *Measure for Measure* explores the incompatibility of patriarchal and comic structures. The world of patriarchy, antithetical to the world of comedy throughout Shakespeare's works, comes closest here to overthrowing the comic world. Far from the one-dimensional representative of morality that critics have perceived her to be, Isabella is a key part of a dramatic environment in which the forces of patriarchy and comedy clash. In this context, her dramaturgical powerlessness becomes a variable in an equation in which the pervasiveness of chauvinism and the possibility of comic resolution are indirectly proportional. In other words, the stronger the forces of patriarchy, the less likely—or at least less convincing—comic resolution becomes.

Generically, Isabella is Shakespeare's pivotal female

[40]Joel Fineman, "Fratricide and Cuckoldry: Shakespeare's Doubles," *The Psychoanalytic Review* 64 (1977): 426
[41]Hans Sachs, "The Measure in *Measure for Measure*," in *The Design Within*, ed. M. Faber (New York: Science House, 1970), pp. 495–96.

figure. She simultaneously links the dramatically effective early comic women to the victimized tragic women, even while her sympathetic portrayal anticipates the revival of influential women in the later plays. If Isabella's voice is lost in *Measure for Measure*—to remain mute throughout Shakespeare's tragedies, in which male misfortune and misogyny explode into significantly linked central issues[42]—that voice is rediscovered in the romances, Shakespeare's most mature creations, in which patriarchal and misogynistic values, if present at all, are, as in the early comedies, subverted, and in which the imaginative environment once again allows female characters, like Paulina in *The Winter's Tale*, for example, to exert a powerful, positive force in shaping dramatic action.

RUTH NEVO

Complex Sexuality

We need to consider more closely the complex sexuality
of Isabella. I press the point because I think Isabella is mis-
conceived very often. She slips too easily into reductive
stereotypes of frigidity, hypocrisy, or egoism, whereas what
the drama articulates is the breakdown of a passionate and
sensual nature heroically idealizing a spiritually sanctified
abnegation.

Challenged by Angelo's "What would you do?" (2.4.98)
her immediate response is to imagine a martyrdom willingly
embraced. But it is in erotically masochistic terms that she
pictures martyrdom:

> As much for my poor brother as myself:
> That is, were I under the terms of death,
> Th' impression of keen whips I'd wear as rubies,
> And strip myself to death as to a bed
> That longing have been sick for, ere I'd yield
> My body up to shame. (99–104)

This vision of martyrdom is a cherished idea, not an anticipated actuality, for she has not yet caught the drift of
Angelo's probings. And it enables us to see that what sur-
faces under the pressure of Angelo's "temptation" is a deep-
seated fear, not of sex as such, and not of sin—she knows as
well as Angelo that 'compelled sins' are not blameworthy,[1]
and that chastity is a state of the soul, not the body—but of

From Ruth Nevo, "Measure for Measure: Mirror for Mirror" (*Shakespeare
Survey* 40, Cambridge University Press, 1987), pp 107–22. We reprint pages
116–19, with a new title. Used by permission of the publisher and the author
[1] In the sources the woman is always blameless.

the breakdown of her fragile ideology of a desexualized, an alternative ecstasy.

When Isabella, desperate and frightened, flies to her brother to tell him of the monstrous proposal, she is seeking not so much to reconcile him to his fate as to confirm her own decision, to receive authority for it, to have him say something like "You have done well, my child," and then to embrace him in a loving reciprocal sacrifice—a Christianized *liebestod* of souls. She says

> I'll to my brother.
> Though he hath fall'n by prompture of the blood,
> Yet hath he in him such a mind of honor,
> That, had he twenty heads to tender down
> On twenty bloody blocks, he'd yield them up,
> Before his sister should her body stoop
> To such abhorred pollution   (177–83)

But why tell him, after all? Why torment him with her own anguish? Why does she force him to endure the same agonizing decision that she has been forced to undergo, if not out of her great need for a supporting, confirming, justifying response from him? And she is in deep fear that she will not receive it, as her initial testing of him shows (3.1.64–80). When he does respond with "Thou shall not do't" (103) she is overwhelmingly relieved and cries out in loving magnanimity

> O, were it but my life,
> I'd throw it down for your deliverance
> As frankly as a pin.   (104–6)

This announcement (I am not questioning the genuineness of the feeling) is dramatically ironic, since the sacrifice that one is not asked for invariably appears preferable to the one that is demanded, a point neatly underlined by Claudio's laconic "Thanks, dear Isabel." And it precipitates in Claudio the very natural thoughts about the relativity of values, which follow (110–16). As the dialogue proceeds, Isabella becomes more and more alarmed until, when finally faced with Claudio's plea "Sweet sister, let me live" (133), and with his morally impeccable argument—her own, at an earlier point, to Angelo (2.4.65–6):

> What sin you do to save a brother's life.
> Nature dispenses with the deed so far.
> That it becomes a virtue   (3.1.134–36)

she breaks down in panic-stricken, hysterical repudiation. And her outburst is extremely revealing.

> O you beast!
> O faithless coward! O dishonest wretch!
> Wilt thou be made a man out of my vice?
> Is't not a kind of incest, to take life
> From thine own sister's shame? What should I think?
> Heaven shield my mother play'd my father fair!
> For such a warpèd slip of wilderness
> Ne'er issued from his blood.   (135–43)

Wheeler, quoting Eric Partridge's *Shakespeare's Bawdy*, points out that "vice" is an "anatomical pun."[2] But we hardly need the image of closing, or opening thighs to alert us to the distraught condensation in Isabella's words; the expression (once more) "thou be made a man out of" and "to take life from," on either side of the strange question, "Is't not a kind of incest" make the implicit metaphor an indeterminate composite of birth and intercourse. It is a grotesque figuration which has the nightmarish, revelatory disorder of an imagination under great stress. Isabella defends herself against horror by disowning Claudio, while the displacement of shame—the shame of yielding to Angelo, the shame of Claudio's demand, the shame of her rejection of him—from brother/sister relationships to a hypothetical parental lapse allows her rage an outlet. The passion with which she turns upon him with

> Die, perish! Might but my bending down
> Reprieve thee from thy fate, it should proceed.

[2]Richard P. Wheeler, *Shakespeare's Development and the Problem Comedies* (Berkeley, 1981), p 111.

I'll pray a thousand prayers for thy death,
No word to save thee (144–47)

can surely only be due to the massive energy which has
been required to batten down a powerful desire. The play
thus allows us to gauge the anguish Angelo's attempted
seduction produces in her, and to understand her need for
the armor-plated "More than our brother is our chastity"
(2.4.185). But the more we understand her frantic repudiation of her brother, her defensive, panic-stricken rage, the
collapse of her heroic self-control:

O fie, fie fie!
Thy sin's not accidental, but a trade.
Mercy to thee would prove itself a bawd,
'Tis best that thou diest quickly (3.1.148–51)

the less will we be able to understand or accommodate her
response to the bed-trick proposal.

The bed-trick is the crux of the matter. Technically it is
the "well-tied knot" which, in Renaissance theory of tragicomedy, must mediate between extreme peril and happy
solution. It even provides an extra bonus: a happy solution
for a jilted lady we haven't yet become acquainted with, and
who does not appear in any of the sources. But the substitution of Mariana for Isabella in Angelo's bed turns out to be
the most baffling of all the play's anomalies. Claudio got
Juliet with child when she was "fast" his "wife" (1.2.150) by
common-law statute, which accepted betrothal contracts as
binding, and pregnancy as still more so. The canonical sol-
emnizing of ceremony had been postponed, not unreason-
ably, in real-life Elizabethan terms, till the dowry was
forthcoming. Angelo, on the other hand, had broken off his
betrothal contract with Mariana because her dowry had been
lost at sea with her brother, who was bringing it to her; and
he will not, so far as he knows, be sleeping with a fiancée
but raping a ransom hostage. Neatly, the bed-trick makes
Angelo do exactly what he sentenced Claudio to death for,
but in circumstances morally far more blackening to his
character. Isabella's ready acceptance of the Duke's plan,
therefore, strains credibility. The bed-trick foils both the sets

of generic expectations which are entangled in *Measure for Measure*: it prevents the tragic outcome the play prepares for, but it does not mediate a harmonizing comic resolution. So far from being a knot which binds the "serious" with the "comic order of things" (Guarini, in Lever p. lxi), it has been felt to be the chief stumbling block which breaks the play into two incommensurable, disrelated and dissonant parts.

But Humpty Dumpty might be put together again. I want to propose a reading which might do this, for audiences in our time, alert to subtexts, to the oneiric, the subterranean in discourse, to what can be meant, what can be read, and what language can be up to. It has, I believe, the additional advantage of being, conceivably, presentable in the theatre.[3] Certainly in the cinema, with the aid of a director as gifted and dextrous as Alain Resnais, for example. I have in mind the remarkable film *Providence*, in which, it will be recalled, a dying author projects his own anxieties, paranoias, obsessions, guilts through a reconstruction, or construction, or interpretation, or imagination of his family circle. In the film fictional "real" people play fictional imaginary roles, in circumstances invented by the fictional waking dreamer-narrator; characters split and coalesce, plays embed themselves within plays in infinite regression, and fact and fantasy shift and interpenetrate, mask each other and mock each other in a bewildering and enthralling phantasmagoria of the interior life.

My hypothesis is simple: let us suppose that from the moment in 3.1 when the Duke comes forward and draws Isabella aside, when the play changes gear, as it were, in every respect: tone, style, diction, direction, the play can be read as the replay—only this time with escape possible—in Isabella's wishful fantasy, of the traumatic events that are happening to her, and in which she is so terribly trapped. To pursue the cinematic analogy: let us imagine a frozen still of faces and gestures at a moment of high drama, break, pause,

---

[3]In a recent RSC production Isabella and Mariana were dressed alike, and indeed looked rather alike, to excellent effect. This visual semiotic could be extended: after the switch in Act 3 characters would wear the same clothes in a contrasting color; the prison scene décor could be lit contrastingly before and after the break; Lucio's costume could be conspicuously different, so that he appears a gallant in the beginning and a foppish grotesque in Act 4. In sum, efforts could be made, not to slur, or to try to ignore the differences between the two halves of the play, but precisely to foreground them.

and, while that representation stops, another reel continues to unwind, with flashbacks, reminiscence—it is often done—gradually taking the place of the original image as that fades out. Isabella's trauma meshes with the Duke's proposal to produce a wish fulfillment dream sequence, in which the fantasy of escape is shot through by what Freud calls "counter-dreams" of pain and punishment. Read in this way, moreover, Act 4, as we shall see, would correspond to Shakespeare's preceding explorations and discoveries in the forms of comic catharsis.

The replay is first of all, structural. Where the first part moves from Lucio's plea to Isabella for help, through the monstrous proposal, to Isabella's threat to expose Angelo, and her flight to her brother, the second part moves from the Duke's offer of help, through the actualization of the monstrous proposal, to the exposure scenes of Act 5 and the reunion of Isabella with her brother. Moreover, the fatherly Friar steps into Isabella's life, with his remedy, just at the moment when her own (as she had hoped) fatherly brother had desperately let her down.

This in itself is disarming, and promotive of a willingness to be swayed by him. But there are deeper reasons for her "content." Mariana is Isabella's double in a sense more profound than that of mere technical substitution. She is, I suggest, her deeply wished-for double, in a situation that is, as has already been noted, the replica of her brother's with Juliet.

Juliet, as was observed, is the Isabella the novice has chosen not to be; Mariana is the woman Isabella the extortion victim has chosen not to be. But if Mariana to Angelo is the equivalent of Juliet to Claudio, an equivalence the Duke's explanation brings out, then the bed-trick substitution can offer to Isabella the occasion for a repressed wish-fulfillment fantasy. We recall the warmth of her feelings for Claudio, and we recall her outburst when she repudiates him: "Is't not a kind of incest" (3.1.138). However, Mariana is also, since she will double for Isabella, at one and the same time the sexual victim of Angelo's lust. This is exactly the point upon which naturalistic interpretations of Isabella's response stumble. But the unconscious knows no contradiction, as we know. The deep ambivalences that must be denied in consciousness appear in dreams in defiant simultaneity. The role to be played by Mariana could be doubly, triply satisfying to Isabella's exacerbated imagination: she is the permitted, semi-legitimized marriage partner in a fantasy replica of Juliet's (unconsciously envied) misdemeanor with her brother; she is sexual victim of the man who has tried to seduce her, and might well therefore have triggered the underlying masochism already observed, the more especially since in a culture of shame such as Isabella's, disguise, a kind of absence, is a potent enabling factor for sexual fantasizing. And finally, the man who has tried to seduce her is, at the censored level of intellectual and conscious values, her avowed ideal, a spiritual double. The bed-trick, stumbling block to rational or moral interpretation, thus appears as keystone in the overdetermined, polyphonic figurations of fantasy: "The image of it," says Isabella, "gives me content already, and I trust it will grow to a most prosperous perfection" (3.1.264–66).

Measure for Measure on Stage and Screen

The earliest evidence of a performance of the play is an entry in the Revels Accounts, which says that *"Mesur for Mesur"* by "Shaxberd" was acted at Whitehall on December 26, 1604, St. Stephen's Night, by His Majesty's Players. We next hear of a performance in 1662 in Sir William Davenant's adaptation *The Law Against Lovers.* Davenant's sweeping changes in the plot and characterizations reduce greatly the seriousness of Shakespeare's play. He introduced characters from *Much Ado About Nothing,* and rewrote many speeches to suit Restoration ideas of decorum and clarity of expression. Samuel Pepys, who characterized this adaptation as "a good play" when he saw it at The Duke's House in Lincoln's Inn Fields on February 18, 1662, singled out for praise the dancing and singing of the girl who played one of the new roles created by Davenant.

The next recorded performance is of another adaptation, Charles Gildon's *Measure for Measure, or Beauty the Best Advocate,* in 1700, at Lincoln's Inn Fields. This version, with Thomas Betterton playing Angelo and Mrs. Bracegirdle as Isabella, was performed eight times during the season of 1699–1700. There is a little more of Shakespeare in Gildon than in Davenant, but substantial alterations still make this bear only a remote resemblance to Shakespeare's play. Gildon omitted the bawdry of the play, and introduced in its place an operatic interlude by Henry Purcell, *The Loves of Dido and Aeneas* with libretto by Nahum Tate. He gave a love speech to the Duke to reduce the abruptness of his proposal of marriage to Isabella.

Between 1701 and 1750 the play (or an adaptation) was

enacted sixty-nine times, being, according to C. B. Hogan (cited in the *New Variorum* edition p. 468), "the sixth most frequent among Shakespeare's comedies." (The 1720 performance restored Shakespeare's text to the stage.) In 1737 Mrs. Cibber appeared as Isabella and remained unchallenged in the role till she retired in 1759. We do not hear of the play on the London stage again till 1770, although it was occasionally played in the provinces and in Dublin. Between 1751 and 1800 there were sixty-four performances in London. After Mrs. Cibber had retired, the role of Isabella was played by Mrs. Siddons at David Garrick's Drury Lane. (She was later joined by her brothers, John Philip Kemble and Charles Kemble.) Mrs. Siddons's Isabella was "noble, high-principled, idealistic and even fierce, but understandable and lovable as well. It was the sort of part [she] loved to play and people raved about it" (K. Mackenzie, *The Great Sarah*, 1968, p. 70). Her style was somewhat declamatory, but she could feel her way into the part, and make it sympathetic. She was seen for the last time in 1812 when she was so weak with age (although she was only fifty-seven) and ill health that she had to be helped up in the last act after kneeling to the Duke. (To hide the fact, Mariana was also helped up.) After Mrs. Siddons, the role passed on to Elizabeth O'Neill at Covent Garden. Regarded as a worthy successor, she was praised for adding the grandeur of lofty declamation to the pathos of intense feeling and harmonizing sublimity of expression with tenderness of thought.

In the nineteenth century there were (according to the *New Variorum*) only twenty-two performances. In 1824 Macready played the Duke at Drury Lane; the richness of the costumes was particularly remarked. But the usual nineteenth-century emphasis on spectacle, including illusionistic sets that took considerable time to erect and to strike, meant that the text had to be cut. Samuel Phelps, who in 1846 produced *Measure for Measure* at Sadler's Wells with himself as the Duke, especially deserves to be remembered, because he did more than any one else before William Poel to restore Shakespeare's text.

Poel produced *Measure for Measure* in 1893 at the Royalty and again in 1908 at the Gaiety in Manchester. A pioneer in his insistence that Shakespeare could be appreciated

only on the unlocalized stage for which he wrote and that
dramatic speech should be both swift and musical, Poel
declared that if the actor "got the tunes right" and observed
certain principles of deportment, the rest would follow. (It
did not do so always.) He coached his cast in the art of
rhythmic speech and the value of the word to be emphasized.
C. E. Montagu has described how in Poel's productions the
short scenes and the long ones flowed into one another and
the stage arrangement never froze the imagination as reconstructed scholarship often does. The dresses were quaint but
rich and some attempt was made to achieve historical accu-
racy. As for the scenery, one simply did not think about it.
Scenes were changed by the drawing of a curtain. Because
the settings were simple, the full text could be given in the
original sequence of the scenes, revealing Shakespeare's art
of construction. At the production of 1893 gentlemen in
Elizabethan costume sat on the sides of the stage, as in some
theaters in Shakespeare's day, and during the intervals they
smoked Elizabethan claypipes. In 1908, at the end of the performance, the company made a great impression when they
knelt in line on the stage and recited the King's Prayer from
the pre-Shakespearean play of *Ralph Roister Doister.* Poel
had his faults, of course. He was still sufficiently Victorian
to bowdlerize the text. In the line "By yielding up thy body
to my will," "body" became "self," though the line became
unmetrical thereby; "He has got a wench with child" became
"He will shortly be a father." (The bawdry of the play has
always been objected to till recently.) Poel sometimes carried his dislike of elaborate scenery too far, and his emphasis
on natural intonation led him to ignore the variations
demanded by different circumstances. Nevertheless our debt
to Poel remains great. We owe the swiftness and continuity
of modern productions to him.

Poel, who took the part of Angelo in both of the productions, argued that Angelo should not be seen as a moral
reprobate, for he had, after all, won the heart of Mariana. He
was the one instance in Shakespeare of a man who fell while
contemplating virtue. In the Manchester production Sara
Allgood played Isabella as a character of passionate truth.
She did not wear any religious habit because if she did,
argued Poel, the Duke could not very well offer to marry

her. Poel cast the Duke (James Hearne, in 1908) as a man of about forty, alert, full of resource and energy, adored for his kindly ways and far too witty and wise for anyone to feel bored in his company. Poel insisted that his speech to Claudio on death should be given with ease and spirit, for in Poel's view the Duke was not a conventional religious man. (Samuel Johnson, it will be recalled, thought that the description of death as sleep is impious in the Friar, foolish in the reasoner, and trite and vulgar in the poet.)

With Poel begins the modern stage history of the play, characterized by the determined attempts of producers to give a modern reading of the characters and of the general significance of the play. The play is seen either in modern psychological terms or in theological (or anti-theological) terms. The division of critical opinion that the play has occasioned is seen in the theater also, for instance, in the interpretation of the characters of the Duke and Isabella. The play itself is read sometimes either as a dramatic enactment of Christian charity, or, at the other extreme, as a satire on the arbitrary ways of human and divine authority. Isabella's response to the Duke's proposal of marriage is also variously interpreted.

Passing over productions in 1924 (in one of which Ernest Milton played a memorable Angelo) and 1925, we may consider Tyrone Guthrie's production at the Old Vic in 1933. (He had produced the play earlier, in 1930, at Cambridge.) This production was remarkable for Charles Laughton's Angelo as an outright sensualist, a precisian dressed in a black water-silk robe who paced the stage in restless torment and spoke his lines "as if," said one reviewer, "he were drawing a garden-rake across intractable soil." Guthrie himself has written that Laughton's Angelo was "a cunning oleaginous monster whose cruelty and lubricity could have surprised no one, least of all himself" (*A Life in the Theater* [1960], pp. 109–10). Flora Robson as Isabella gave a moving performance, although Guthrie himself thought she made the character too pure. James Agate saw in her acting sensuality under tempestuous restraint (*First Nights*, p. 236). Roger Livesey, Guthrie wrote, made "a glittering and commanding Duke suggesting glamor and the sinister power of absolute authority."

Guthrie came back to the play in 1937, again at the Old Vic, with Emlyn Williams now as a proud, pale, and disturbed deputy struggling to keep his sensuality down. Although his movements betrayed his lust for power, the agony of his temptation was real, and Williams made both the struggle and remorse moving. Isabella was played by Marie Ney. While Agate found her a scold (*The Amazing Theatre* [1939], p. 41), Audrey Williamson admired the intensity of her feeling and the intellectual maturity and poise of her bearing (*Old Vic Drama* [1948], p. 72). (The latter qualities lapsed, however, in her conduct with her brother.) Stephen Murray played a middle-aged Duke, and Sylvia Coleridge presented a Mariana whose forgiveness of Angelo struck many reviewers as truly sublime.

Departing from chronology, we may note that Guthrie produced the play again in 1966 at the Bristol Old Vic. But there was a difference, for he had come to accept the Christian interpretation of the play. (This is chiefly associated with the essay of Professor Wilson Knight included in the Signet Classic edition, but as early as 1908 Charlotte Porter had advanced a similar interpretation in a First Folio edition by herself and Helen A. Clarke.) Guthrie made the Duke the central figure of the production now, describing him in the program note as a figure of Almighty God and even comparing him to the Heavenly Bridegroom in the last scene. "Shakespeare is permitting himself," wrote Guthrie, "a theological comment upon an all-wise, merciful Father-God who permits the frightful and apparently meaningless disasters which unceasingly befall his children." The theme of the play was justice tempered by mercy and authority tempered by love. (Nevertheless the production did not lack an element of fun.) John Franklyn Robbins played the part in a habit and manner that evoked the popular image of Christ. Not everyone was impressed; one critic irreverently said that the Duke was a vulgar-minded man gratifying himself by playing Christ in a water-spaniel wig. However, the comedy was enjoyable, and the tension of the Angelo (Richard Pasco)–Isabella (Barbara Leigh-Hunt) debates was realized.

There were productions of the play at Stratford in 1940 (by Iden Payne) and in 1946 (by Frank McMullan of the

Yale Department of Drama). (For differing views of Mc-Mullan's production, see Professor Wilson Knight's *Shakespearian Production* [1964], pp. 255–58 and T. C. Kemp and J. C. Trewin in *The Stratford Festival* [1953].) The play was again seen at Stratford in 1947 produced by Ronald Giffen with Beatrix Lehmann as Isabella, Paul Scofield as Lucio, and Michael Golden as the Duke.

Nineteen fifty saw what many regard as the best production of the play: Peter Brook's at Stratford in England. Derek Granger, reviewing Anthony Quayle's 1956 production in *The Financial Times*, recalled that Brook's production had the effect of an important discovery, as if "a dark and rarely seen canvas had been suddenly stripped of dirty varnish and newly presented with unexpectedly brilliant highlights."

Brook believes that designing the stage and directing the play are inseparable responsibilities. With the assistance of Michael Northen and Kegan Smith he devised an adaptable set consisting of a circle of gray stone pillars and arches. Downstage on either side stood a heavy postern gate. This permanent set gave coherence to the production and permitted the action to flow swiftly and continuously. It could be an image both of the material prosperity of Vienna and the severity of its penal system. Even the little details were significant. There was, for instance, a tarboosh on a prisoner's head suggesting that Turkey was not far away. This simple setting allowed the actors and the text to assume their rightful importance. In the stage business Brook made a distinction between the religious and the comic parts. Brook recognized that the play was religious in thought and suggested a morality play in its symmetrical pattern and balance. Although the director was free to improvise stage action for the comedy, which is in prose, he did not have the same freedom in the poetic part of the play, which deals with the weightier themes. Thus, Brook's Pompey distributed advertisements for Mistress Overdone's establishment, a piece of business for which there is no authority in the text. But in the non-comic scenes Brook was very restrained. Brook has said that the meanings of the play will emerge only if the comic and the serious—the Rough and the Holy, as he calls them—are both accepted in good faith. (Whether Brook himself did so has been questioned by Professor

Herbert Weil in *Shakespeare Survey 25*, 1972. Weil argues
that in Brook's text the ambivalence of the play was significantly diminished. Later directors have fully played up this
ambivalence.)

Brook's Angelo was played as a repressed, sensual
Puritan by John Gielgud, who had not somehow played that
role at all in his long and distinguished Shakespearean
career. Wearing a close-fitting black cap that made him look
"spiritually clean-shaven, unromantic and very strict," he
brought what one observer called a "thin-lipped hauteur" to
the part. His Angelo was not a hypocrite, but a self-ignorant
man who thought himself incorruptible till he met Isabella
and discovered how unscrupulous he could be under the
impulse of sudden lust. Gielgud made him a near-tragic
figure, for whom one felt some pity when he said in the last
scene, "Immediate sentence then, and sequent death, is all
the grace I beg." Barbara Jefford, who was only nineteen and
was making her debut, played Isabella, proving equal to the
double challenge of the role and her place opposite Gielgud.
Her Isabella was an emotionally restrained and innocent
young novice for whom it was entirely natural to prefer
chastity to the life of her brother. She conveyed Brook's own
conviction (reported in *The Times* March 10, 1950), that
Isabella's preference was consistent with the tradition of the
age, her calling, and her faith. She spoke the "proud man"
speech with an air of discovery rather than in cynical denunciation. Several times she stopped Angelo from leaving the
chamber by kneeling to him and clutching his arm. At one
point Gielgud showed subtly the response of the awakened
Angelo. His voice became ever so slightly less sure and
steady. The audience was aware of the change, but Isabella
was not. Her attractiveness had begun to work on him,
though of course she had not set out to exploit it. The scenes
of Angelo's attempted seduction of Isabella were highly
effective. The actress Gwen Watford has described the first
meeting as follows: "It was a purely mental process, he
made no physical movement at all, but seemed as if a
tremendous force had suddenly gripped every muscle in his
body and numbed his brain. There was a timeless pause as
the shock lessened and he found sufficient strength to move
down to the table and sit. And then the tremendous relief

when he heard his own voice speaking steadily and under control. I must confess I found myself gasping under the impact." At the difficult line, "More than our brother is our chastity," Isabella turned toward the wall, as if "she was herself ashamed that her intellect could find no more adequate expression of her heart's certainty" (Richard David, in *Shakespeare Survey 4* [1951], pp. 136–37). There was an agonized excitement in her voice. Her anger against her brother was not the hysterical outburst of a sexually repressed woman, as in many productions, but "anger with her own failure as a witness to truth, her own inability to communicate it to others" (David, p. 137). The most memorable moment of the performance came when she had to plead for Angelo. After the Duke's definitive-sounding "He dies for Claudio," there was a long pause, for two minutes. (Brook had instructed Miss Jefford to prolong the pause till she felt the audience could take it no longer.) Then she slowly moved across the stage and knelt before the Duke. "Her words came quiet, and as their full import of mercy reached Angelo, a sob broke from him" (David, p. 137). Robert Speaight felt that this Angelo deserved to be pardoned, and Brook himself has said in *The Empty Space* (p. 89) that in the silence of the long pause the abstract notion of mercy became concrete to all those who were present.

But it was the Duke who held the central place in Brook's production. Harry Andrews presented him, says Richard David, as the Friar turned Duke rather than as the Duke turned Friar. He maintained an exact measure of aloofness and conveyed Authority and Benevolence without any supernatural overtones. When his proposal was accepted by Isabella the audience did not feel any sense of incongruity in the characters. Maxine Audley presented Mariana as a woman who might honestly love and admire Angelo. The comic characters (Leon Quartermaine as a sprightly Lucio, George Rose as an amiable vigorous spiv with his own brand of integrity, Rosalind Atkinson as Mistress Overdone) were all played as natural English characters. Alan Badel made a genuinely terrified Claudio. Brook's production has become a classic of the stage and a landmark in the stage history of the play.

In 1951 the Berliner Ensemble of Brecht (who regarded
Measure for Measure as Shakespeare's most progressive
play) staged a version under a title that translates as "Round
Heads and Pointed Heads." Juliet is made an Aryan girl
whom Claudio (renamed Guzman) has seduced. He is condemned to death. His sister Isabella agrees to the Police
Chief's proposal, which is the same as Angelo's. When she
goes to a prostitute for advice on how to conduct herself
during the assignation, the brothel-keeper is shocked that a
lady should take this job upon herself and for a handsome
payment deputes one of her girls. The girl is, however, paid
her usual time-rate while Madam pockets the difference.
Margot Heinemann explains that Brecht's point is that "the
gentry can usually find someone else to suffer the unpleasant
experiences for them" (Jonathan Dollimore and Alan Sinfield: *Political Shakespeare* [1985], p. 220). This, according
to Ms. Heinemann, is hinted at in Shakespeare's play. Mariana is vulnerable because she has lost the dowry, and the
Duke seeks to substitute Barnardine for Claudio. "Beneath
the surface of Shakespeare's reassuringly happy ending
lurks a very nasty underworld of sexual and commercial
exploitation of inferiors which is never cleaned up, only
played down and obscured. In Brecht's rewriting this side of
the contradiction becomes the central impression" (Heinemann). A similar political interpretation was given to a
Polish production in 1956 in which a parallel was drawn
between Vienna under Angelo and Poland on the eve of the
Poznan riots.

In 1954 the play was produced by Cecil Clarke at the
Ontario Stratford festival as an exploration into the com-
plexities and inconsistencies of human nature. But perhaps
the production in 1956 at the English Stratford by Anthony
Quayle is better known. Quayle made the Duke the central
figure of his production, with Anthony Nicholls playing him
as a human figure, forceful, noble and reassuring. (Quayle
cut out lines that could be interpreted against this interpretation.) Emlyn Williams played Angelo again, but his performance this time was considered inferior to his earlier one of
1937 with Guthrie, for now he made Angelo too obviously a
hypocrite, with only occasional glimpses of the tortured
soul, and in the central scenes his restlessness was too self-

conscious. Isabella, played by Margaret Johnston, was a girl utterly dedicated to the religious life. (This made her acceptance of the Duke's proposal rather out of character.) In the scene with her brother (Emrys Jones), she conveyed the impression that her denunciation of him reflected her own moral agony. Alan Badel's Lucio made corruption attractive and venial, and conveyed the view that man's instincts represented the basic truth of human nature. Patrick Wymark's Pompey was a Cockney with a music-hall touch in his gestures and miming. The sets (of Tanya Moisewitsch) showed a permanent vault which suited the play's moods in many of the scenes, but they did not capture the corrupt Vienna of the play.

In 1957 Margaret Webster produced the play at the Old Vic. Miss Webster saw a Heaven-Earth-Hell pattern in the play, with the characters having a threefold identity: as they liked to appear; as they liked to think they were; and as they really were (*Don't Put Your Daughter on the Stage*, New York [1972], pp. 303–305). The play was concerned, in her reading, with the use and abuse of power. She postponed the second Isabella-Angelo encounter in order not to lose sight of Angelo for too long. Barry Kay designed a unit set for her with the Duke entering at the highest level and "Hell" being the dungeons. Angelo first wore a scholar's black gown; then the robes of public office; and at the end he was stripped. (Miss Webster would have liked to strip him completely.) Lucio's wig of golden hair came off when he was arrested, revealing a bald, scabrous skull. Anthony Nicholls again played the Duke as a human figure. Miss Webster believed that the character could be humanized and given a variety of thought and feeling by the actor. John Neville's Angelo was a precisian swept off his feet by temporary lust. Isabella was again played by Barbara Jefford as a warm-blooded young woman devoted to chastity and possessing a strong sense of right. She accepted the Duke's proposal.

In 1962 the allegorical Duke reappeared in John Blatchley's production at the English Stratford. Blatchley felt that the preference for chastity could not be made the main theme in a modern production of the play. Nor sex; Brook had already done that. He chose the problem of evil as his cohesive idea: how to reconcile the existence and prevalence of evil in a world created by an omnipotent, omniscient, and good God. The Duke (Tom Fleming) was the pivot of the performance. He was omnipresent. He knew all about Angelo, and like a schoolmaster who has conceived a dislike for the clever boy of the form, set a trap for him (*The* [London] *Times,* April 11, 1962). But the star performance was Marius Goring's Angelo. Goring presented Angelo as a neurotic, though sincere, Puritan who happened to make a sudden and appalling discovery of his own corruption. He became hysterical; scourged himself; fell prone on the ground; and writhed at Isabella's feet in the second meeting. Isabella, played by Judi Dench, was too robust a figure for some reviewers. She did not make her passion, her sense of vocation, or the agony of her dilemma convincing. (Incidentally, her dress, an uncommonly low-cut gown, remained secular throughout the performance.) The set consisted of a backwall made of large pieces of stone, a slightly raised platform that filled more than half the stage, and a section of cobblestones. This bare setting agreed with the central conception of the production.

It is probably an index of the improved critical and theatrical fortunes of the play that Michael Elliott should have selected it for the last night of the Old Vic on April 3, 1963, before that theater closed down. The program notes were prepared by Professor Nevill Coghill of Oxford, who had earlier written on the underlying medieval comic form of the play (*Shakespeare Survey 8,* 1955) and had himself produced it in 1956 for the Bristol University Union. James Maxwell made a severe but just Duke, dignified, saintly, and aloof. He was a mysterious, semidivine personage, and there was a strong suggestion that the final scene was a kind of Day of Judgment. Dilys Hamlet played Isabella as a fiery-tempered and passionate girl suddenly confronted with a reality different from what she had expected. She screamed at her brother for exposing her to one more glimpse of ugly reality. Lee Montagu played a nonascetic, virile-looking Angelo, unbuttoned to his chest hair in his second meeting with Isabella.

There were interesting productions in 1965 by John

Neville (who had earlier played Angelo) at the Nottingham Playhouse and in 1969 by David Giles in Stratford in Canada, but the landmark of 1970 was John Barton's controversial production at Stratford in England. Barton made some cuts in the text and shifted some scenes and speeches. He recognized that the background of the play was religious, but he opted for a human Duke. Barton thinks that allegorical, symbolical, or metaphysical interpretations are not easy to realize in stage terms; besides, the acting tradition in England has always favored the exploration of character ("Directing the Problem Plays: John Barton Talks to Gareth Lloyd Evans," in *Shakespeare Survey 25* [1972], pp. 63–71). Although very well-informed about the criticism of the play, Barton did not wish to illustrate any particular critical view of the play in his production. For instance, many critics (e.g., Tillyard) think that the play breaks up or changes its characters in the middle. Barton disagrees. If the actors bring the characters to life in the first part of the play, the so-called division of the play is hardly apparent in the theater. There is a change of emphasis with the entry of Mariana, but that is a different matter. The play is open-ended, and an honest production must also be open-ended. The controversy was whether Barton's own production was open-ended.

Barton's Duke, played by Sebastian Shaw, was a philosopher statesman—his dusty table was piled with books—but he was an ineffectual ruler. Shaw captured all aspects of the Duke except his authority. Juliet was indignant when he questioned her, and Claudio went on with his prison meal without paying any attention to the Duke-Friar's consolation. (On the first night there was an unnecessarily vulgar piece of stage business when Barnardine threw the crucifix given to him into a chamber pot and noisily urinated into it. The audience was not amused, and the business was dropped after a few performances.) His proposal of marriage evoked a shocked silence from Isabella. "After a long pause of silence, he uttered a resigned 'So,' put on his glasses, and departed with all the others leaving a bewildered Isabella alone on the stage looking out on the audience" (Jane Williamson, "The Duke and Isabella on the Modern Stage," in *The Triple Bond*, ed. Joseph G. Price, University Park, Pa. [1975], pp. 149–69). From the heights of royalty and divinity (says Ms. Williamson), the character had slid down in Barton's production into a pathetic, ineffective bumbler, lost and confused in the real world of men and affairs.

Barton's Angelo was played by Ian Richardson, handsome and physically well cast for the part. He portrayed Angelo as rather nervous to begin with, but once installed in office, he became proud, arrogant, and cold. His impatience and superciliousness were shown when he pulled a chair with his foot for Isabella. He looked at the Duke's dusty table with obvious distaste, and when *he* came to sit at it, it was spotlessly clean. He was constantly wiping his hands. He was a hypocrite, aware of all things sexual. When Isabella entered his presence, he was busy with papers. Then he lifted up his head and saw her, and there was a small pause. It conveyed much. In the second meeting he left the table and went toward her while she moved into action, reversing roles, as it were. When he proposed his condition, he grabbed her by the hair, pulled her over the table, and caressed her body. (This piece of violence, suggested by the actress herself, helped her to utter the difficult line, "More than our brother is our chastity.") Barton also improvised a scene in which the Provost silently showed Angelo the head of Claudio in a bag. Angelo broke down and wept, unable to confront the consequences of his own cruelty.

In Barton's view the play was Isabella's. His Isabella was played by Estelle Kohler, a very youthful actress. There was an air of uncertainty about her performance, and it was hard to make out whether it belonged to the actress or to her interpretation of the character. The program note (written by Professor Anne Barton of Cambridge) spoke of Isabella's purity as concealing an hysterical fear of sex. When she spoke the line about chastity, she flung her arm out, like a general waving his troops on into action, said Harold Hobson. And in "the proud man" speech, she stressed the word "man," intimating that women were different. When her brother accepted the sentence, she sat by his side, but when he showed signs of weakening, she leaped away to denounce him. When the Duke proposed to her, she stared at him. Was it incredulity, dislike, or disgust? She remained on the stage after all the others had left, pondering the strange ways of men, perhaps recalling what she had told Angelo—that men always try to take advantage of a woman's weakness at the slightest chance. She seemed to have realized the power of sex, that everything goes down before it—authority, justice, piety, even decency. The whole business of concealing the fact that her brother was alive had only one aim: to rush her into marriage in a freshet of gratitude. Barton made the ending ambiguous in this way. Sara Kestelman played Mariana and was the dominant presence in the last act. (The program note said that she was the only character in the play who existed in "an uncriticized absolute.") She was portrayed as "a pale, auburn-haired pre-Raphaelite beauty whose dejection [had] produced in her no hesitancy" (Peter Thomson in *Shakespeare Survey 24* [1971], p. 124). The lower characters were, in general, not well realized, though Terence Hardman made a ratlike Lucio. Timothy O'Brien's sets of wall blocks of paneled wood, with semiparquet flooring and wooden ceiling, conveyed claustrophobic puritanical cleanliness, but not the corruption of Vienna.

Peter Thomson in *Shakespeare Survey 24* summed up the difference between Brook and Barton in the following way: Barton looked for ways of revealing the text while Brook preferred to make his crucial discoveries in rehearsal, believing that theatrical revelation must not be anticipated but "risked." On this interpretation Brook's approach was more open-ended than Barton's.

The next production, Dr. Jonathan Miller's in February 1974 for the National Theatre, was equally interesting. Miller set the play in the pleasure-loving Vienna of Freud, who was the invisible, brooding presence of the production. The society of the play was characterized by bureaucratic rule and petty bourgeois professionalism. The performance was intended to throw light on the history that followed the 'thirties. Miller has argued in *Subsequent Performances* that a great play has an "after-life"; each performance is incomplete in itself but contributes to the development of the play. "If works of art are discovered after a long period of being lost or neglected, it is as if they are perceived and valued for reasons so different from those held originally that they virtually change their character and identity. There comes a point in the life of any cultural artefact, whether a play or a painting, when the continued existence of the physical token that represents it does not necessarily mean that the original identity of the work survives." It is this aesthetic that has guided many recent productions of the play.

The stage for Miller's production was designed by Bernard Culshaw, who set a long corridor with a row of doors nailed together without any stretches of wall to separate them. Miller has explained (in *Subsequent Performances*) that at the moment when any one door in the facade represented a door, none of the others did so. Though these doors were representational, referring to exits and entrances mentioned in the text, the overall style was dictated by the now-familiar idiom of an empty (rather than highly localized) space within which an action can occur without having to be slavishly pictorial. The only furniture was a table. Carl Davis's imitation classical music helped to realize the Viennese setting.

Angelo, played by Julian Curry, was angular, pear-faced, bespectacled, and went about always with a briefcase. He constantly referred to the law book on the table even while he was fondling Isabella's "holy-knee." Gillian Barge's Isabella was a highly professional Sister who had sacrificed her emotions for the sake of her calling. She shared Angelo's disgust at what her brother (played by David Bradley) had done. Angelo rather than the Duke was her man, and she cast a series of "furtive, longing" glances at him. Alan Macnaughten as the Duke projected the ambiguities of the character, principally his "meddlesome cruelty" (Miller's own phrase) and pleasure in other men's miseries. His disregard of Barnardine was brutal, and he stage-managed the denouement in a bluff and callous way. He did not reenter the city with the traditional fanfare, but slipped in after giving an oily handshake to the persons gathered around him (Peter Ansorge in *Plays and Players*, March 1974, p. 45). He looked like a thirties politician whose dirty deeds were to plunge the world soon into a world war. When he proposed to Isabella, she drew back in horror.

This interpretation was taken further in the production that followed: Keith Hack's at Stratford in England, also in 1974. Hack followed Edward Bond's reading of the play, printing it in the program note: the play is an arraignment of all authority; Angelo is a lying self-deceiving fraud; the

Duke is a vain, face-saving hypocrite; and the saintly Isabella is a vicious sex-hysteric. As Michael Billington pointed out in his *Guardian* review (September 5, 1974), the production became dull because such a reading does not permit any psychological growth. Michael Pennington presented a virile Angelo who, at the second meeting with Isabella, dropped to his knees, supplicating her and trembling with lust. This was the only scene which proved acceptable in the production. Otherwise it was regarded as a dismal failure. A charitable judgment was that it had the negative virtue of demonstrating that *Measure for Measure* cannot be treated as Jonsonian satire, only more nihilistic.

Hack's attempt at updating the play was put in the shade by the adaptation of Charles Marowitz produced at the Open Space in London in 1975. Marowitz omitted characters, rearranged scenes, and rewrote the plot. For instance, in Marowitz's version Isabella goes to bed (not altogether unwillingly) with Angelo.

In a modern-dress production in 1975 at the Ontario Stratford festival Robin Phillips saw the core of the play as consisting of sex, misuse of power, and the exploitation of women. It was the least Elizabethan of Shakespeare's plays, requiring a place where both low-life gaiety and freedom and sophisticated upper-class life obtained and outward piety went hand in hand with unspoken sexuality. Venereal disease was a widespread problem, indicating massive sexual repression. The Vienna of 1912 was the obvious choice. (Besides, one could also think of a Duke as Head of State in 1912.) In Phillips's production the Duke (William Hutt), more a monster than a sage, was totally insensitive to others and thought only of himself. Isabella (Martha Henry) was dressed in the white costume of her order, but the soft jersey of her dress revealed clearly the female form underneath. The costume gave the clue to her character: sexuality overlaid with its transparent negation. She was aware of the contradiction, and the awareness gave a touch of sorrow and self-contempt to her tone and behavior. After Angelo had stated his condition and left, she dipped her hand in a water jug and splashed the cold water on her forehead. At the end, after the Duke had left with the other characters, she remained on the stage, turned around, removed her headdress and her steel-rimmed glasses, and placed the back of her hand on her forehead. Her face showed her revulsion and anguish at the prospect of marriage to the Duke. Some reviewers received the impression that she accepted the Duke's proposal in a spirit of fatalistic resignation, but the director himself told Professor Ralph Berry that she neither accepted nor rejected the proposal (*On Directing Shakespeare* [1977], p. 103). Angelo (Brian Bedford) welcomed the office bestowed on him with a self-satisfied smirk on his face as a belated recognition of his merit. When self-discovery overtook him, he was horrified at himself. Richard Monette made a brash, cynical Lucio, and Lewis Gordon made a hearty Pompey.

The play was produced in 1978 at the English Stratford by Barry Kyle. Kyle saw *Measure for Measure* not as a parable of justice but as an essay on appearance and reality. The key image was that of dissembling. The stage showed a black box with numerous exits and entrances suggesting corridors and a warren of offices. The box flattened out at the back to display cubicles where the whores carried on their brisk business. The cubicles also served as prison cells. The walls swung inward to enclose Angelo and Isabella during their second interview. The sword of justice rested conspicuously on Angelo's knee while he was examining Pompey, and after he left, Escalus leaned it against the table. Angelo wore a long white robe decorated with red motifs that looked like tiny leaping flames. These motifs were also seen on the uniforms worn by the prison staff and the prisoners. Both Escalus and the Justice removed their robes of office after Pompey had left as if they were glad to be rid of them. Isabella arrived at the convent with a suitcase. She wore her nun's habit when going to meet Angelo.

The central figure in Kyle's production also was the Duke, played by Michael Pennington. He saw him neither as *deus ex machina* nor as a Christ figure. He was not much older than Isabella, for a marriage proposal from him would otherwise be incongruous. Pennington believed that the Duke not only guided Isabella but traveled in the play toward self-discovery, achieving humility. Pennington praised the Duke's relationship with Isabella as a real one, different from what is found in Romantic comedy. In the finale he was

testing Isabella. Wearing his Friar's robes with arms outstretched, and looking at Isabella all the while, he delivered
his "measure for measure" speech in a voice of authority. He
ended the play on a note of harmony and self-knowledge.
Angelo was played by Jonathan Pryce as a symbol of "emergent lust" (J. C. Trewin, *Shakespeare Quarterly*, Spring
1979, p. 154). He was an efficient career man, who knew
nothing of his own sexuality. Nervous and fidgety, he was
always plaiting his fingers. When he had to state the vile
condition for saving Claudio, he turned toward the wall as if
he was afraid of facing Isabella. The scenes of Isabella
(Paola Dionisetti) with Angelo lacked the necessary element
of erotic tension, but she successfully suggested that she had
also undergone a gradual process of self-awakening. She felt
drawn to the Duke and accepted his proposal with alacrity.
Majorie Bland played Mariana with very few sentimental
overtones. Richard Griffiths made an excellent Pompey who
lectured the officers on civic morality, and John Nettles was
"an unctuously unsnubbable" Lucio (Irving Wardle, *The
Times*, June 28, 1978). Kyle repeated the production in 1979
at the Aldwych. David Suchet played Angelo as a precise
man of affairs suddenly overcome by temptation. Pennington was the Duke in full control of his part, giving the
impression in the final scene that he was enjoying it as the
sequel to his masquerade. Miss Sinead Cusack made a rather
light Isabella.

In 1981 Michael Rudman produced the play for the
National Theatre. The cast was all West Indian because, said
Rudman, there were plenty of very good West Indies actors
available. According to Rudman, all the leading characters
behave very oddly, and he wanted to devise a political context that would explain such behavior. He chose a mythical
Caribbean island that has just attained independence and
that has not yet learned how to govern itself. A leader can be
changed overnight, for instance. High-minded laws have
been passed that cannot be put into practice. There is no distinction between private and public behavior because everybody knows everybody. Warm friendliness jostles with
physical cruelty. The action of the play began during an official reception at what had obviously been the governor's

place before independence. The new regime had two connections with the old, a worldly Escalus (Leslie Sands) and
the Provost in khaki (Anthony Brown). Eileen Diss had
erected colonnades to represent the marketplace where the
local population sang, danced and drank (hardly a picture of
corruption, was the wry comment of Roger Warren in
Shakespeare Survey 35, 1982). Stefan Kalipha as the Duke
tended to bury the emotion while Yvette Harris as Isabella
merely stated it. Norman Beaton made an uncompromising
Angelo (a bishop in this production) brooding over his temptation without any inner turmoil—like a bureaucrat. Oscar
James played Pompey as a Lord of Misrule. Peter Straker's
Lucio sang an interpolated song describing how Angelo's
repressive measures had led to increased pimping. The verse
was treated with excessive reverence. In general, opinion on
the production was divided.

The next production in Stratford, England, took place in
1983. Adrian Noble saw the play as a comedy in its structure
with a situation that could have come from a Buñuel film or
from the Surrealists. The challenge of the play was that it
had characters like Isabella as well as Mistress Overdone,
and then there was the whole discussion about the development of government and autocracy. These features of the
play indicated that it should be set in a recognizable period
and have a clear social definition. Noble set the play in a
Vienna of gilt mirrors, white wigs, and brocade coats, but
underneath this seventeenth-century elegance seethed a
world of moral anarchy. With the aid of Bob Crowley he set
the stage to bring out the contrast between the secluded, opu-
lent court and the teeming city. Two bisecting white carpets
formed a crucifix pattern on the floor with a tottering, ba-
roque campanile encrusted with candles, crosses, and legal
scales suggesting a world gone awry. The carpeted strip was
used for scenes in which a choice had to be made: Angelo's
acknowledgement of his desires, or Isabella's response to
his condition. It was also used for passages where characters
from different strands of the play passed each other, almost
touching each other but in reality oblivious of each other's
existence. The music of Ilona Sekacz, sensuously blending
with the setting, sounded like the deformed echo of some
classical piece. The play opened to a woman's singing of

sacred music which had a vague suggestion that she was simultaneously enjoying sexual pleasure. Daniel Massey played the Duke as a ruler who is aware of his authority but who still has to learn that self-knowledge is essential to a ruler. Angelo was presented by David Schofield as a repressed personality whose moral equilibrium is upset by sudden unsuspected passion. His knees buckled and his fingers began to flex and unflex involuntarily. Juliet Stevenson, whose emotional directness and vocal range were praised by many reviewers, portrayed Isabella as a moral absolutist who learns that compassion is superior to cloistered virtue. Her final acceptance of the Duke seemed right and proper. Noble repeated the production at the Barbican in 1984.

David Thacker produced the play twice (in modern dress on both occasions) at the Young Vic in 1985 and in 1987. He projected the court of the Duke as a banker's boardroom where nothing counted but economics, and men with serious flaws of character encouraged dogma and repression in the name of sound and sensible administration. In 1985 Peter Guinness played a "grouchy and saturnine" Duke while in 1987 he was played by Matthew Marsh. John Gillett's 1985 Angelo was a figure of frigid virtue and serious demeanor, while in 1987 Corin Redgrave played the part with impressive control and precision, his torment when he realized his corruption being eloquent. Joanna Foster's Isabella in 1985 displayed a sincere belief in the value of chastity. (She accepted the Duke's proposal.) Saskia Reeves's 1987 Isabella showed a "rising passion of spiritual self-righteousness, flat-footed grace and awkward innocence of the world" (John Vidal in the *Guardian*, *London Theatre Record*, VII, 10, 609). Rod Edwards played Lucio on both occasions, though in 1987 there was less fun. Margaret Leicester was Mariana on both occasions. She sang her own song, and in general appeared as a forsaken middle-aged woman. The sober Escalus was given an affair with his secretary.

The play was also seen in 1985 at the Canadian Stratford festival directed by Michael Bogdanov with designs by Chris Dyer. The general aim of this production was to convey the disturbing qualities of the play to our more open society whose extremely relaxed attitude in sexual matters makes the audience somewhat shockproof. The director therefore introduced many innovations, such as a cabaret scene. "Vienna was corrupt, and the Duke was at the center of the corruption. In the final scene Isabella let the Duke take her hand, but broke away, to be left out on the stage for a blackout, punctuated by flashing cameras. When the lights came up she was standing in front of the prison, looking stunned. This ending marked her entry into a corrupted spiritual condition in which she, like everyone else, is imprisoned in a decadent society." (For details, see Mary Ellen Lamb, *Shakespeare Studies* XX, 1988, p. 144.) In the same year Robert Egan produced *Measure for Measure* at the Mark Taper Forum in Los Angeles. He found that the play illustrated Freud's concepts of acquisitive, violent, and sexually aggressive instincts as well as Jung's archetypes. Its wholesome moral was that the "instinctual drives must be confronted, brought to consciousness and controlled" to achieve harmony and survival. Egan made the play into a psychodrama of the Duke (Ken Ruta) with Lucio (Kelsey Grammer) being a part of his own personality. The production suggested that all the women who were married at the end were victims of exploitation by men who were using marriage as a respectable form of whoredom. Isabella was left alone on the stage. She took off her wimple and outer garment, but retained her rosary. She moved to the palace gates to be embraced by Eros, a character added to the cast.

The next production at Stratford took place in 1987 when Nicholas Hytner made his debut as producer with a competent (but not particularly remarkable) production. Roger Allam presented the Duke as a human character who has to find instant solutions to unexpected developments. He conveyed the impression that as Friar he was discovering the city he had long governed, or rather, failed to govern. Sean Baker played Angelo as a close-cropped, white-faced precisian, cast in marble. Isabella was played by a black actress, Josette Simon, who made the preference for chastity credible. When the Duke proposed to her, she stared at him—without actually rejecting him.

Trevor Nunn produced the play for the RSC at The Other Place in Stratford-upon-Avon in 1991. He set the play in Freud's Vienna, and made sexuality its central concern. Nunn focused on Angelo (David Haig), who became uncon-

trollably aware of his sexuality as soon as he set eyes on
Isabella. Peter Holland, who reviewed the performance in
Shakespeare Survey 45 (pp. 137–39), reports that Haig pur-
sued every twist and turn of Angelo's psychology with an
intelligence and power that was quite extraordinary. Angelo
maintained this posture till the last moments of the final
scene when he was embraced by Mariana. Robert Smallwood, in *Shakespeare Quarterly 43*, felt that this was
perhaps the only false note "in a splendidly coherent performance, a slight sentimentalization of an otherwise powerful presentation of the stultifying effects of inhibition and
of the destructive results of its relaxation" (p. 355). Isabella
(Claire Skinner) appeared very vulnerable. "Her repugnance
to sexuality strongly suggested some abhorrent past experience" (Smallwood, p. 354). She could display a frightening
temper as when she pounded her brother's chest when he
proposed that she should yield to Angelo. There was quiet,
benevolent authority in Allan Mitchell's Escalus. The Duke
was played by Philip Madoc—very much a Freudian figure.
In all his experiments, he played the role of the detached
observer-physician. When he made his proposal of marriage, there was a long pause. Patiently the Duke waited and
(as he had clearly diagnosed) up came her hand, slowly
joining his; in spite of the long delay, however, she had obviously not been able to think of anything to say. They made a
most curious couple. . . . (Smallwood, p. 356). Nunn added
several realistic details to the action such as a slopping-out
parade of bucket-carrying prisoners in the first jail scene.
There was also a large clock on the stage that marked the
exact timing of each scene, occasionally whizzing around
between scenes to mark the passage of time. Peter Holland
(in *Shakespeare Survey*) found the production a challenge
to traditions of English Shakespearean production (though
he also expressed the hope that the style would not become
"a new orthodoxy," p. 139). In Smallwood's opinion, this
was a "profoundly engaging and constantly interesting *Measure for Measure*, full of sharp and challenging insights,
deliberately eschewing the elements of myth and religious
allegory . . . in favor of a closely focused, psychological
investigation . . ." (p. 356).

There were two major productions of the play in England

in 1994—by Declan Donellan for Cheek by Jowl and by
Stephen Pimlott for the Royal Shakespeare Company (RSC).
(Peter Holland reviewed both the productions in *Shakespeare Survey 48* [1995], pp. 217–22, and Russell Jackson
reviewed the RSC production for *Shakespeare Quarterly*
[1995], pp. 355–57.) Both the productions emphasized the
modernity of the play, though in different ways. While
Donellan made the play immediate and contemporary, Pimlott gestured at the development of British society from the
nineteenth century to the present. For Donellan, the play
exhibited the moral relativism of the modern state. For Pimlott, the play recapitulated the male ethos of the modern
Establishment.

Objects on the stage took on different meanings as the
occasion demanded. Angelo's office desk became an altar
when Isabella knelt before it and prayed. Thus, when Angelo
came close to raping her, the place of assault signified both
an assault in his office and a sacrilegious act. Donellan made
his actors part of the set; the first line of a scene would be
pitched loudly "across the final image of a previous one
before the tableau broke, the furniture was rearranged and
the next scene properly began" (Holland, 217). First lines
became prominent, and the technique became part of "the
simultaneity Donellan was exploring" (Ibid). Several characters were left onstage for scenes that they had no part in as
"silent reminders of the play's problems" (Ibid). Donellan
introduced many realistic touches such as Escalus offering
a cigarette to Pompey, which he tucked behind his ear for
later. Among the characters, three stood out: the Duke
(Stephen Boxer), Isabella (Anastasia Hille) and Angelo
(Adam Kotz). Isabella clung to her virtue rather desperately
in a context of universal corruption. But she could be passionate and physical also as when she placed her head on
Angelo's breast to say, "Go to your bosom" (2.2.136). She
was rejected at the end by her brother, who turned his back
to her as he embraced Juliet. Isabella herself was dragged
back to the stage at the end and forced to hold the Duke's
hand as the couples stumbled from the stage. Peter Holland
found Hille's performance "too lush in its emotions"
(*Shakespeare Survey*, p. 222), but Russell Jackson (in *Shakespeare Quarterly*) thought that she gave the part warmth and

sensuality without suggesting that the character was given to
masochistic fantasy or that her declaration, "More than our
brother is our chastity" was anything less than axiomatic.
She was a mature and thoughtful woman rather than an innocent with fundamentalist views. In the final scene she was in
masculine dress, as if she had decided that these men had to
be taken on their own terms. Only with Mariana (Tanya
Moodie) did she find companionship. (Donellan's Mariana
drank vodka in large gulps; Pimlott's Mariana took to
Expressionist painting, throwing handfuls of paint at the
canvas when she remembered Angelo.) Donellan's Angelo
and the Duke were of course opposites, but they were one in
their attitude to Isabella and the exercise of power without
responsibility. There was not much difference either between Angelo's assault on Isabella and the Duke's fixing of
things. When the Duke proposed the bed trick, Isabella was
shocked and walked around the auditorium. She was at the
end acquiescent rather than enthusiastic. In the fifth act both
the women were made to speak into a microphone fixed
center stage by the Duke, who was directing them. Donellan
also assembled some citizens of Stratford as citizens of
Vienna, all clad in wigs, gowns, and mortarboards. They
were obviously in sympathy with Angelo and laughed rau-
cously and smuttily when Isabella confessed her apparent
sexual act with Angelo to save her brother.

Pimlott's fifth act was particularly striking. When the
Duke proposed, Isabella slapped his face, kissed him, and
unexpectedly rejected him sharply and stood apart in tears,
twitching. As the stage darkened, a very nervous Duke stood
beside her helpless crying, looking rather shifty. In Jackson's opinion, "there can have been few productions in
which the deviousness of the Duke has been so tautly plotted
or the consequences so dissatisfying to its beneficiaries or
victims" (*Shakespeare Quarterly 46*, pp. 355–57). The Duke
was played by Michael Feast as an ascetic, cultured, and
ironic figure who had clearly no control over his state. Feast
made him a fantastical duke of dark corners (but there was
no support for Lucio's sexual innuendos) and "a voyeur of
suffering." Jackson writes that Feast's Duke had an unholy
enthusiasm for exploring the emotions of others. His interview with the heavily pregnant Juliet made her cry, and the

consolation that he gave to Claudio brought Claudio to despair. He was equally unsuccessful with Barnardine. Except in the last moments of the last scene of the fifth act Lucio had the better of him always. If Isabella did marry him, one feared for her. Alex Jennings played Angelo as an authoritarian, ramrod-stiff bureaucrat. He was anguished by the discovery of passion in himself. There was no suggestion that he had any kind of enlightenment at the end of the play. He could counter every passage from the Bible that Isabella tossed at him—she carried a Bible with her—with a contrasting passage. At "Plainly conceive, I love you" (2.4.141), he fell to his knees. He seemed limitless in his dangerousness, and gave a hint that he might be planning to have the Duke declared insane and take over the State. Peter Holland (in *Shakespeare Survey*) thought that Pimlott succeeded in establishing the moral politics of the play in the English society that he reconstructed, and Jackson found the production "memorable and exciting." The best part of the production was Act 5.

The play has been seen on the North American stage also—at the Shakespeare Theater in Washington, D.C., in 1991, and at Ontario's Stratford festival in 1992. The Washington production by Michael Kahn was described by the *Shakespeare Quarterly* reviewer, Miranda Johnson-Haddad, as "a provocative and intriguing production" that confronted the play's most disturbing implications while providing a hopeful ending that offered passion and romance (*43*, 1992, pp. 462–68). Philip Goodwin as Angelo expressed the character's rigidity and repression as well as the strength of the emotions that were being repressed. He accepted the death sentence without flinching, but when he was forgiven he knelt before the Duke, and seized and fervently kissed the Duke's hand. He exited slowly with Mariana, and when she reached tentatively for his hand, he put his arm around her. "There was hope, after all, for his redemption" (p. 465). Keith Baxter played the Duke as "not only thoughtful and complex but also as full of warmth and humor." He found it difficult to enforce the laws, but he cared deeply about his people, and was obviously relieved to hear Escalus's testimony refuting Lucio's slanders. Baxter convinced the audience that the Duke loved Isabella with a love which developed credibly throughout the course of the play, so that his proposal to her in the final scene came as no surprise. There was also a strong suggestion throughout the play that he was guiding the younger Isabella toward a less judgmental, more forgiving attitude. However, he was never paternalistic or patronizing; he encouraged her to realize her potential capacity for empathy and kindness. Kelly McGillis as Isabella was a radiant figure who was suffused with spiritual happiness. She was very sexy, but totally unaware of the effect she produced when she dealt with Angelo. She was strong and forceful, although she was innocent of the world's ways. In the final scene as Mariana pleaded with her, she stood with her back to the stage crowd and the audience "for a long, long moment of silence—longer than I have ever seen in a production of this play—before she turned and began to implore the Duke to pardon Angelo" (p. 467). The supporting characters—Kate Skinner as Mariana, Daniel Southern as Lucio, Jonathan Lutz as the Provost, David Manis and his understudy, Eric Hoffmann, as Pompey—were very strong in their roles. At the end the Duke and Isabella joined hands and exchanged a passionate and tender kiss. The production was a triumph because it brought out both the humor and the darkness of the play; and it suggested that there are many ways in which men and women can speak with and listen to each other, or refuse to do so. "The final vision offered by this production suggested that men and women are indeed capable of mutual redemption, but only through honest communication and shared devotion. The threat that loomed over this Vienna was that such communication would never occur . . ." (p. 468).

The play was also seen at Ontario's Stratford festival in 1992. (The production was reviewed by C. E. McGee in *Shakespeare Quarterly 44*, pp. 477–79.) Michael Langham opened the play with a scene that showed the ravages of sexually transmitted disease in Vienna and established the point that both Isabella's chastity and the Duke's resignation of his authority to one of Angelo's severity were not unreasonable options. The music and the stylization of the production deepened the dark atmosphere. Stanley Silverman's music, which drew on the work of Arnold Schönberg, went in for what is known as atonality and created tension and darkened the atmosphere of the play. "The throbbing music provided the through-line to the production's most shocking bit of violence: Angelo's tearing from Isabella's head her novice's veil" (p. 478). Elizabeth Marvel made a disingenuous Isabella who was particularly vulnerable. Colm Feore's Angelo was a bureaucrat for whom justice had more to do with paperwork than people; he was lost in his papers. Isabella had to tug at his sleeve to attract his attention. When the Duke made his proposal of the bed trick, she thanked him with a hug. Brian Bedford gave a look to the audience which suggested that her expression of hope and gratitude was being taken by the Duke as something more than that—a sign of more intimate contact to come. "In the world of this *Measure for Measure*, men sexualized all forms of physical contact so as to obliterate significant refinements in the expression of emotion" (p. 479). The production ended on a happy note. The Duke's schemes succeeded; Isabella and Claudio were reunited; Lucio was put down; Juliet was married. Only Angelo refused to smile—not even when the cast took its bows. The Duke's proposal of marriage remained unanswered: "the lights went out before she took the hand that he held out—if she took it at all" (Ibid).

The play has been seen on the European stage also (at Peter Brook's theater in Paris, for instance) in translations that have been often described as excellent. There was also a Chinese production at the Beijing People's Art Theatre in 1981, described by Carolyn Wakeman in *Shakespeare Quarterly*, Winter 1982. (This may be supplemented by the following information provided by Consulting British Director of the production, Mr. Toby Robertson and by Mr. Charles Aylmer of Cambridge University, who kindly translated from the Chinese an article by the director, Ying Ruo Cheng.) The director himself translated and adapted the play for the stage. Some 500 lines containing references to God, prostitution, and beliefs that were inadmissible in 1981 were omitted. A new title was given: *Please Step into the Pot*, which recalled a well-known Chinese folktale about a corrupt official who was asked to enter a red-hot pot, which he had himself indicated was the proper punishment for corrupt officials. The Chinese director saw the play as a realistic portrait of a society in transition, though the characterization is not based on actuality. In the production the principal features of the Shakespearean stage were adopted: no drop curtain, close contact between actors and audience, swift and continuous action and a quick tempo of speech. The Chinese players had to change their style of acting to adopt these innovations. They did so with great success. The stage setting (of Alan Barrett) showed an old broken-down gray wall symbolizing decadent Vienna, while a large lace doily at the rear suggested the refinement of the court. There were different hangings for the different locales of action. At the rear, painted in red on a panel of white cloth, a leering, frowning face looked down on the audience. One eye looked up at the sky and another downward. A wavy line at the neck suggested the Puritan's ruffled collar. This face was the emblem of the play's contradictions and duality, and it warned the Chinese audience not to expect straight lessons. Sound and lighting also contributed to the tragic-comic conception of the production. At the beginning and at intervals "a ghoulish, maniacal, demonic" laugh (Wakeman) echoed across the stage. It faded into the mirth of the disguised Duke as he explained to the Friar why he had disguised himself. The shadow of a cross sometimes loomed large on the stage, suggesting judgment. Throughout there were menacing shadows on the stage that disappeared only at the end, replaced by "a warm red-tinged glow that bathed the characters in a mellow golden light and assured the audience that the threat to happiness and to harmony had finally been extinguished" (Wakeman, p. 501).

The Duke (Yu Shizhi) was lavishly costumed in ocher velvet when he was the Duke and in plain black sack cloth when he played the Friar. (Originally the company had hoped to use modern dress, but this was almost the first production of Shakespeare in Chinese after 1940, and it was felt that there were many other innovative features for the cast and the audience to get used to.) The Duke was cunning and insinuating, genial and benevolent, as occasion demanded. Angelo (Ren Baoxian) wore a black doublet, white ruff, and silver-cross pendant. He was stern and arrogant, and his tone was uniformly unyielding. Li Rong played Isabella in a simple gray surplice and appeared pure and innocent. When the Duke proposed to her, she stood silent on the platform

stage with her back to the spectators. Then she turned and
walked with graceful steps toward them, her face serene and
unreadable. Finally she went up to the Duke and accepted
his proffered hand. The tension-filled silence erupted into
joyful music and the couples ran hand in hand from the
stage. Justice, mercy, and love had triumphed, if only barely.
Wakeman felt that the Chinese audience was fully aware of
the serious issues of the play, and could sympathize with the
predicament of Isabella when Angelo defied her to denounce
him, or with Claudio's humiliation as he was paraded in
the streets. These were experiences not unknown during
the Cultural Revolution. The director had instructed his cast
to play naturally, as if the characters were Chinese. Mr.
Robertson has praised (private communication) Ying Ruo
Cheng's outstanding contribution and the team spirit of the
company.

The play has also been seen on TV. The BBC and *Time-
Life* collaborated to produce the play on TV in 1979 as part
of a complete Shakespeare on TV. The producer, Cedric
Messina, has stated that the aim of the series was to make the
plays available as entertainment for a potential audience of
the very young who have probably no experience of the theater or of Shakespeare. The director was Desmond Davis. In
the text of the production some lines rendered superfluous
by the TV medium have been omitted; minor characters
have been dropped or merged, and stage directions have
been realigned. Most of the action takes place at sunset,
night, or dawn, only the last scene being in sunshine. Many
scenes are visually effective. For example, Angelo sits at a
large desk in front of a throne with armorial bearings. While
he appears large, Isabella in a corner looks tiny. The desk in
the vast judgment hall constricts the movements of those
who come to see him. He himself sits at the other end of the
hall with its whole length behind him. Tim Piggott-Smith
has played him as an efficient, arrogant, and overbearing
bureaucrat. The antagonism between him and Isabella is the
center of this production. Isabella is played by Kate Nel-
ligan, who has declared that the school of thought that considers Isabella a sexual neurotic and the play a study in
repressive sexuality is "absolute nonsense." She has presented Isabella as a girl for whom Heaven, Hell and eternal

life are realities superior as existential values to anything that this life has to offer. The Duke (Kenneth Colley) is a recognizable human being with just a touch of divinity about him and a certain prankishness in his ways. The last scene is staged as a show on an Elizabethan platform stage with the courtiers and the people watching. The translation of a Shakespeare play into the very different medium of television presents some problems, but in this production they are imaginatively surmounted.

After this brief (and regrettably selective) survey of the stage interpretations of *Measure for Measure*, certain general reflections may be offered. *Measure for Measure* continues to be a controversial play, and there is no prospect of its losing that status! But it is no longer an unpopular or infrequently seen play. It has attracted full and appreciative audiences and some very distinguished and imaginatively gifted directors and players. It has provoked as many interpretations on the stage as in the study, perhaps more so. A stage interpretation can be more varied, more subtle and nuanced, certainly more immediate in its impact, with a longer life in one's imaginative memory than a critical book. Jonathan Miller has declared that a text has no definitive or exhaustible meaning:

> I don't believe that any human utterances beyond engineering instructions have got that sort of quality. I think that every play which describes people talking to one another is very vague, very permissive, very noncommittal except in moments of very, very stringent commitment. . . . The greater the play, the more alternative and mutually contradictory versions are possible . . . all of which are at least minimally compatible with the text from which they spring. (*Shakespeare Quarterly*, Winter 1976, p. 12)

(He has reiterated this point of view in his interview with Ralph Berry, *On Directing Shakespeare* [1977], and presented it at length in his own book *Subsequent Performances* [1986].) The limits of interpretation cannot be set in advance with theoretical precision. Tact and good sense are essential, but it must be remembered that these are virtues that hug the coastline, whereas the wild sea that Shakespeare represents requires a daring Columbus, an actor or director for whom Shakespeare is the natural element. Another fact that has emerged is that the director has become independent of the critic and the scholar. He consults them, but is no longer content to follow meekly in their footsteps. Some trends may of course be discerned—the recent human Duke, for instance—but the only safe generalization that one can make is that somehow *Measure for Measure* is felt to be a modern play—though there is little agreement on what constitutes modernity. Perhaps the chief value of the play and the use of its critical and theatrical history is that together they promote what Keats called "negative capability," when a man can remain in "uncertainties, mysteries, doubts without any irritable reaching after fact and reason." It may be that to take part in the drama of life we need some convictions and principles also, but their stability and worth will depend on a prior cultivation of negative capability. At any rate the study of *Measure for Measure* can help very considerably in understanding the art and vision of Shakespeare in the tragedies and the final plays.

Bibliographical Note: There is no book-length comprehensive study of the stage history of *Measure for Measure*. I have depended on the calendar of productions (up to 1977) given by Mark Eccles in his *New Variorum* edition, pages 467–77. Eccles also gives titles of books and articles that discuss the listed productions. For post-1977 productions I have depended chiefly on reviews in the daily and weekly press and the more detailed accounts in the learned periodicals. Excerpts from press reviews are generally available in the *London Theatre Record*. First-night reviews are often written in a hurry, and do not always agree with one another, but they are fresh and vivid. A performance may settle down after the first night and may even change in significant ways. Reviews in the learned journals, especially *Shakespeare Quarterly* and *Shakespeare Survey*, are written with greater deliberation and perhaps after more than one viewing. On William Poel's productions, see Robert Speaight's *William Poel and the Elizabethan Revival* (1954); on Peter Brook, see Ralph Berry's *On Directing Shakespeare* (1977); on John Gielgud, see Gielgud's *An Actor and His Time* (1979) and Ronald Hayman's *John Gielgud* (1971). Other works on the stage history of *Measure for Measure* include: Joseph G. Price's *The Triple Bond* (1975) (This contains an essay by Jane Williamson on "The Duke and Isabella on the Modern Stage," pp. 149–69.); Philip Brockbank's *Players of Shakespeare*, First Series (1958); Russell Jackson and Robert Smallwood's *Players of Shakespeare*, Second Series (1988) and Third Series (1993); Faith Evans' *Clamorous Voices* (1989); Penny Gay's *As She Likes It* (1994); and Jonathan Bate and Russell Jackson's *Shakespeare: An Illustrated Stage History* (1996).

Suggested References

The number of possible references is vast and grows alarmingly. (The *Shakespeare Quarterly* devotes one issue each year to a list of the previous year's work, and *Shakespeare Survey*—an annual publication—includes a substantial review of biographical, critical, and textual studies, as well as a survey of performances.) The vast bibliography is best approached through James Harner, *The World Shakespeare Bibliography on CD-Rom: 1900–Present.* The first release, in 1996, included more than 12,000 annotated items from 1990–93, plus references to several thousand book reviews, productions, films, and audio recordings. The plan is to update the publication annually, moving forward one year and backward three years. Thus, the second issue (1997), with 24,700 entries, and another 35,000 or so references to reviews, newspaper pieces, and so on, covered 1987–94.

Though no works are indispensable, those listed below have been found especially helpful. The arrangement is as follows:

1. Shakespeare's Times
2. Shakespeare's Life
3. Shakespeare's Theater
4. Shakespeare on Stage and Screen
5. Miscellaneous Reference Works
6. Shakespeare's Plays: General Studies
7. The Comedies
8. The Romances
9. The Tragedies
10. The Histories
11. *Measure for Measure*

The titles in the first five sections are accompanied by brief explanatory annotations.

1. Shakespeare's Times

Andrews, John F., ed. *William Shakespeare: His World, His Work, His Influence,* 3 vols. (1985). Sixty articles, dealing not only with such subjects as "The State," "The Church," "Law," "Science, Magic, and Folklore," but also with the plays and poems themselves and Shakespeare's influence (e.g., translations, films, reputation)

Byrne, Muriel St. Clare. *Elizabethan Life in Town and Country* (8th ed., 1970). Chapters on manners, beliefs, education, etc., with illustrations.

Dollimore, John, and Alan Sinfield, eds. *Political Shakespeare: New Essays in Cultural Materialism* (1985). Essays on such topics as the subordination of women and colonialism, presented in connection with some of Shakespeare's plays.

Greenblatt, Stephen. *Representing the English Renaissance* (1988). New Historicist essays, especially on connections between political and aesthetic matters, statecraft and stagecraft.

Joseph, B. L. *Shakespeare's Eden: the Commonwealth of England 1558–1629* (1971). An account of the social, political, economic, and cultural life of England.

Kernan, Alvin. *Shakespeare, the King's Playwright: Theater in the Stuart Court 1603–1613* (1995). The social setting and the politics of the court of James I, in relation to *Hamlet, Measure for Measure, Macbeth, King Lear, Antony and Cleopatra, Coriolanus,* and *The Tempest.*

Montrose, Louis. *The Purpose of Playing: Shakespeare and the Cultural Politics of the Elizabethan Theatre* (1996). A poststructuralist view, discussing the professional theater "within the ideological and material frameworks of Elizabethan culture and society," with an extended analysis of *A Midsummer Night's Dream.*

Mullaney, Steven. *The Place of the Stage: License, Play, and Power in Renaissance England* (1988). New Historicist analysis, arguing that popular drama became a cultural institution "only by . . . taking up a place on the margins of society."

Schoenbaum, S. *Shakespeare: The Globe and the World*

(1979). A readable, abundantly illustrated introductory book on the world of the Elizabethans.

Shakespeare's England, 2 vols. (1916). A large collection of scholarly essays on a wide variety of topics, e.g., astrology, costume, gardening, horsemanship, with special attention to Shakespeare's references to these topics.

2. Shakespeare's Life

Andrews, John F., ed. *William Shakespeare: His World, His Work, His Influence*, 3 vols. (1985). See the description above.

Bentley, Gerald E. *Shakespeare: A Biographical Handbook* (1961). The facts about Shakespeare, with virtually no conjecture intermingled.

Chambers, E. K. *William Shakespeare: A Study of Facts and Problems*, 2 vols. (1930). The fullest collection of data.

Fraser, Russell. *Young Shakespeare* (1988). A highly readable account that simultaneously considers Shakespeare's life and Shakespeare's art.

———. *Shakespeare: The Later Years* (1992).

Schoenbaum, S. *Shakespeare's Lives* (1970). A review of the evidence and an examination of many biographies, including those of Baconians and other heretics.

———. *William Shakespeare: A Compact Documentary Life* (1977). An abbreviated version, in a smaller format, of the next title. The compact version reproduces some fifty documents in reduced form. A readable presentation of all that the documents tell us about Shakespeare.

———. *William Shakespeare: A Documentary Life* (1975). A large-format book setting forth the biography with facsimiles of more than two hundred documents, and with transcriptions and commentaries.

3. Shakespeare's Theater

Astington, John H., ed. *The Development of Shakespeare's Theater* (1992). Eight specialized essays on theatrical companies, playing spaces, and performance.

Beckerman, Bernard. *Shakespeare at the Globe, 1599–1609* (1962). On the playhouse and on Elizabethan dramaturgy, acting, and staging.

Bentley, Gerald E. *The Profession of Dramatist in Shakespeare's Time* (1971). An account of the dramatist's status in the Elizabethan period.

———. *The Profession of Player in Shakespeare's Time, 1590–1642* (1984). An account of the status of members of London companies (sharers, hired men, apprentices, managers) and a discussion of conditions when they toured.

Berry, Herbert. *Shakespeare's Playhouses* (1987). Usefully emphasizes how little we know about the construction of Elizabethan theaters.

Brown, John Russell. *Shakespeare's Plays in Performance* (1966). A speculative and practical analysis relevant to all of the plays, but with emphasis on *The Merchant of Venice, Richard II, Hamlet, Romeo and Juliet,* and *Twelfth Night.*

———. *William Shakespeare: Writing for Performance* (1996). A discussion aimed at helping readers to develop theatrically conscious habits of reading.

Chambers, E. K. *The Elizabethan Stage*, 4 vols. (1945). A major reference work on theaters, theatrical companies, and staging at court.

Cook, Ann Jennalie. *The Privileged Playgoers of Shakespeare's London, 1576–1642* (1981). Sees Shakespeare's audience as wealthier, more middle-class, and more intellectual than Harbage (below) does.

Dessen, Alan C. *Elizabethan Drama and the Viewer's Eye* (1977). On how certain scenes may have looked to spectators in an Elizabethan theater.

Gurr, Andrew. *Playgoing in Shakespeare's London* (1987). Something of a middle ground between Cook (above) and Harbage (below).

———. *The Shakespearean Stage, 1579–1642* (2nd ed., 1980). On the acting companies, the actors, the playhouses, the stages, and the audiences.

Harbage, Alfred. *Shakespeare's Audience* (1941). A study of the size and nature of the theatrical public, emphasizing the representativeness of its working class and middle-class audience.

Hodges, C. Walter. *The Globe Restored* (1968). A conjectural restoration, with lucid drawings.

Hosley, Richard. "The Playhouses," in *The Revels History of Drama in English*, vol. 3, general editors Clifford Leech and T. W. Craik (1975). An essay of a hundred pages on the physical aspects of the playhouses.

Howard, Jane E. "Crossdressing, the Theatre, and Gender Struggle in Early Modern England," *Shakespeare Quarterly* 39 (1988): 418–40. Judicious comments on the effects of boys playing female roles.

Orrell, John. *The Human Stage: English Theatre Design, 1567–1640* (1988). Argues that the public, private, and court playhouses are less indebted to popular structures (e.g., innyards and bear-baiting pits) than to banqueting halls and to Renaissance conceptions of Roman amphitheaters.

Slater, Ann Pasternak. *Shakespeare the Director* (1982). An analysis of theatrical effects (e.g., kissing, kneeling) in stage directions and dialogue.

Styan, J. L. *Shakespeare's Stagecraft* (1967). An introduction to Shakespeare's visual and aural stagecraft, with chapters on such topics as acting conventions, stage groupings, and speech.

Thompson, Peter. *Shakespeare's Professional Career* (1992). An examination of patronage and related theatrical conditions.

———. *Shakespeare's Theatre* (1983). A discussion of how plays were staged in Shakespeare's time.

4. Shakespeare on Stage and Screen

Bate, Jonathan, and Russell Jackson, eds. *Shakespeare: An Illustrated Stage History* (1996). Highly readable essays on stage productions from the Renaissance to the present.

Berry, Ralph. *Changing Styles in Shakespeare* (1981). Discusses productions of six plays (*Coriolanus*, *Hamlet*, *Henry V*, *Measure for Measure*, *The Tempest*, and *Twelfth Night*) on the English stage, chiefly 1950–1980.

————. *On Directing Shakespeare: Interviews with Contemporary Directors* (1989). An enlarged edition of a book first published in 1977, this version includes the seven interviews from the early 1970s and adds five interviews conducted in 1988.

Brockbank, Philip, ed. *Players of Shakespeare: Essays in Shakespearean Performance* (1985). Comments by twelve actors, reporting their experiences with roles. See also the entry for Russell Jackson (below).

Bulman, J. C., and H. R. Coursen, eds. *Shakespeare on Television* (1988). An anthology of general and theoretical essays, essays on individual productions, and shorter reviews, with a bibliography and a videography listing cassettes that may be rented.

Coursen, H. P. *Watching Shakespeare on Television* (1993). Analyses not only of TV versions but also of films and videotapes of stage presentations that are shown on television.

Davies, Anthony, and Stanley Wells, eds. *Shakespeare and the Moving Image: The Plays on Film and Television* (1994). General essays (e.g., on the comedies) as well as essays devoted entirely to *Hamlet, King Lear*, and *Macbeth*.

Dawson, Anthony B. *Watching Shakespeare: A Playgoer's Guide* (1988). About half of the plays are discussed, chiefly in terms of decisions that actors and directors make in putting the works onto the stage.

Dessen, Alan. *Elizabethan Stage Conventions and Modern Interpretations* (1984). On interpreting conventions such as the representation of light and darkness and stage violence (duels, battles).

Donaldson, Peter. *Shakespearean Films/Shakespearean Directors* (1990). Postmodernist analyses, drawing on Freudianism, Feminism, Deconstruction, and Queer Theory.

Jackson, Russell, and Robert Smallwood, eds. *Players of Shakespeare 2: Further Essays in Shakespearean Performance by Players with the Royal Shakespeare Company* (1988). Fourteen actors discuss their roles in productions between 1982 and 1987.

————. *Players of Shakespeare 3: Further Essays in Shake-

spearean Performance by Players with the Royal Shakespeare Company (1993). Comments by thirteen performers.

Jorgens, Jack. *Shakespeare on Film* (1977). Fairly detailed studies of eighteen films, preceded by an introductory chapter addressing such issues as music, and whether to "open" the play by including scenes of landscape.

Kennedy, Dennis. *Looking at Shakespeare: A Visual History of Twentieth-Century Performance* (1993). Lucid descriptions (with 170 photographs) of European, British, and American performances.

Leiter, Samuel L. *Shakespeare Around the Globe: A Guide to Notable Postwar Revivals* (1986). For each play there are about two pages of introductory comments, then discussions (about five hundred words per production) of ten or so productions, and finally bibliographic references.

McMurty, Jo. *Shakespeare Films in the Classroom* (1994). Useful evaluations of the chief films most likely to be shown in undergraduate courses.

Rothwell, Kenneth, and Annabelle Henkin Melzer. *Shakespeare on Screen: An International Filmography and Videography* (1990). A reference guide to several hundred films and videos produced between 1899 and 1989, including spinoffs such as musicals and dance versions.

Sprague, Arthur Colby. *Shakespeare and the Actors* (1944). Detailed discussions of stage business (gestures, etc.) over the years.

Willis, Susan. *The BBC Shakespeare Plays: Making the Televised Canon* (1991). A history of the series, with interviews and production diaries for some plays.

5. Miscellaneous Reference Works

Abbott, E. A. *A Shakespearean Grammar* (new edition, 1877). An examination of differences between Elizabethan and modern grammar.

Allen, Michael J. B., and Kenneth Muir, eds. *Shakespeare's Plays in Quarto* (1981). One volume containing facsimiles of the plays issued in small format before they were collected in the First Folio of 1623.

Bevington, David. *Shakespeare* (1978). A short guide to hundreds of important writings on the subject.

Blake, Norman. *Shakespeare's Language: An Introduction* (1983). On vocabulary, parts of speech, and word order.

Bullough, Geoffrey. *Narrative and Dramatic Sources of Shakespeare*, 8 vols. (1957–75). A collection of many of the books Shakespeare drew on, with judicious comments.

Campbell, Oscar James, and Edward G. Quinn, eds. *The Reader's Encyclopedia of Shakespeare* (1966). Old, but still the most useful single reference work on Shakespeare.

Cercignani, Fausto. *Shakespeare's Works and Elizabethan Pronunciation* (1981). Considered the best work on the topic, but remains controversial.

Dent, R. W. *Shakespeare's Proverbial Language: An Index* (1981). An index of proverbs, with an introduction concerning a form Shakespeare frequently drew on.

Greg, W. W. *The Shakespeare First Folio* (1955). A detailed yet readable history of the first collection (1623) of Shakespeare's plays.

Harner, James. *The World Shakespeare Bibliography*. See headnote to Suggested References.

Hosley, Richard. *Shakespeare's Holinshed* (1968). Valuable presentation of one of Shakespeare's major sources.

Kökeritz, Helge. *Shakespeare's Names* (1959). A guide to pronouncing some 1,800 names appearing in Shakespeare.
———. *Shakespeare's Pronunciation* (1953). Contains much information about puns and rhymes, but see Cercignani (above).

Muir, Kenneth. *The Sources of Shakespeare's Plays* (1978). An account of Shakespeare's use of his reading. It covers all the plays, in chronological order.

Miriam Joseph, Sister. *Shakespeare's Use of the Arts of Language* (1947). A study of Shakespeare's use of rhetorical devices, reprinted in part as *Rhetoric in Shakespeare's Time* (1962).

The Norton Facsimile: The First Folio of Shakespeare's Plays (1968). A handsome and accurate facsimile of the first collection (1623) of Shakespeare's plays, with a valuable introduction by Charlton Hinman.

Onions, C. T. *A Shakespeare Glossary*, rev. and enlarged by

R. D. Eagleson (1986). Definitions of words (or senses of words) now obsolete.

Partridge, Eric. *Shakespeare's Bawdy*, rev. ed. (1955). Relatively brief dictionary of bawdy words; useful, but see Williams, below.

Shakespeare Quarterly. See headnote to Suggested References.

Shakespeare Survey. See headnote to Suggested References.

Spevack, Marvin. *The Harvard Concordance to Shakespeare* (1973). An index to Shakespeare's words.

Vickers, Brian. *Appropriating Shakespeare: Contemporary Critical Quarrels* (1993). A survey—chiefly hostile—of recent schools of criticism.

Wells, Stanley, ed. *Shakespeare: A Bibliographical Guide* (new edition, 1990). Nineteen chapters (some devoted to single plays, others devoted to groups of related plays) on recent scholarship on the life and all of the works.

Williams, Gordon. *A Dictionary of Sexual Language and Imagery in Shakespearean and Stuart Literature*, 3 vols. (1994). Extended discussions of words and passages; much fuller than Partridge, cited above.

6. Shakespeare's Plays: General Studies

Bamber, Linda. *Comic Women, Tragic Men: A Study of Gender and Genre in Shakespeare* (1982).

Barnet, Sylvan. *A Short Guide to Shakespeare* (1974).

Callaghan, Dympna, Lorraine Helms, and Jyotsna Singh. *The Weyward Sisters: Shakespeare and Feminist Politics* (1994).

Clemen, Wolfgang H. *The Development of Shakespeare's Imagery* (1951).

Cook, Ann Jennalie. *Making a Match: Courtship in Shakespeare and His Society* (1991).

Dollimore, Jonathan, and Alan Sinfield. *Political Shakespeare: New Essays in Cultural Materialism* (1985).

Dusinberre, Juliet. *Shakespeare and the Nature of Women* (1975).

Granville-Barker, Harley. *Prefaces to Shakespeare*, 2 vols. (1946–47; volume 1 contains essays on *Hamlet, King*

Lear, Merchant of Venice, Antony and Cleopatra, and *Cymbeline;* volume 2 contains essays on *Othello, Coriolanus, Julius Caesar, Romeo and Juliet, Love's Labor's Lost*).

————. *More Prefaces to Shakespeare* (1974; essays on *Twelfth Night, A Midsummer Night's Dream, The Winter's Tale, Macbeth*).

Harbage, Alfred. *William Shakespeare: A Reader's Guide* (1963).

Howard, Jean E. *Shakespeare's Art of Orchestration: Stage Technique and Audience Response* (1984).

Jones, Emrys. *Scenic Form in Shakespeare* (1971).

Lenz, Carolyn Ruth Swift, Gayle Greene, and Carol Thomas Neely, eds. *The Woman's Part: Feminist Criticism of Shakespeare* (1980).

Novy, Marianne. *Love's Argument: Gender Relations in Shakespeare* (1984).

Rose, Mark. *Shakespearean Design* (1972).

Scragg, Leah. *Discovering Shakespeare's Meaning* (1994).

————. *Shakespeare's "Mouldy Tales": Recurrent Plot Motifs in Shakespearean Drama* (1992).

Traub, Valerie. *Desire and Anxiety: Circulations of Sexuality in Shakespearean Drama* (1992).

Traversi, D. A. *An Approach to Shakespeare,* 2 vols. (3rd rev. ed, 1968–69).

Vickers, Brian. *The Artistry of Shakespeare's Prose* (1968).

Wells, Stanley. *Shakespeare: A Dramatic Life* (1994).

Wright, George T. *Shakespeare's Metrical Art* (1988).

7. The Comedies

Barber, C. L. *Shakespeare's Festive Comedy* (1959; discusses *Love's Labor's Lost, A Midsummer Night's Dream, The Merchant of Venice, As You Like It, Twelfth Night*).

Barton, Anne. *The Names of Comedy* (1990).

Berry, Ralph. *Shakespeare's Comedy: Explorations in Form* (1972).

Bradbury, Malcolm, and David Palmer, eds. *Shakespearean Comedy* (1972).

Bryant, J. A., Jr. *Shakespeare and the Uses of Comedy* (1986).

Carroll, William. *The Metamorphoses of Shakespearean Comedy* (1985).

Champion, Larry S. *The Evolution of Shakespeare's Comedy* (1970).

Evans, Bertrand. *Shakespeare's Comedies* (1960).

Frye, Northrop. *Shakespearean Comedy and Romance* (1965).

Leggatt, Alexander. *Shakespeare's Comedy of Love* (1974).

Miola, Robert S. *Shakespeare and Classical Comedy: The Influence of Plautus and Terence* (1994).

Nevo, Ruth. *Comic Transformations in Shakespeare* (1980).

Ornstein, Robert. *Shakespeare's Comedies: From Roman Farce to Romantic Mystery* (1986).

Richman, David. *Laughter, Pain, and Wonder: Shakespeare's Comedies and the Audience in the Theater* (1990).

Salingar, Leo. *Shakespeare and the Traditions of Comedy* (1974).

Slights, Camille Wells. *Shakespeare's Comic Commonwealths* (1993).

Waller, Gary, ed. *Shakespeare's Comedies* (1991).

Westlund, Joseph. *Shakespeare's Reparative Comedies: A Psychoanalytic View of the Middle Plays* (1984).

Williamson, Marilyn. *The Patriarchy of Shakespeare's Comedies* (1986).

8. The Romances (*Pericles, Cymbeline, The Winter's Tale, The Tempest, The Two Noble Kinsmen*)

Adams, Robert M. *Shakespeare: The Four Romances* (1989).

Felperin, Howard. *Shakespearean Romance* (1972).

Frye, Northrop. *A Natural Perspective: The Development of Shakespearean Comedy and Romance* (1965).

Mowat, Barbara. *The Dramaturgy of Shakespeare's Romances* (1976).

Warren, Roger. *Staging Shakespeare's Late Plays* (1990).

Young, David. *The Heart's Forest: A Study of Shakespeare's Pastoral Plays* (1972).

9. The Tragedies

Bradley, A. C. *Shakespearean Tragedy* (1904).

Brooke, Nicholas. *Shakespeare's Early Tragedies* (1968).

Champion, Larry. *Shakespeare's Tragic Perspective* (1976).

Drakakis, John, ed. *Shakespearean Tragedy* (1992).

Evans, Bertrand. *Shakespeare's Tragic Practice* (1979).

Everett, Barbara. *Young Hamlet: Essays on Shakespeare's Tragedies* (1989).

Foakes, R. A. *Hamlet versus Lear: Cultural Politics and Shakespeare's Art* (1993).

Frye, Northrop. *Fools of Time: Studies in Shakespearean Tragedy* (1967).

Harbage, Alfred, ed. *Shakespeare: The Tragedies* (1964).

Mack, Maynard. *Everybody's Shakespeare: Reflections Chiefly on the Tragedies* (1993).

McAlindon, T. *Shakespeare's Tragic Cosmos* (1991).

Miola, Robert S. *Shakespeare and Classical Tragedy: The Influence of Seneca* (1992).

——. *Shakespeare's Rome* (1983).

Nevo, Ruth. *Tragic Form in Shakespeare* (1972).

Rackin, Phyllis. *Shakespeare's Tragedies* (1978).

Rose, Mark, ed. *Shakespeare's Early Tragedies: A Collection of Critical Essays* (1995).

Rosen, William. *Shakespeare and the Craft of Tragedy* (1960).

Snyder, Susan. *The Comic Matrix of Shakespeare's Tragedies* (1979).

Wofford, Susanne. *Shakespeare's Late Tragedies: A Collection of Critical Essays* (1996).

Young, David. *The Action to the Word: Structure and Style in Shakespearean Tragedy* (1990).

——. *Shakespeare's Middle Tragedies: A Collection of Critical Essays* (1993).

10. The Histories

Blanpied, John W. *Time and the Artist in Shakespeare's English Histories* (1983).

Campbell, Lily B. *Shakespeare's "Histories": Mirrors of Elizabethan Policy* (1947).

Champion, Larry S. *Perspective in Shakespeare's English Histories* (1980).

Hodgdon, Barbara. *The End Crowns All: Closure and Contradiction in Shakespeare's History* (1991).

Holderness, Graham. *Shakespeare Recycled: The Making of Historical Drama* (1992).

————, ed. *Shakespeare's History Plays: "Richard II" to "Henry V"* (1992).

Leggatt, Alexander. *Shakespeare's Political Drama: The History Plays and the Roman Plays* (1988).

Ornstein, Robert. *A Kingdom for a Stage: The Achievement of Shakespeare's History Plays* (1972).

Rackin, Phyllis. *Stages of History: Shakespeare's English Chronicles* (1990).

Saccio, Peter. *Shakespeare's English Kings: History, Chronicle, and Drama* (1977).

Tillyard, E. M. W. *Shakespeare's History Plays* (1944).

Velz, John W., ed. *Shakespeare's English Histories: A Quest for Form and Genre* (1996).

11. *Measure for Measure*

For works concerning the play on the stage and screen, see above, pages 210–11. For the play in the contexts of the comedies, see the titles cited earlier in Section 7, The Comedies.

Editions: For fuller annotations and editorial discussions, consult the following editions: J. W. Lever (Arden edition, 1965); J. M. Nosworthy (New Penguin, 1969); R.E.C. Houghton (New Clarendon, 1970); Mark Eccles (New Variorum, 1980); Brian Gibbons (New Cambridge, 1991); N. W. Bawcutt (Oxford, 1991); Barbara Mowatt and Paul Werstine (New Folger, 1997).

Critical and Historical Studies: For a bibliographic essay on the problem plays, see John Wilders, in *Shakespeare: A Bibliographic Guide,* new ed. (1990). In the list that follows, most of the books, especially the study by Harriet Hawkins, contain full bibliographies. Annual reviews of current scholarship and criticism are available in *Shakespeare Survey* and *The Year's Work in English Studies*.

Alexander, Nigel. *Shakespeare's "Measure for Measure"* (1975).

Bennett, Josephine Waters. *"Measure for Measure" as Royal Entertainment* (1966).

Berry, Ralph. *Shakespeare in Performance* (1993).

———. *Shakespearean Structures* (1981).

Bradbrook, M. C. *Artist and Society in Shakespeare's England.* Vol. I. (1982).

———. *Muriel Bradbrook on Shakespeare* (1984).

———. *Shakespeare and Elizabethan Poetry* (1951).

Brennan, Anthony. *Shakespeare's Dramatic Structures* (1986).

Brockbank, Philip. *On Shakespeare* (1989).

Chambers, R. W. *Man's Unconquerable Mind* (1939).

Desense, M. C. *The Bed-Trick in English Renaissance Drama* (1994).

Desmet, Christy. *Reading Shakespeare's Characters: Rhetoric, Ethics, and Identity* (1992).

Dollimore, J. and Sinfield, A., eds. *Political Shakespeare* (1985, 1994).

Drakakis, J., ed. *Alternative Shakespeares* (1985).

Empson, W. *The Structure of Complex Words* (1957).

Evans, Bertrand, *Shakespeare's Comedies* (1960).

Fabricius, J. *Syphilis in Shakespeare's England* (1994).

Foakes, R. A. *Shakespeare: The Dark Comedies to the Last Plays* (1971).

Friedman, Michael. "Oh let him marry her." *Shakespeare Quarterly* 45 (1995): 454–64.

Frye, Northrop. *The Myth of Deliverance: Reflections on Shakespeare's Problem Comedies* (1983).

Geckle, G. L. (ed.) *Twentieth Century Interpretations of "Measure for Measure"* (1974).

Gibbons, B. *Shakespeare and Multiplicity* (1993).

Gless, Darryl J. *"Measure for Measure," The Law and the Convent* (1979).

Goldman, Michael. *Shakespeare and the Energies of Drama* (1972).

Greenblatt, S. (ed.) *The Power of Forms in the English Renaissance* (1982).

Hawkins, Harriet. *"Measure for Measure"* (1987).

Hellman, Richard. *William Shakespeare: The Problem Plays* (1993).

Honigman, E. A. J. *Myriad-Minded Shakespeare: Essays*, 2nd ed. (1997).

Hunter, Robert G. *Shakespeare and the Comedy of Forgiveness* (1965).

Lawrence, W. W. *Shakespeare's Problem Comedies* (1931).

Leavis, F. R. *The Common Pursuit* (1952).

Mahood, M. M. *Bit Parts in Shakespeare* (1992).

Marcus, Leah. *Puzzling Shakespeare and Local Reading* (1988).

McCandless, D. *Gender and Performance in Shakespeare's Problem Comedies* (1997).

McGuire, Philip. *Speechless Dialect: Shakespeare's Open Silences* (1985).

Miles, Rosalind. *The Problem of "Measure for Measure": A Historical Investigation* (1976).

Muir, Kenneth and Wells, Stanley, eds. *Aspects of Shakespeare's Problem Plays* (1982).

Nicholls, Graham. *"Measure for Measure": Text and Performance* (1986).

Ornstein, Robert, ed. *Discussions of Shakespeare's Problem Comedies* (1961).

Rabkin, Norman. *Shakespeare and the Common Understanding* (1984).

Rosenberg, Marvin. *The Adventures of a Shakespeare Scholar* (1997).

Ross, Lawrence J. *On "Measure for Measure"* (1997).

Rossiter, A. P. *"Angel with Horns" and Other Shakespeare Lectures*, ed. Graham Storey (1961).

Schanzer, Ernest. *The Problem Plays of Shakespeare* (1963).

Seiden, Melvin. *"Measure for Measure," Casuistry, and Artistry* (1990).

Shell, Marc. *The End of Kinship: "Measure for Measure" Incest, and the Ideal of Universal Siblinghood* (1988).

Soelner, Rolf. *Shakespeare's Patterns of Self-Knowledge* (1972).

Stevenson, D. L. *The Achievement of "Measure for Measure"* (1966).

Taylor, Gary and Jowett, John. *Shakespeare Reshaped, 1603–1623* (1993).

Tennenhouse, Leonard. *Power on Display: Politics and Shakespeare's Genres* (1986).

Thomas, Vivian. *The Moral Universe of Shakespeare's Problem Plays* (1950).

Tillyard, E.M.W. *Shakespeare's Problem Plays* (1950).

Watts, Cedric. *"Measure for Measure"* (1986).

Wheeler, Richard P. *Shakespeare's Development and the Problem Comedies* (1981).